Steven Callahan's fight for survival began abruptly, near midnight on the 4th of February 1982, when his small sailboat sank beneath him in rough Atlantic seas. He was cast adrift on a rubber raft, thousands of miles from the nearest landfall, with few supplies, a single gallon of fresh water, and very little clothing to protect him from the elements.

As you can imagine, his battle to live was a brutal encounter with hunger and exposure, but it centered, more than anything else, on his ability to capture fresh drinking water, and on his discipline when it came to conserving those supplies. The fact that he survived is a testament to human will, resourcefulness, and simple endurance. His experience illustrates one of the ultimate lessons presented in the activities and case studies of *Conserve Water*. Namely, that we are all living on a life raft and that we are all adrift on an intergalactic ocean with limited supplies. Our life raft is called Planet Earth, and among the most essential resources necessary to our survival is our need for fresh water that we drink, use to manufacture materials, flush wastes away, play on, irrigate our vegetables, and are tethered to in a far more fundamental way than we normally realize.

The Watercourse is a not-for-profit water science and education program based at Montana State University, Bozeman. Specializing in the development of educational materials on water and water-related management issues, The Watercourse distributes these materials through training workshops and institutes. The goal is to promote and facilitate public understanding of atmospheric, surface, and ground water resources and related management issues through publications, instruction, and networking. The scope of The Watercourse is international, its delivery unbiased, and its mission is to build informed leadership in resource decision-making.

The Watercourse
201 Culbertson Hall
Montana State University
Bozeman, Montana 59717-0570
Phone: (406) 994-5392
Fax: (406) 994-1919
e-mail: Watercourse@montana.edu

Educators' Guide

Water Conservation Activities & Case Studies

The Watercourse
Montana State University
Bozeman, Montana

United States
Department of the Interior
Bureau of Reclamation

International Project WET
Montana State University
Bozeman, Montana

Production Team, Contributors, and Reviewers

The Watercourse Staff, 2000
Dennis Nelson, *Executive Director*
Sandra Chisholm DeYonge, *Associate Director*
Chandra Morris, *Publication and Production Coordinator*
Stephanie Ouren, *Accountant*
Linda Hveem, *Administrative Assistant*

Production Team for *Conserve Water Educators' Guide*
Production Managers/Writers: Dennis Nelson, Sandra Chisholm DeYonge, and Chandra Morris
Writers: Sandra Chisholm DeYonge, Alan Kesselheim, George Robinson, and Jennie Lane
Production Business Manager: Chandra Morris
Researchers: Sally Unser and Kristen Limb
Copy Editor: Lee Esbenshade
Support Services: Linda Hveem, Sally Unser, and Kristen Limb
Art Direction/Design/Production: Chandra Morris
Logo Design: Chandra Morris
Cover Design: Chandra Morris
Illustrator: James Lindquist
Additional Illustration: Robert Rath ("Water Conservation Celebration")
Photography: Shell Beck. *Cover Photo*: Don Unser. All others as credited.

Financial Sponsors
The publication of the *Conserve Water Educators' Guide* was funded by the United States Department of the Interior, Bureau of Reclamation. Special thanks to:
·Leonard Duberstein, Water Conservation Coordinator, Great Plains Region of the U.S. BOR
·Christy L. Bridges, Water Policy Analyst, U.S. BOR–Denver Office
·Jeanette Campbell, formerly Water Conservation Specialist, Great Plains Region of the U.S. BOR.

Acknowledgments

On behalf of The Watercourse, I would like to thank everyone who contributed to the development and publication of the Conserve Water Educators' Guide.

In researching and writing Conserve Water, *The Watercourse staff contacted literally thousands of educators and water resources managers for input and guidance. The real world of using water wisely and more efficiently involves a full range of discipline and is truly complex.*

From individual water users to diplomats of great countries who are negotiating water use treaties with other nations, the solutions to meeting future water needs must include water conservation education. The people and organizations acknowledged are pioneers in the water conservation field.

From an organizational level, I would like to thank my staff for making this an outstanding publication, the Project WET network (U.S.A., Canada, and Mexico) for countless contributions and support, and the U.S. Bureau of Reclamation for funding this much needed project.

Dennis Nelson
Executive Director

Acknowledgments, continued

Fieldtesters:
Nicole Clegg, *New Hampshire Project WET*
Janice Conner, *South Carolina Project WET*
Jerry de Bin, *Alabama Project WET*
John Etgen, *Montana Project WET*
Alex Falig, *Northern Marianas Project WET*
Petey Giroux, *Georgia Project WET*
Cindy Grove, *Maryland Project WET*
Don Hollums, *Colorado Project WET*
Sandra Jurban, *Florida Project WET*
Monica Kilpatrick, *Georgia Project WET*
Sara Kneipp, *Texas Project WET*
Jim Lafley, *Massachusetts Project WET*
Brooke Levey, *Nebraska Project WET*
Diane Maddox, *Kansas Project WET*
Sue McWilliams, *Oregon Project WET*
Dave Parsons, *Connecticut Project WET*
Sue Perin, *Wyoming Project WET*
Amy Picotte, *Vermont Project WET*
Joe Pitts, *Missouri Project WET*
Nancy Rolli, *Delaware Project WET*
Julie Scanlin, *Idaho Project WET*
Susan Schultz, *Indiana Project WET*
Marcy Seavey, *Iowa Project WET*
Kristina Smitten, *Minnesota Project WET*
Eileen Tramontana, *Florida Project WET*

Case Study Contributors:
Warren Liebold, City Conservation, *New York Department of Environmental Protection*
Vivian Brooks, Public Affairs, *Friendly's Ice Cream*
Dana Porter, *Texas Agricultural Experiment Station: Lubbock*
Leon New and Jim Bordovsky, *Texas Agricultural Experiment Station: Amarillo*
Jenny Mendez-Isenburg, Public Affairs, *MWRA*
Liz Gardiner, *Denver Water*
John Parsons, Water Systems Manager, and Marilyn Smith, *Irvine Ranch Water District*
Tom Kiah, Architect, *Deel Mechanical Corporation*
Shawna Lockhart, Civil Engineering, *Montana State University-Bozeman*
Jeff Dickerson, Manager, *OPUS Center Irvine*
Joe Weatherly, owner, and Gail Sams, *Heritage Beef*
Panhandle Plains Historical Museum
Ann Runley, *Brookwater Irrigation*
James Hartsfield, Public Affairs Representative for the Shuttle, *NASA*

Activity Contributors
Leonard Duberstein, *Bureau of Reclamation*
Christy Bridges, *Bureau of Reclamation*
John Etgen, *Project WET*
Gary Cook, *Project WET*
Eileen Tramontana, *St. Johns River Management District*
Marcey Seavey, *The Iowa Academy of Science*
Kristen Limb, *The Watercourse*
Dr. Eric Grimsrud, *Montana State University*
Chris Beytes, *GrowerTalks Magazine*
Denise Rendina, *Kansas City Zoo*
Chad Yelton, *Cincinnati Zoo*
Ann Noble, *Museum of New Mexico Foundation*
Tony Marinella, *Museum of Northern Arizona*
Barton Wright, *Natural History Writer*
Liz Gardiner, *Denver Water*
Courtney Grafa, *Fort Worth Zoo*

Special thanks to librarians at:
Montana State University—Bozeman
Bozeman Public Library

Table of Contents

Introductory Material

Introduction to Water Conservation

Essay by Dennis Nelson, Executive Director, The Watercourse and Project WET

Conserve Water Activities

First Things First

Fixed, Finite & Fickle

Water Use, Water Users

Nothing New Under the Rainbow

Meeting the Challenges

Our Water Future

Table of Contents, continued

The Watercourse

History of The Watercourse

Since its inception in 1989, The Watercourse has expanded to accommodate the varied interests of water users nationwide. Watercourse programs provide opportunities for young people and adults to learn about water through materials that are educationally sound, interdisciplinary, interactive, and creative and can be used immediately in the field, classroom, or home.

The Goal of The Watercourse

The goal of The Watercourse is to promote and facilitate public understanding of atmospheric, surface, and ground water resources and related management issues through publications, instruction, and networking.

The Watercourse's scope is international, its delivery is unbiased, and its mission is to build informed leadership in resource decision making. The Watercourse responds to the information needs of many diverse groups. Above all, The Watercourse relies on cooperation with other public, private, and NGO resource managers, policy makers, water educators, and citizens.

The Watercourse Believes...

· Water is important for all water users (e.g., energy producers, farmers and ranchers, fish and wildlife, manufacturers, recreationists, rural and urban dwellers).
· Wise water management is crucial for providing tomorrow's children social and economic stability in a healthy environment.
· Awareness of, and respect for water resources, can encourage a personal, lifelong commitment of responsibility and positive community participation.

Wetlands · WOW! the Wonders Of Wetlands Teachers' Guide	Healthy Water, Healthy People · Water Quality Education Program	Discover a Watershed Series · Rio Grande/Rio Bravo · Columbia · Everglades · Missouri	International Project WET · USA · Canada · Peace Corps · Mexico	Childrens' Cultural Books · The Rainstick, a Fable · Spring Waters, Gathering Places
Ground Water · Flow Model · Teachers' Guide · Geothermal Teachers' Guide				Student Booklets · Conserve Water · Celebrate Wetlands · Big Rivers · The Water Story · Fish & Fishing · Explore Oceans · Discover Ground Water/Spring Water
Conserve Water Program · Teachers' Guide		**The Watercourse and Project WET** (Water Education for Teachers) **Programs and Project Divisions**		Native Waters Program · Teachers' Guide · Student Guide
Reference · Water Festivals · Water Rights · Water Photo Essay				Childrens' Fishing Series · Bass · 9 Other Fish Species
Water Management · Watershed Management Educators' Guide · Flooding (Future)	Water History · Lewis and Clark Bicentennial Project · Liquid Treasure Trunk Guide	Life Box Books (Future) · Natural Resources Publications	Water Works Series (Future)	Getting to Know Series · Yellowstone · Everglades

Introduction

Conserve Water Educators' Guide for teachers of students in grades six through twelve, is a collection of innovative activities and case studies that are easy to use, interactive, challenging, and fun! Depending upon grade level, interests, or curricular needs, educators and students simulate the management of the water resources of a community; create a Xeriscape landscape; play an irrigation innovation game; or perform in a turn of the century play to learn early lessons in water conservation. *Conserve Water* includes many opportunities for teachers to engage their students in exploring the issues and information that encompass the topic of water conservation.

The full-length activities, that have been field tested by educators and students, are in-depth treatments of various aspects of water conservation. They are presented according to a proven and practical format for classroom use, and are entirely self-contained. Each activity begins with an information sidebar that includes: subject areas, grade level, preparation and activity time, setting, vocabulary, and skills. (See Activity Format.) To assist teachers in incorporating activities into their existing curricula, a Cross Reference and Planning Chart in the appendix correlates subject areas

with activities. Also, in the appendix, lessons and activities are matched with case studies that provide relevant examples of the content and concepts explored in the lesson.

Activities that move students beyond the classroom and engage community members are outlined in the section, "Water Conservation Celebrations." Educators are provided with in-depth information to organize and implement celebrations that increase a school or community's awareness and appreciation of water conservation topics, practices, and issues. These events may comprise exhibits, presentations, games, music, performances, and student contests that relate to water conservation.

The case study section of *Conserve Water* has been developed to illustrate concepts and issues in real-life terms. These have been oriented toward small group work sessions, and are set up to mimic the process of evaluation and decision-making that actually face water users. These case studies put students in the position of a rancher trying to make a living in the Texas panhandle, of a water authority official responsible for supplying several million water users, or of a space shuttle engineering team that determines the role water

will play on the voyage. Embedded in each of the case studies is a prediction problem. The real-life story is interrupted at a certain point, and students are asked to assess the problem as if they were in the shoes of the NASA space shuttle team, the industry official, or the ranch owner. Before students go on to the conclusion of the story, they work through the process of brainstorming and strategizing to engage intellectually in the same dilemma that faced these individuals in real life.

Activities and case studies were designed to be thought provoking and challenge students to exercise decision-making and higher level thinking skills. Following is a list of thinking and process skills utilized when learning about water conservation concepts and issues. The skills listed are based on those advocated by the Association for Supervision and Curriculum Development and the American Association for the Advancement of Science.

· Gathering information includes: reading, observing, listening, collecting, researching, interviewing, measuring, computing, calculating, recording.
· Organizing information includes: matching, plotting data, graphing, sorting, arranging, sequencing, listing, classifying,

categorizing, estimating, mapping, drawing, charting, manipulating materials.

· Analyzing information includes: identifying components and relationships among components, identifying patterns, comparing, formulating questions, contrasting, discussing.

· Interpreting information includes: generalizing, summarizing, translating, relating, inferring, making models, drawing conclusions, defining problems, identifying cause and effect, confirming.

· Applying learned information includes: planning, designing, building, constructing, composing, experimenting, restructuring, inventing; predicting, hypothesizing, proposing solutions; problem solving, decision making, developing and implementing investigations and action plans.

· Evaluating application of learned information includes: establishing criteria, verifying, testing, assessing, and critiquing results.

· Presenting evidence of learning from application and evaluation processes includes: demonstrating, writing, drawing, describing, public speaking, reporting, persuading, debating.

Through activities, case studies, and school and community celebrations, educators and students explore the concepts, practices, and issues of water conservation. *Conserve Water* offers young people the information and tools to become responsible stewards of our water resources and one day, to be informed leaders and decision-makers within their own communities.

Word Usage, Grammar, and Writing Style

The writing style within the guide follows *The Chicago Manual of Style*, 14th edition; spelling is based on *The Random House Unabridged Dictionary*, 2nd edition. The term ground water is presented as two words within *Conserve Water* based on the recommendation of the United States Geological Survey (USGS), the primary water management data agency for the country. Ground water (two words) correlates with surface water (two words). When referring to Earth, the planet, a capital *E* is used and the article *the* is omitted. The word earth, with a lowercase *e*, is used to designate soil and rock materials.

Activity Summaries

Alligators, Epiphytes, and Water Managers
Students identify plants, animals, and their water conservation behaviors by analyzing clues that describe water-related adaptations of aquatic and terrestrial organisms. 75

Blue Traveller (The)
With a roll of the die, students simulate the movement of water within and between natural and constructed systems. 43

Conservation Choices
Students confront a variety of water conservation dilemmas and choose courses of action to deal with them. In the process they face ethical, financial, and practical issues. 115

Get the Ground Water Picture
Students will "get the ground water picture," learning about basic ground water principles as they create their own geologic cross section or earth window. 65

Hydrologic Primer (A)
Students apply their understanding of basic water science to real-world conservation problems. 31

Ins and Outs of Water Conservation (The)
Concept maps and other assessment tools indicate students' interests, ideas, experiences, and knowledge related to water conservation concepts prior to, during, and following participation in activities and lessons. 23

Irrigation Innovation
Students apply their knowledge of irrigation systems to determine the appropriate method of water application for diverse crops and topography through a simple card game; simulate the four methods of irrigation; and solve an irrigation mystery from the past. 131

Mrs. Alderson: Early Lessons in Water Conservation
Students study water artifacts from the early 1900s and impart a message about water conservation through an interactive play. 101

Pass the Jug
Students simulate and analyze different water rights policies to learn how water availability and people's proximity to the resource influence how water is allocated. 123

Water Audit
Students conduct a home water audit and compare and contrast results with and without the implementation of water conservation practices. 147

Activity Summaries, continued

Case Study Summaries

© The Watercourse

Case Study Summaries, continued

Planning With Vision

Problem With Silt (The)

Shuttle Water

TRP in NYC

Used Up Country

Water Trouble on the High Plains

Activity Format

Grade Level:
Suggests appropriate learning levels; Upper Elementary (3-5), Middle School (6-8), and High School (9-12).

Subject Areas:
Disciplines to which the activity applies.

Duration:
Preparation time: The approximate time needed to prepare for the activity. NOTE: Estimates are based on first-time use. Preparation times for subsequent uses should be less.

Activity time: The approximate time needed to complete the activity.

Setting:
Suggested site.

Skills:
Skills applied in the activity.

Vocabulary:
Significant terms defined in the glossary.

Summary
A brief description of the concepts, skills, and affective dimensions of the activity.

Objectives

The qualities or skills students should possess after participating in the activity. NOTE: Learning objectives, rather than behavioral objectives, were established for *Conserve Water* activities. To measure student achievement, see Assessment.

Materials

Supplies needed to conduct the activity. (Describes how to prepare materials prior to engaging in the activity.)

Background

Relevant information about activity concepts or teaching strategies.

Procedure

Warm Up

Prepares everyone for the activity and introduces concepts to be addressed. Provides the instructor with preassessment strategies.

The Activity

Provides step-by-step directions to address concepts. NOTE: Some activities are organized into "parts." This divides extensive activities into logical segments. All or some of the parts may be used, de-pending on the objectives of instruction. In addition, a few activities provide Options. These consist of alternative methods for conducting the activity.

Wrap Up

Brings closure to the lesson and includes questions and activities to assess student learning.

Assessment

Presents diverse assessment strategies that relate to the objectives of the activity, noting the part of the activity during which each assessment occurs. Ideas for assessment opportunities that follow the activity are often suggested.

Extensions

Provides additional activities for continued investigation into concepts addressed in the activity. Extensions can also be used for further assessment.

Resources

Lists references providing additional background information. NOTE: This is a limited list. Several titles are suggested, but many other resources on similar topics will serve equally well.

A-14 © The Watercourse

Introduction to Water Conservation

The 4 Rs of Water Use
Essay by Dennis Nelson, Executive Director, The Watercourse and Project WET

I watched my grandfather study the cloud-less sky. As he turned to my grandmother, the silent look that passed between them spoke of years of hard work and hope coupled with the uncertainty of weather, pests, and prices. Another month without rain and the crops, their growth already stunted from the lack of moisture, would perish. No rain, no crops, no money to pay the bills. Standing in my grandfather's long shadow, I looked up into his face with boyish faith. My grandfather was a strong man; surely he could make it rain. But as he bent down and scooped up a handful of dry, barren earth, his helplessness showed in the weary slump of his shoulders. I knew then that even my grandfather could not make it rain.

In the face of drought, my grandmother was concerned about the family well. If the well went dry, the family's daily water needs, as well as those of the thirsty livestock, would not be met. During the great depression and the drought of the 1930s, my grandmother had been forced to pack up the family belongings and to look for the last time upon a house that had been transformed by a family's love and energy into a home. Now she looked at the simple, neat farmhouse in which she and grand-father had finally raised their lively brood. Surely, so late in her life, she would not be forced to give up this home too, where so many family memories kept her company.

Fortunately, before the week was up the rains came. I have often looked back and wondered what would have happened if they had not.

I learned many things from my grandparents, among them a great appreciation and respect for water. They used water carefully and wisely; conserving water was not a matter of choice, but of survival. Indeed, water conservation was a way of life.

Water Conservation Basics
An understanding of water use must precede any understanding of water conservation. All living things, wherever they live on earth, need water to survive and flourish. Water is life.

A core belief of The Watercourse and Project WET (Water Education for Teachers) is the importance of water for all water users (i.e., energy producers, farmers and ranchers, fish and wildlife, manufacturers, recreationists, navigators, rural and urban dwellers) and for natural systems. Each water user group needs water to provide a myriad of products. In this context, water "works" for all of us and sustains economies. However, meeting the water needs of all water users, all the time, and under all circumstances—while maintaining natural systems—is a daunting challenge. Still, countries around the world are embracing the task.

The 4 Rs of Water Use
The fact that water is essential for life gives it extraordinary importance. Throughout time, individual organisms have developed unique ways to meet their water needs. The cottonwood seed that lies dormant for years in the parched soil along a river will germinate only when water conditions are right. The mature cottonwood tree that stands strong and tall near the sprouting seed is a testament to the species' ability to survive during times of drought and through challenges presented by diverse environmental factors.

Each water user has specific needs. The concept of the 4 Rs of water use classifies these needs into four general categories: the right amount of water, at the right time, of the right quality, and for the right cost. Indeed, all four of these "rights" or conditions must be met to ensure an organism's survival. The priorities and balance among the four conditions vary as each species adapts to its habitat and the prevailing conditions. An imbalance in any one of the 4 Rs must precipitate an action or death may occur.

The Right Amount

Each species requires a specific minimum amount of water to survive. Humans need roughly eight glasses of water per day. A kangaroo rat feeds only on dry seeds to meet its water needs; the rat metabolizes proteins and fats in a manner that provides all the fresh water it requires. An elephant consumes large amounts of water to meet its needs. Although the quantities are vastly different, the human, the kangaroo rat, and the elephant must each consume the right amount of water in order to survive.

The Right Time

To ensure the survival and procreation of plants and animals, water must be available at the right time. People generally consume water based on thirst. Nutritionists have set the minimum amount of water required to keep most people hydrated at eight glasses per day. The timing is critical; if the duration of consumption expands to eight glasses every three days, the individual may eventually suffer the effects of dehydration.

In some cases, an organism's growth or reproduction may be severely affected by a lack of water at the right time; in other cases, an organism may not achieve life until water is available. With the addition of water, a dry, dormant area may erupt with plant and animal life. Temporary wetlands usually appear during the wet season, then dry up again later in the year.

In some places, such wetlands appear in the spring and are called vernal pools. Where do all the grasses, mosquitoes, and frogs, come from? Buried in the soil, many wait for the essential ingredient that allows them to become active—water! These temporary wetlands teem with frogs, toads, salamanders, fairy shrimp, and microorganisms—a whole world of life.

The Right Quality

Water quality is an important aspect of meeting water needs. Water quality requirements vary from species to species. The quality of water suited for human consumption in the United States is set by the U.S. Environmental Protection Agency, state Natural Resources Management Agencies, and local health authorities. Humans have the technology to clean water before distributing it for consumption. But not all people have the luxury of simply turning on a tap to receive clean drinking water. Some people live in areas where water is not piped into their homes. Daily, these individuals carry their drinking water from the nearest available source. In other cases, humans live in areas where the water that is piped into their homes is not treated first to remove pollutants or other substances. Untreated water may carry disease-causing bacteria, chemicals, or heavy metals, all of which can pose serious health risks.

Most plants and animals use water directly from its source within their environment. Water that contains a healthy balance of dissolved oxygen and nutrients—and few contaminants—can support abundant and diverse aquatic life, including algae, microscopic organisms, and macroinvertebrates. These organisms form the cornerstone of the aquatic food chain: the algae produces food from the sun's energy and the macroinvertebrates feed on the algae. Larger animals, such as fish, feed on the macroinvertebrates and are in turn preyed upon by birds and mammals. When water becomes polluted, for example through sediment, abrupt

temperature changes, or direct human intervention, the healthy balance of oxygen and nutrients is altered, threatening the survival of some aquatic life. Often the diversity and abundance of organisms decreases when water becomes polluted. In some cases, pollution-tolerant organisms, such as snails and leeches, come to dominate these altered waters. They out-compete other species, posing a serious threat to the survival of the original inhabitants. When altered conditions prevail, organisms at the top of the food chain must often seek new habitats where the water is of sufficient quality to support a diversity of aquatic life.

The Right Cost

The cost of obtaining water may be measured in terms of economics and energy consumption. All living organisms exert energy to secure and consume water. When the water conditions in a given environment change, an organism's energy expenditure may also have to change, sometimes to an extreme degree. Severe drought conditions cause many animals to migrate, a journey that "costs" energy. If a plant is water stressed, it closes its stomata to conserve moisture. But the plant receives carbon dioxide through its stomata, and if the plant is not taking in carbon dioxide, photosynthesis is limited and plant growth slows. For humans, a change in the water quality of rural or urban systems may necessitate increased treatment costs.

Humans are particularly ingenious in their efforts to ensure that they have water. In some areas of the United States, extensive rural water systems have been constructed to deliver reliable supplies of high quality water to rural water users. Although the cost of building such a system is high, the benefits of bringing this precious resource to a water-stressed area outweigh the costs.

The 4 Rs bring water use and the concept of water conservation to an individual level. Each species is a water manager, uniquely altering its behavior and biology to meet its water needs. A beaver will build a dam across a river to create a pool of water. If the stream dries up, the pool of water will sustain the beaver. If the pool dries up, the beaver will search until it finds the water it needs.

The Rationale for Water Conservation

The decision to conserve water is sometimes made by an individual water user. A homeowner who wants to reduce her monthly water bill reduces water use. Often the impetus to conserve water comes from external sources. A drought or a sudden increase in population can motivate a municipal water department to implement the city's water conservation plan. These are common and compelling reasons why people conserve water. Regardless of the prompting, the wise or efficient use of water resources makes sense. However, this knowledge alone does not ensure that individuals or organizations will take action.

The idea of conserving water and still meeting your water needs may seem simple, but in reality, it is not! Using less water to satisfy the needs of an individual, a family, a farm, an industrial plant, a city, an irrigation district, or a region doesn't happen by chance. Conserving water resources requires considerable discipline, thought, planning, and, ultimately, action. It may necessitate a new way of thinking and operating. It may involve financial investment in new and improved water-saving equipment and/or research and development in crops that are more drought tolerant.

During the twentieth century, the world population tripled, while water use for human purposes multiplied sixfold. Although our basic need for water is the same today as it was in the past, the way water is located, collected, distributed, and used has changed drastically.

It is not a coincidence that many Native American tribes and early settlers lived near reliable water sources like springs, rivers, and lakes. Not only did these locations supply water for drinking and other domestic uses—they also provided essential habitat for fish and wildlife. The Native Americans and early settlers knew they could not afford to live great distances from year-round water sources. They expended neither the energy nor the time to procure long-distance water. The discovery of ground water as another reliable source of water allowed settlers to live farther from surface water sources.

In most modern societies, water is available with the turn of a tap. However, in North America less than 100 years ago, many people had to pump and haul water for washing, cooking, bathing, and other needs. Imagine how differently we might feel about water if we had to pump and carry it by hand. Today the average household consumes an estimated 200 gallons (760 l) of water per day. Water weighs about eight pounds per gallon. The idea of hauling 1,600 pounds of water every day may give you a new appreciation for the people who conceived and built your water system.

Today, many major cities are located far from water sources. Through elaborate water collection and distribution systems, they have become thriving metropolitan areas and centers of commerce. The fruits and vegetables city-dwellers enjoy often come from distant farms and orchards that irrigate with water collected and distributed from even farther away.

Climate, geography, economics, access to technology, population growth, water management laws and policies—all can affect the availability of water. Overall, meeting the needs of all water users is an ongoing challenge. How many people have thought about water conservation?

Ask a water department superintendent if her agency has a plan for conserving water during a looming shortage, and you will likely be over-whelmed with information, issues, and options. The water department's number one goal is to meet the water needs of its constituents. The mayor of a city does not want to tell a potential new business that in a few years the city's water supply may not be able to meet the needs of new enterprises.

Ask 100 homeowners in a new subdivision if they are willing to use less water and you will likely get 100 different responses. Ask your family to conserve water and you will need to answer some very practical questions: Who says we need to conserve water? Why do we need to conserve water? How can we conserve water? How much will it cost? Will it really matter if I use less water? Who is keeping track? These are legitimate questions and the answers will vary from family to family, city to city, and region to region. The idea of water conservation becomes reality when you, your family, or your business are asked to take action and reduce water use.

Ask an irrigation district board of directors about water conservation and if the district has a water conservation plan. You will learn about settlement, surface or ground water hydrology, soils, crop science, irrigation technology, law, economics, and water management. The district's number one goal is to consistently meet the water needs of the district members. This is not an easy task during water shortages or if new water needs arise from external sources. Ask an individual farmer living in the district to conserve water and you will be asked some familiar questions. Who says we need to conserve water? Why do we need to conserve water? How can we conserve water? How much will it cost? Will it really matter if I use less water? Who is keeping track? The farmer knows that if the water needs of his crops are not met, revenue will be less. And if every farmer suffers a loss of revenue, the local economy may be impacted.

Ask the director of a state game and fish agency about water conservation. If he is from a region of the United States that periodically faces low flow conditions in popular fishing rivers and lakes, you will learn about hydrology, fish and habitat needs, and the value of outdoor recreation to the state's economy. The agency's number one priority is to make sure the fish have sufficient clean water to survive.

This line of thinking could be applied to the navigation industry, a business or manufacturing plant, an energy producer, a nature preserve, or a rancher. Many people have considered water conservation and many others have not. The bottom line is that water is critically important to all water users.

The Future

There is little doubt that water will continue to be of critical importance. We will need to devote more and more effort in order to meet the needs of all water users worldwide. In March 2000, the World Water Congress met in Australia and the World Water Forum met in The Netherlands to discuss global water issues. Participants discussed the growth of "mega" cities in regions of the world with limited fresh water supplies and shared ideas about how to use water more efficiently, drawing upon technologies of the future and simple, but effective traditions from the past.

The question now becomes: how can people think globally when their individual water needs must be met first? Negotiating the resources of rivers that flow through countries of diverse cultures and needs will require high levels of diplomacy. We will need to configure creative watershed partnerships that address the critical water needs of downstream users. The concept of being a good water neighbor takes on new meaning in a watershed of multiple countries and languages. How do we connect people and their water needs through cooperative processes?

Education will play a pivotal role in helping families and communities satisfy their water needs through peaceful and productive technologies and traditions throughout the world. We will have to focus particular attention on transferring information and technology to people with the most pressing needs. Investing in solutions that are economically feasible, practical, and relevant to a myriad of water situations is key to resolving water issues. The problems may be global, but the solutions must work within the sphere of the local community, business, or family unit within a megacity or a small village.

As we look to the future, we cannot forget the voices from the past. My grandparents showed me our dependence on water and taught me to appreciate and respect this valuable resource. The choice to conserve our water resources must be built on respect—for our ancestors, for our children, for ourselves, and ultimately, for the planet.

Conserve Water

Activities

First Things First

What Do We Know About Water Conservation?

The Ins & Outs of Water Conservation

Grade Level:
Middle School, High School

Subject Areas:
All

Duration:
Preparation time: depends on activity

Activity time: depends on activity

Setting:
Depends on activity

Skills:
Depends on activity

Vocabulary:
pre-assessment, concept map

Summary
Concept maps and other assessment tools indicate students' interests, ideas, experiences, and knowledge related to water conservation concepts prior to, during, and following participation in activities and lessons.

Objectives
Students will:
· contribute to and generate classroom concept maps to assess their knowledge, skills, and attitudes (and connections with the knowledge, skills, and attitudes of others) before, during, and after participation in activities and lessons concerning water conservation.
· analyze *Water Surveys* to determine if they experience any changes in attitude or behaviors related to water conservation practices after participating in lessons and activities.

Materials
Option 1
· index cards (3 per student)
· markers
· masking tape
· large sheets of flip chart paper or butcher paper
Option 2
· large sheet of paper (1 per classroom)
· markers (at least three different bold colors)
Option 3
· *Water Survey* Student Copy Page (2 copies per student)

Background
Learning is an interconnected, interdependent, and ordered process. Assessing students' prior knowledge or preconceptions is a vital component of effective teaching. Students' preconceptions may be accurate and facilitate learning, or they may be misconceptions that can impede learning. Students' prior knowledge related to water conservation can be used to plan activities and to make concepts more relevant to the learner. Teachers introducing new concepts or nonformal educators who are contacting students for the first time need to assess the class's level of understanding of the topic to be presented. The lessons and activities of *Conserve Water* include a variety of pre-assessment strategies, allowing teachers to determine what students know and think about water conservation before introducing a new aspect of the topic.

Procedure
Warm Up
The *Warm Up* section of each *Conserve Water* activity includes suggested methods for assessing what students

currently think and feel about the forthcoming water-related concepts. These approaches include the following: asking students thought-provoking questions; having students create diagrams to illustrate their perceptions; providing students with a demonstration and encouraging discussion.

These strategies can help educators determine if students already have an understanding of the topic. If they do, further study may not be necessary, or the activity could be conducted for reinforcement. On the other hand, students may have limited information and may require additional instruction prior to the activity.

The Activity
Option 1
"Concept Maps are drawings or diagrams showing the mental connections that students make between a major concept the instructor focuses on and other concepts they have learned." *Classroom Assessment Techniques* by Thomas A. Angelo and K. Patricia Cross

1. Inform students that they will be involved in lessons and activities related to water conservation. Give each student three index cards and ask him or her to write or draw one idea related to water conservation on each card. Students should limit their writing to a few words or a single sentence.

2. Ask a student to describe or read aloud one of his or her cards. Ask the class if anyone has a similar description. Collect related cards and tape them in a group on the wall. Repeat the procedure and continue forming groups until all the cards are posted. The number of groups generated will depend on the size of the class.

3. Draw or tape a circle around each group and ask students to suggest a title that describes the common element among the cards in a group. Write this on a card and attach it to the surrounding circle. Explain that each group is a separate "idea pool" (a collection of related ideas, topics, or concepts). Students may note overlaps among pools.

4. Have students describe the links among pools. Record these links on the map. Discuss the network of idea pools.

5. Challenge groups of students to create a story or write a paragraph using all of the idea pools. Encourage them to present their story using a variety of techniques, such as role-playing, storytelling, or pantomime.

6. Ask students to evaluate their stories or presentations. What information did they feel confident in using? What connections seemed weak? Have them identify what they think is factual information about water conservation and note topics that they would like to

learn more about.

Option 2
"An ideal use of this technique [concept maps] is to employ it before, during, and after lessons on critical concepts." Angelo and Cross

1. Another method for creating a classroom concept map is to write the topic in the center of a large sheet of paper posted in front of the group.

2. Ask students to contribute any words or ideas they associate with this concept. Request that they link ideas by drawing lines between them. They can often add verbs to the lines to clarify relationships among their thoughts.

3. Record the initial words or ideas in one distinct color. During a unit on water conservation, assess changes in student knowledge and attitudes by inviting them to contribute to the map again. Record student responses in a color different from the one used in the initial session. Create a key to show the relationship of the color to the order of sessions (such as blue before, green during, and red following instruction).

4. After the final lesson or activity, ask students to contribute to the concept map and to draw connections among ideas. Point out to students how the different colors demonstrate the growth of their ideas and understanding about water conservation.

Moving from idea to idea, discuss with students why their attitudes may have changed over time. Was there any relationship between their growth in knowledge and understanding and their change in attitude and behavior?

Option 3

1. Before teaching activities and lessons from *Conserve Water*, distribute the *Water Survey* to students. This sample survey is a list of behaviors related to water conservation. Add or delete questions to tailor it for your specific use.
2. Ask students to complete the survey, then collect it.
3. In order to assess changes in behavior related to water conservation, after completing a number of activities, lessons, and supplementary case studies, distribute the survey again.
4. After students have completed the form a second time, hand back their original survey. Have them compare and contrast their responses on the two surveys.
5. Ask them if there were any changes in their behavior related to water conservation. What do they believe contributed to the changes?
6. It may be interesting to tabulate the changes for the entire class and see if there were any trends. It may be possible to assign this task to one or two students. To protect students' anonymity, forms could be numbered and a key retained to match student names and numbers.

Wrap Up

The *Wrap Up* of *Conserve Water* activities is used to bring closure to activities; however, it can also confirm acquisition of knowledge. One approach is to compare students' responses in the *Wrap Up* to similar questions found in the *Warm Up*. Further, in all activities, each objective is matched with an assessment.

Assessment

Have students:
· present what they currently know about water conservation in the form of concept maps (**Option 1**, steps 1-4)
· contribute to a classroom concept map before, during, and after instruction to indicate their acquisition of knowledge and changes in attitude and behavior (**Option 2**, steps 2-4)
· have students complete a Water Survey before and after instruction to assess changes in attitude and behavior related to the conservation of water resources. (**Option 3**, steps 1–4)

Extensions

Teachers may wish to review the publication *Classroom Assessment Techniques* written by Thomas A. Angelo and K. Patricia Cross. This resource offers fifty classroom assessment techniques. Most of these techniques can be modified to assess changes in student knowledge, interests, attitudes, and behavior related to water conservation. By understanding what students are learning and how well they are learning it, educators can modify the teaching process to accommodate the needs and interests of the learners. As you find ways to modify the activities, if you would be willing to share with other educators, please send your changes to: The Watercourse (Attention: *Conserve Water*) 201 Culbertson Hall, Montana State University, Bozeman, Montana 59717-0570.

Resources

Angelo, Thomas A., and K. Patricia Cross. 1993. *Classroom Assessment Techniques.* San Francisco: Jossey-Bass Publishers.

Biehler, Robert F., and Jack Snowman. 1986. *Psychology Applied to Teaching*, 5th ed. Boston: Houghton Mifflin Company.

Gagne, Ellen D. 1985. *The Cognitive Psychology of School Learning.* Boston: Little, Brown & Company.

Novak, J. D., and D. Bob Gowin. 1986. *Learning How to Learn.* New York: Cambridge University Press.

Novak, Joseph. 1991. "Clarify with Concept Maps, a Tool for Students and Teachers Alike."

The Science Teacher. 58 (7): 45—49.

Saunders, Walter L. 1992. "The Constructivist Perspective: Implications and Teaching Strategies for Science." *School Science and Mathematics* 92 (3): 136–141.

Water Conservation Concept Map (Example)

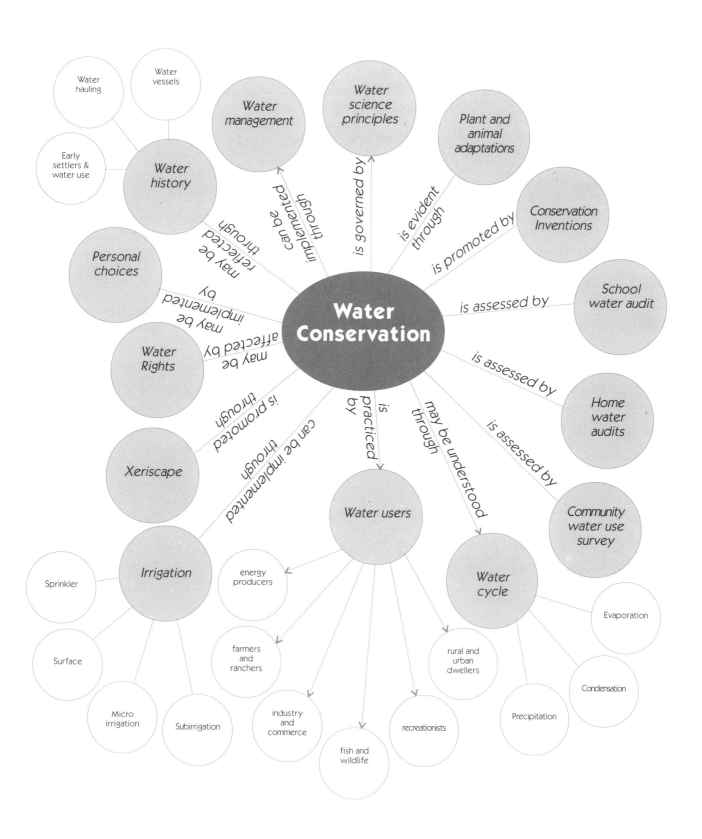

The Ins & Outs of Water Conservation
Water Survey

Directions

Following is a list of water-related behaviors. Record your responses based on what activities you currently participate in. Do not respond based on what you think you should probably do or what others tell you to do. Please indicate yes, no, don't know (?) or N/A. If you place a check under the column N/A, it means "this does not apply to me." There are no right or wrong answers. You will not be graded on this.

	Yes	No	(?)	N/A
While brushing my teeth, I turn the water off and on as needed.	___	___	___	___
I limit the length of my showers so they are three to five minutes.	___	___	___	___
When washing my hands, I turn the water off and on as needed.	___	___	___	___
I wash my clothes when there is a full load of laundry.	___	___	___	___
I run the dishwasher when there is a full load of dishes.	___	___	___	___
I turn the hose off and on as needed while I wash the car.	___	___	___	___
When asked to clean the sidewalk, I sweep it instead of hosing it down.	___	___	___	___
When asked to water the lawn, I do it when I can, at any time of day.	___	___	___	___
When changing the oil in my car or my family's car, I take the dirty oil to a disposal center.	___	___	___	___
When washing dishes in the sink, I allow the water to run so it is easy to rinse them.	___	___	___	___
When I want a glass of water, I let the water run so it will get cold.	___	___	___	___
If I saw a leaking water pipe in my community, I would report it to my parents or the appropriate authority.	___	___	___	___
If there was an oil leak from my (or my family's) car, I would get it fixed as soon as possible.	___	___	___	___
I encourage my family to install water-saving devices (such as water-saving shower heads) in the bathroom and kitchen.	___	___	___	___
I keep a bottle of drinking water in the refrigerator so I don't need to run the water from the faucet to get it cold.	___	___	___	___
I would help my school design and change the school grounds into a water-conservative landscape.	___	___	___	___

Fixed, Finite & Fickle

Water Science and Hydrology

A Hydrologic Primer

Grade Level:
Middle School

Subject Areas:
Earth Science and
Environmental Science

Duration:
Preparation time:
   Part I: 10 minutes
   Part II: 15 minutes

Activity time:
   Part I: 50 minutes
   Part II: 50 minutes (25
   minutes more if lab is
   conducted)

Setting:
Classroom

Skills:
Gather, Organize, Analyze,
Interpret, Apply, Evaluate,
Present

Vocabulary:
hydrogen bonding,
evaporation, condensation,
transpiration, density,
adhesion, cohesion,
Xeriscape, reservoir,
osmosis, reverse osmosis,
desalinization

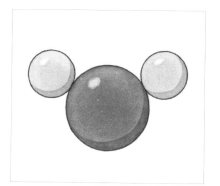

Water molecule.

Summary
Students apply their understanding of basic water science to real-world conservation problems.

Objectives
Students will:
· demonstrate water science principles.
· apply principles to real-world conservation problems.

Materials
· 1 set of *Water Conservation Challenges* Student Copy Pages (1 challenge per group)
· simple lab equipment (depends upon student investigation) (optional)

Background:
In order to comprehend water conservation and related issues, it is important to have an understanding of the basic characteristics of water. Following is a primer of hydrologic principles organized by topic.

The Water Molecule
Water is made up of molecules. Each water molecule contains two hydrogen atoms and one oxygen atom. This is indicated by the formula H_2O. Hydrogen bonding is a weak attraction between water molecules. When water is in the vapor state, the molecules are separate and independent. In the liquid state, the weak attraction between water molecules—hydrogen bonding—provides the properties of liquid water. In the solid state or ice, hydrogen bonding firmly holds the molecules in a six-sided lattice pattern.

States of Water
Molecules constantly move. Heat energy contributes to the motion of molecules. The motion of molecules determines the state of water. In the gaseous state (water vapor), water molecules have a large amount of heat energy and move rapidly. The molecules in liquid water move more slowly. In ice, the molecules contain the least amount of heat energy, so their movement is even slower.

Water changes from one state to another when heat energy is added or lost. Heat travels from areas of high temperature (rapidly moving molecules) to low temperature (slower-moving molecules). For example, ice melts in your hand because the heat from your body transfers to the colder material. Sometimes when molecules near the surface of liquid water move very rapidly, they break away or evaporate, becoming water vapor. Eventually water vapor will lose energy and return to liquid form; steam condensing on a cold bathroom mirror is an example of this.

Hydrogen Bonding

Water molecules have poles; like magnets, one end has a negative charge and the other has a positive charge. The positive end of one molecule is attracted to the negative end of another molecule. When the molecules stay in contact with each other, a bond—called a hydrogen bond—forms between the two molecules. The structure and nature of the water molecule give it various properties that are critical to life. Examples follow.

1. **Water dissolves a number of substances**. More things dissolve in water than in any other substance. Compounds such as sugar that are also polar dissolve easily in water. If water could not dissolve sugar, sugar molecules could not travel through our blood to our cells. However, some materials like oils and fats are not charged (nonpolar). These do not dissolve or mix in water because hydrogen bonds do not form. Cells within our body are made of fatty substances. If fat and oil dissolved in water, we would all end up like mush!

2. **Water cools as it evaporates**. Water is constantly evaporating from the surface of our skin, as it does from the skin of other animals. If it didn't, the body, which constantly produces energy, would overheat. Water in the body is heated by the metabolism of digested nutrients.

Sweat glands excrete the heated water to the skin's surface. Because the water molecules contain heat energy, they move quickly, making it difficult for them to form hydrogen bonds. Individual water molecules break away or evaporate, becoming gas molecules. Gas molecules take heat energy with them, leaving behind the slower moving molecules that make the body feel cooler.

3. **Water expands when it freezes**. One might expect the slower moving molecules of frozen water to be closer together than liquid water molecules; however, in ice, water molecules are actually farther apart from each other than they are in liquid form. Hydrogen bonds easily form when water molecules have little heat energy and are moving slowly. The strong hydrogen bonds force water molecules into a pattern, holding them apart from each other. This is important for life on earth. If ice were denser than water, ponds would freeze from the bottom up and plant and animal life would be affected each winter. A physical demonstration of freezing water's effects is the fracturing of rocks by water. Water that seeps into the fissures of rocks may freeze and melt as often as 70 times a year in some regions. Freezing water expands and exerts a force of about 30,000 pounds per square inch

on the surrounding rock.

Density

One difference among the three states of water is density—how close water molecules are to each other. The amount of particles (mass) within a certain space (volume) determines the density of a substance. Water vapor is the least dense of water states because the molecules are farthest apart from each other. What factors affect the density of water?

1. **Heating and cooling water affect the density of water**. Heating water speeds up the movement of water molecules. As they move faster, the molecules bounce off each other more frequently and move farther apart, decreasing the molecular density. When their movement is increased, water molecules are less able to stay near each other. Therefore, warm water is less dense than cold water. As water cools, the molecules lose heat energy and move more slowly. This allows the water molecules to move closer together, making the water more dense. Therefore, cold water sinks and warm water rises.

2. **Adding certain materials to water such as salt increases its density**. If salt is added to fresh water, the amount of material within the space the water occupies increases. Whereas only water molecules previously

Three States of Water

Gas

Note: When water evaporates, it becomes a gas you cannot see.

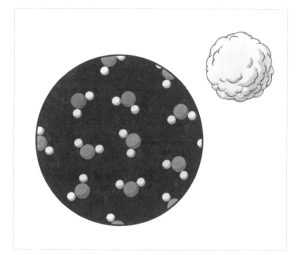

Liquid

Solid

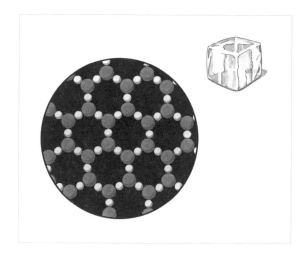

consumed space, now salt molecules are crowded into the same space. This makes salt water denser than fresh water.

3. **Pressure increases the density of water**. Deep water has greater pressure than surface water because the weight of the water molecules above pushes down on the deeper molecules, forcing them closer together and making deeper water denser.

Adhesion and Cohesion

Because of its polar nature, a water molecule is attracted to other water molecules and also to molecules of other substances. The attraction between water molecules is called cohesion and the attraction of water molecules to other materials like glass or soil, is called adhesion. Without these characteristics, plants could not get water (capillary action) and blood would have difficulty traveling through the body.

Evidence of water's attraction to itself can be seen by simply looking at its surface. If a glass is filled to the brim and more water is added gently, the level of the water will exceed the top of the glass. The cohesive force between water molecules causes the water surface to behave as though it is a thinly stretched membrane that is always trying to contract. This phenomenon is called **surface tension**. In many ways, surface tension is like water's "skin."

The same forces that cause water molecules to be attracted to each other cause them to adhere to other substances. If this didn't happen, water would slide off everything like water off a duck's back. Water appears to defy gravity as it moves up a paper towel, through spaces among soil particles, or along a piece of yarn at an angle to the ground. This is called **capillary action**; it results from water molecules being attracted to the molecules of the towel, soil, or yarn and to each other. However, the molecules can only travel so far before the force of gravity overcomes the force of the attraction.

Evaporation, Condensation, and Transpiration: The Water Cycle

Evaporation, condensation, and transpiration are the all-important processes that move water through the water cycle. Evaporation is the conversion of a liquid (specifically water) into a vapor (a gaseous state), usually through the application of heat energy. Water may evaporate from the ocean, a river, a reservoir, or a glacier. The opposite of evaporation is condensation: the process by which a vapor becomes a liquid. Clouds form when water vapor in the atmosphere condenses into tiny ice crystals or water droplets. When droplets

or crystals merge, they become larger and heavier, and gravity pulls them to the ground. Because the upper atmosphere is so cold, precipitation usually starts as snow and melts to rain as it falls nearer Earth's warm surface.

The processes of evaporation and condensation result in a form of natural water purification. When water evaporates, salts and other solids that may be dissolved in the liquid are left behind. (Scientists involved in laboratory work produce chemically pure water through distillation, the process of boiling water and recondensing the vapor.) Only the water molecules leave the surface of the liquid water. Therefore, when this water condenses, it is purified. However, rain water is not necessarily pure. As condensed water falls through the air it may pick up pollutants. (An example is acidic precipitation, which occurs when certain chemicals mix with atmospheric water and form sulfuric acid and nitric acid.)

Transpiration is the evaporation of water from pores, or stomata, on trunk, stem, and leaf surfaces. Transpiration helps plants transport water upward through their tissues. Root pressure, the cohesive and adhesive qualities of water (capillary action), and evaporation all contribute to water's circulation through a plant.

However, the plant's loss of water through the stomata can be dramatic. For example, a field of corn in a single growing season may transpire "an equivalent of a field-sized layer of water 17 inches (43 cm) deep." (*Environmental Science, The Way the World Works*) In contrast, some plants are characteristically frugal water users. They generally have smaller leaves, deeper root systems, thick waxy surfaces, or other qualities that limit water loss.

Procedure
Warm Up
Tell students that they are going to role-play the three states of water. Explain how water is made up of molecules and that the molecules constantly move. Ask students what contributes to the motion of molecules (heat energy). Request six volunteers to come to the front of the room. Tell the class that you

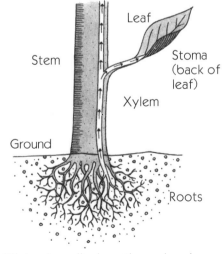

Water is pulled up the xylem by the process of transpiration.

are changing the six students into single water molecules. Assemble the six volunteers into a huddle, and ask them to spread out and move vigorously as they are role-playing water as a gas. In the form of a gas, water molecules are separate and independent. Ask the rest of the class to guess what state of water the volunteers are demonstrating.

Reassemble the volunteers and ask them to hold on to the back of someone's shirt (to simulate hydrogen bonding) and to move more slowly. Request that they move from person to person, holding and then releasing the back of each shirt. Again ask the class to indicate what state of water is being demonstrated. This represents the liquid state of water in which hydrogen bonds keep breaking and reforming among different molecules.

Now ask the volunteers to clump together and move very slowly. The class will likely guess "ice," an incorrect answer. If water molecules continued to move proportionately closer together in the transition from gas to liquid to ice, life as we know it would not exist on Earth. If this configuration were correct, then ice would be more dense than liquid water. What would this mean? Ice cubes would sink to the bottom of a glass and ponds in winter would freeze

from the bottom up.

Water molecules in ice are moving so slowly that strong hydrogen bonds are able to form. These strong bonds actually force the molecules apart into a six-sided lattice pattern. This configuration causes ice to be less dense than water—a property that is fundamental to life on earth.

The Activity
Part I
1.   Organize students into small cooperative learning groups.
2.   Distribute one challenge card from the Student Copy Page, *Water Conservation Challenges* to each group.
3.   Ask students to study the definition of the scientific principle on their card and to do

additional research if necessary in order to understand the concept.
4.   Request that students design a one-minute skit that illustrates the concept for the rest of the class. (Remind them of the *Warm Up*.)
5.   Have students perform their skits for the class.
6.   At the conclusion of each skit, briefly discuss the principle the students have enacted.

Part II
1.   Have students remain in their original cooperative learning groups.
2.   Refer each group to the challenge on their card and have students design an investigation that connects the scientific principle with the real-world problem described in the challenge.

Water Cycle

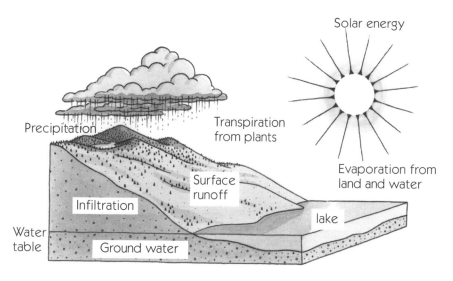

3. After the students design their investigations, if you have access to the appropriate equipment, have them conduct their research. Be sure you have approved their design before they begin working in the lab or classroom. (Most of these investigations can be designed to use materials readily available in a classroom or kitchen.)

4. After students have designed and, if appropriate, conducted their investigations and believe they have answered the challenges, have them share their research and its application with the rest of the class.

Wrap Up

After all groups have had an opportunity to present their findings, discuss the following questions with students. Do students believe it is necessary to understand the basics of water science when trying to solve real-world problems? What may be the consequences of not understanding the science? Did students learn new ideas that may contribute to solving water resource management problems?

Assessment

Have students:
· design and present skits to demonstrate basic water principles (**Part I**, steps 3—5).
· design a lab or field experiment to demonstrate basic water-science principles (**Part II**, step 2).

· conduct the approved lab or field experiment (**Part II**, step 3).
· present the results of their work to the class (**Part II**, step 4).
· relate their investigations to the real-world water conservation challenge they were assigned (**Part II**, step 4).

Extensions

Have students research whether any of the practices discussed in this activity are used in their own communities such as water conservation landscaping or Xeriscaping, reverse osmosis, or desalinization. Ask students to discuss how effective these practices have been in solving water quantity and quality issues.

Resources:

Doran, Rodney. 1998. *Science Educator's Guide to Assessment.* Arlington, Va.: National Science Teachers Association.

Niebel, Bernard J., and Richard T. Wright. 1996. *Environmental Science, The Way the World Works.* Upper Saddle River, New Jersey: Prentice Hall.

Simon, Paul. 1998. *Tapped Out.* New York: Welcome Rain.

The Watercourse. 1999. *Project WET Curriculum and Activity Guide.* Bozeman, Mont.: The Watercourse.

Water in the West: Challenge for the Next Century. 1998. Springfield, Va.: National Technical Information Service. Copies of this publication may be obtained from the National Technical Information Service, 5285 Port Royal Road, Springfield, VA, 22161.
Tel. 703-487-4650

Desalinization by means of distillation. ▼

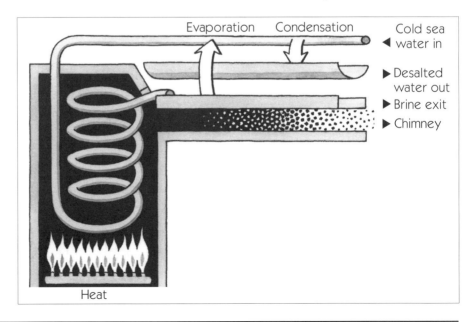

Water Conservation Challenges

#1

Transpiration is the evaporation of water from pores, or stomata, on trunk, stem, and leaf surfaces. Transpiration helps plants transport water upward through their tissues. Root pressure, the cohesive and adhesive qualities of water (capillary action), and evaporation all contribute to water's circulation through a plant.

Plants can absorb large quantities of water; however, they lose most of this water through transpiration. Transpiration coupled with evaporation of surface water is called evapotranspiration. Evapotranspiration returns water to its gaseous state, in which it can be carried by winds through the atmosphere until it condenses and returns to Earth as precipitation.

The rate of transpiration from plants depends on diverse factors such as humidity and the nature of the plants. Some plants require less water to survive than others. Frugal water users may have smaller leaves, deeper root systems, thick waxy surfaces, and other qualities that limit water loss.

* * *

You are a landscape architect in a water-scarce area. You landscape areas around homes, hospitals, industrial complexes, and schools. How could an understanding of transpiration and evapotranspiration be useful to you?

Challenge

· Design an investigation to compare the characteristics of plants that require a lot of water to survive with the characteristics of those that are frugal water users.

(The following questions may require additional research on the topic of Xeriscaping or water-conserving landscaping.)
· If your clients wanted to conserve water and wanted their yard landscaped, how would a knowledge of drought-tolerant plants and native plants be useful? (Almost any plant can be a Xeriscape plant if it is placed where it can thrive in the landscape. Therefore, what type of plants would you place in a sunny, dry area or in a depressed, wet area of the landscape? Native plants have evolved with the climate and rainfall distribution of the area. Why would it be important to consider the use of native plants in water-conserving landscaping?)
· How would a knowledge of groundcover and mulch be useful? (Think about surface evaporation.)
· What other characteristics of plants would you have to take into consideration if you were landscaping a home or school? (Think about safety, maintenance, and so forth.)
· Do you think all of your clients would agree to water conserving landscaping? What would affect their attitudes about Xeriscaping? What strategies would you use to help educate a client about this type of landscaping?

Water Conservation Challenges, continued

#2

Evaporation is the conversion of a liquid (specifically water) into a vapor (a gaseous state), usually through the application of heat energy.

* * *

Imagine that you are responsible for managing a reservoir. A reservoir is a human-made body of fresh water, often created by damming a river. Reservoirs are constructed to capture, store, and release water in a controlled manner. There are two major kinds of reservoirs. Flood detention reservoirs are built only to control floods. Multipurpose storage reservoirs are built not only for flood control, but for many other purposes as well: municipal and agricultural water supply, recreation, downstream fisheries management, hydroelectric power production, and release flows for navigation. As a reservoir manager, why would you find knowledge of evaporation useful?

Challenge

· Design an investigation to demonstrate water loss through evaporation.
· If you are responsible for maintaining sufficient water in the reservoir to satisfy the needs of urban and downstream water users, but also for enabling the reservoir to accommodate floodwaters, do you need to be concerned with the rate of evaporation?
· Can anything be done to reduce the rate of water loss through evaporation?
· Think of how you use water in the area outside your home (i.e., lawn, garden). Are there things that you can do to reduce the loss of water through evaporation?

Water Conservation Challenges, continued

#3

Clouds form when water vapor in the atmosphere condenses into tiny ice crystals or water droplets. When droplets or crystals merge, they become larger and heavier, and gravity pulls them to the ground. Because the upper atmosphere is so cold, precipitation usually starts out as snow and melts to rain as it falls nearer Earth's warm surface.

* * *

If you were responsible for allocating water in the West, why would the variability of precipitation be a problem? It is your responsibility to let farmers and others know how much water they will receive each year. You monitor rainfall and measure snowpack in early winter to predict the amount of moisture that will be available for water users like farmers in the spring. In October and November, the precipitation is average. In December and January, a series of massive storms hits. You have to release water from the reservoir to maintain safe flood storage space. You know that if the precipitation is average for the remainder of the spring, the yearly totals will approach record high levels. In February, you tell farmers and other water users that they will get 100 percentof their allocation. In April, however, you announce that water users will only get 90 percent of their allotment. Farmers have already purchased seed, fertilizer, and other materials based on what you told them in February. Why are the farmers upset? And what happened? Why were you forced to reduce the allocation?

Challenge

· Design an investigation to measure precipitation and develop a means to record it for a significant period of time such as one year. Why is it important to have historical records of snowpack and precipitation? Compare your investigation to the methods that meteorologists currently use to measure precipitation.
· Why is precipitation such a critical factor in water resource planning, especially in the West?
· How could water conservation measures be helpful for communities that receive variable precipitation?

Water Conservation Challenges, continued

#4

Osmosis is a physiological process in which substances enter and leave cells across a semipermeable membrane. When a semipermeable membrane separates two water volumes, water will move from the side of low solute concentration to the side of high solute concentration. Imagine two volumes of water separated by a semipermeable membrane, one containing a large amount of dissolved salt, the other containing little or no salt. The water containing little or no salt will move through the membrane to the side containing a large concentration of salt.

However, if pressure is applied to the volume of water containing a high concentration of salt, water will move from the more-concentrated to the less-concentrated side. This process is called reverse osmosis.

* * *

You are a water planner in a coastal community. Over the last ten years, the community has experienced a tremendous increase in population. You predict that in five years, if the population continues to grow at the current rate and no changes occur in existing water supplies, the population will exceed its water supply. You can institute water conservation measures; in addition, how could the knowledge of reverse osmosis help solve your community's water shortage problems? Remember that as a coastal city, you have access to great quantities of salt water.

Challenge

· Design an investigation to demonstrate osmosis.
· Discuss how reverse osmosis works.
· How could reverse osmosis help coastal communities to increase their fresh water supply?
· What might be the drawbacks to using reverse osmosis? (Think of cost, disposal of waste products, etc.)
· If a community built a reverse osmosis system, would it still be necessary to use water conservation measures?
· Are you aware of communities that use reverse osmosis to help supply fresh drinking water?

Water Conservation Challenges, continued

#5

The paths water takes as it moves through its various states—solid, liquid, and gas—and travels throughout Earth's systems (oceans, atmosphere, ground water, streams, etc.) is the water cycle. This continual movement of water collects, purifies, and distributes water around the world.

The processes of evaporation and condensation result in a form of natural water purification. When water evaporates, any salts and/or solids that may be dissolved in the liquid are left behind. Only the water molecules leave the surface of the liquid water. Therefore, when this water condenses, it is purified.

* * *

You are a water manager in a coastal area with an increasing population. The main industry of your community is tourism. Your community is exploring options to increase their water supplies. How would knowledge of the hydrologic cycle (the water cycle) assist you in designing sea water desalting (desalinization) systems?

Challenge

· Design an investigation to demonstrate how the processes of the water cycle (evaporation and condensation) could purify sea water.

· Draw a diagram to illustrate this process.

· The cost of desalinized water is about $3 per 1,000 gallons (4,000 l). This is three to six times the cost that the typical urban dweller in the United States pays for water. Although desalinization might help solve the drinking-water problem, why might this system be economically impractical for irrigation? (Think of the amount of water needed and the distance it may have to be transported.)

· If this is a resort area with high visitation, what conservation measures could be adopted in hotels and restaurants to help conserve water resources?

· Why do you think processes to purify sea water (reverse osmosis and desalinization) are being explored so actively, despite the costs involved? (Think of population distribution.)

The Blue Traveller

Summary

With a roll of the die, students simulate the movement of water within and between natural and constructed systems.

Grade Level:
Upper Elementary, Middle School

Subject Area:
Earth Science

Duration:
Preparation time: 50 minutes

Activity time:
Part I: 50 minutes
Part II: 50 minutes

Setting:
A large room or playing field

Skills:
Organize, Analyze, Interpret

Vocabulary:
condensation, evaporation, electromagnetic forces, hydrologic cycle

Objectives

Students will:
· identify water users in natural and constructed systems.
· describe specifically the movement of water within and between natural and constructed systems for urban and rural use.
· discuss how an understanding of how water moves on the planet supports water conservation measures.

Materials

· 19 large pieces of paper (for **Part I** and **Part II**)
· marking pens
· 19 boxes, about 6 inches (15 cm) on a side (Boxes are used to make dice for the game. Gift boxes used for coffee mugs are a good size, or you can inquire at your local mailing outlet for suitable boxes. There will be one die [or box] per station of the water cycle. The labels for the sides of the die are located in the **Water Cycle Table**. These labels represent the options for pathways that water can follow.
· copies of *Water Journey Map*, Part I and Part II Student Copy Pages
Optional Materials:
· beads, 19 different colors or shapes (see **Part I**, step 7)
· 19 small containers to hold beads
· twine or string, cut in 12" lengths, one per student

Background

The pathways that water follows are part of the hydrologic cycle. Heated by the sun, water evaporates from oceans, rivers, lakes, and soil; water transpired from plants also rises into the air. Cooled in the atmosphere, water condenses. It falls as rain, snow, or hail to the earth, where it can seep into the ground and become ground water, evaporate again from the land, be absorbed by the roots of plants, quench the thirst of animals, or rush or meander in rivers on a course to the sea.

During this incredible journey water can assume the form of solid, liquid, or vapor (gas). The chemical structure of water—two atoms of hydrogen and one atom of oxygen—and the molecules' orientation to each other determine the state of water. Partnered with gravity and other forces, water as a solid, liquid, or gas is a powerful agent of change. Expanding when it freezes, water exerts enough pressure to fracture rock. Raindrops can release tremendous energy. In driving rainstorms, droplets falling on unprotected lands can loosen tons of soil. Runoff carries these sediments into streams and rivers that may eventually find their way to the sea. Beach sand that you sift through your fingers may once have been part of a mountaintop. Water is constantly arranging and rearranging the planet.

Although snow contains less water than rain, snowpack functions like a water bank, and is important in the water cycle. When snow in the high country melts in late spring, the runoff swells streams and rivers and recharges ground water.

Although unseen, water's most dramatic movements take place in its gaseous phase. Water is constantly evaporating—changing from a liquid to a gas. As a vapor, it travels through the atmosphere over Earth's surface. In fact, water vapor surrounds us all the time. Where it will condense and return to Earth depends on loss of heat energy, on gravity, and on the structure of Earth's surface.

The water cycle connects all living and nonliving things on Earth. Living organisms help move water. Humans and other animals carry water within their bodies and transport it from one location to another. Water is either directly consumed by animals or is removed from foods during digestion. Water is excreted as a liquid or leaves the body as a gas, usually through respiration. When

water is present on the skin (for example, as perspiration), evaporation may occur.

Plants, too, take from and contribute to the hydrologic cycle. Water makes up 80 to 90 percent of the weight of herbaceous (green leafy) plants, and about 50 percent of the weight of woody plants. Where temperatures favor plant growth, the availability of water is one of the main factors that determines the distribution of plants. Through transpiration, plants give off water to the atmosphere through pores on their leaves. Plants give up 95 percent of the water they absorb; the remaining 5 percent is used for growth and maintenance. The greatest movers of water among living organisms are plants.

Humans have created additional pathways for water to follow in its journey on the planet. For example, water is often supplied for urban use, from a *public water supply system*. That is, water is withdrawn from large wells or is removed from surface waters such as lakes or rivers. This water is generally treated regardless of where it comes from (surface or ground water). The degree of treatment depends upon the condition of the water. For example, in some areas, ground water from wells is only treated with small quantities of chlorine gas. This

process kills microorganisms that may occur in water lines. However, if surface water is used and it contains silt, algae, microorganisms or other materials, a more elaborate and costly cleaning process is required.

Water is prepared for drinking and other uses in a water treatment plant and generally includes the following steps:

1. **Aeration**: In this process the water is sprayed into the air to release trapped gases and also to absorb oxygen. This generally improves the taste of the water.

2. **Coagulation**: A chemical known as alum is added and mixed into the water. After a certain amount of time, alum breaks into small cohesive particles that are called floc. Does it seem contradictory to add more chemicals to water to clean it? The point of this addition, is that dirt suspended in the water sticks to the floc.

3. **Sedimentation**: The water is allowed to stand (contained with almost no movement) to provide an opportunity for particles of dirt and floc to become heavy and finally to settle to the bottom of the tank. The cleaner water above the sediment is drawn off.

4. **Filtration**: To remove any other impurities, the water is then passed through layers of

© The Watercourse

charcoal, sand, gravel, and rocks. (This imitates the filtration of ground water through layers of sand, gravel, rock, and other materials in nature.)

5. **Chlorination**: To kill any bacteria that may still be in the water, chlorine gas is added in small amounts.

After treatment water may be stored in large tanks. Upon demand it moves through **water mains** or large underground pipes to residences, businesses, industrial complexes, etc.

But what happens to this water after use? Years ago, wastewater was returned directly to rivers and streams. At that time, the volume of wastewater could be accommodated by natural systems. The small amount of waste was diluted by the great amount of fresh water. Also, dissolved oxygen, bacteria, and other organisms acted on the sewage to turn it into mostly harmless products.

However, the quantity of wastewater has greatly increased and the composition of wastewater has changed. Therefore, after use, water is generally treated in wastewater treatment plants.

The process used in contemporary wastewater treatment plants is similar to the natural process by which water is cleaned, while moving through

the water cycle. The simplest form of wastewater treatment (primary treatment) involves filtration and settling procedures. In addition, waste materials that float are skimmed from the top. Primary techniques remove 45 to 50 percent of pollutants. Most developed countries have a secondary process of wastewater treatment. Secondary treatment, mainly a biological process, removes between 85 and 90 percent of remaining pollutants. Helpful microorganisms consume most of the waste materials in aerator tanks. Solids and microorganisms are separated from the wastewater in secondary settling tanks. Adding a disinfectant (such as chlorine) kills any remaining disease-causing organisms. The water is released from the treatment plant into nearby waterways. Some plants even have a third stage of wastewater treatment that removes small amounts of undesirable materials such as nitrates, phosphates, and heavy metals.

In many areas, depending upon the degree of treatment, wastewater is being used for diverse purposes. Often called **reclaimed water**, this is wastewater which has been treated to a level that is acceptable for specific applications. These applications include: watering of golf courses, athletic fields, and parks; cooling and pro-

cessing in industrial systems; irrigation of animal feed crops, cotton, and trees; recharging ground water aquifers; and in some cases, for drinking water.

However, many people do not get their water from public water supply systems. Instead, their water is provided by private household wells. In addition to providing water to residences, well water is also used for irrigating crops, watering livestock, cooling equipment and processing in industrial and commercial operations, and irrigating lawns. (Wells are also drilled to monitor ground water.)

Wells are constructed by professionals who use special machines called well-drilling rigs. Wells are drilled into an aquifer. Well depth varies, but wells can be as much as 600 to 800 feet deep. Electric pumps are used to bring up the water through pipes into private homes. In many cases, this water is directly removed from the aquifer and consumed without treatment. In these situations, it is a good idea to have the well water tested periodically to insure that it is still safe to drink. Consumers can get information from their state health departments to find out how often they should have their well water sampled and tested.

What happens to well water after it is used by the consumer? If public sewer lines are not available, it is the responsibility of homeowners to treat their own wastewater. On-site sewage disposal is defined as "the treatment and disposal of sewage on the same property as the residence." These systems should remove pollutants and disease-causing organisms before wastewater is introduced back into ground and surface waters.

How does a septic system accomplish these objectives? A septic system is comprised of a septic tank and a soil absorption area. Wastewater from the residence flows into the septic tank. In the tank organic solids in the wastewater float to the surface and form a layer called scum. Bacteria act on these solids and convert them to a liquid. Inorganic material sinks to the bottom of the tank and forms a layer called sludge. Between the layers of scum and sludge, clear water passes through the outlet pipe to the soil absorption area. Here the water passes through a filtering system. Leaching fields, filter beds, and cesspools are types of filtering systems.

Individuals can help protect the quality of the water that will enter the natural water cycle by monitoring their septic system. The following may be indicators of septic system failure:
· Water drains slowly from the home

· Plumbing backs up
· Pipes and drains emit a gurgling sound
· The grass is greener over the septic system!
Every few years, homeowners should practice routine maintenance of their septic system by having sludge removed.

As water moves through and connects natural and constructed systems, we recognize the need that all water users have for water of the right quality and quantity, at the right time and cost. Urban and rural dwellers require water for drinking, cooking, cleaning, and watering of lawns and gardens. Agriculturists and ranchers need water for their livestock and irrigation of the fruits, vegetables, and grains we consume. Industrialists use water to produce the materials and goods we use. Energy producers generate the power for the production of goods and the comfort of our homes. Fish and wildlife require clean and abundant water for their survival and proliferation. Recreationists depend on water resources for canoeing, rafting, fishing, surfing, skiing, and other activities that renew the human spirit. As all water users recognize their dependence on this resource, protecting water quality and quantity makes social, economic, and ecological good sense!

Procedure
Warm Up
Ask students to take out a piece of paper and illustrate how they think water moves on the planet. Ask them to identify the different places water can go as it moves through and around Earth and, if possible, to indicate the processes that occur (condensation, evaporation, transpiration). Remind them to include not only the "natural cycle," but also where humans have added to that cycle. As students are drawing, walk around and observe their work. Many students are likely to draw the "water circle:" water rains from the clouds, falls onto the land, runs off into the ocean, and evaporates back into the clouds.

After students have completed their drawings, ask them to identify the different places they indicated that water can go. Discuss with them the processes of condensation, evaporation, and transpiration.

The Activity
Part I
1. Tell students they are going to become water molecules moving through the natural water cycle.
2. Categorize the places through which water can move into nine stations: clouds, plants, animals, rivers, oceans, lakes, ground water, soil, and glaciers. Write these names on

large pieces of paper and put them in locations around the room or field. (On a windy day, choose students to hold the station signs and help others move through the cycle. Students may enjoy making the station signs and illustrating them.)

3. Either assign an even number of students to each station (except for the cloud station) or have all students start in the clouds. Have students identify the different places to which water can travel from the station they were assigned in the water cycle. Discuss the conditions that cause the water to move. Explain that water movement depends on energy from the sun, electromagnetic energy, and gravity. Sometimes water will not move anywhere. After students have generated lists of possible destinations, have each group share their work. Have students compare the die that has been prepared for their station with the lists they wrote. The **Water Cycle Table** provides an explanation of water movements from each station.

4. Have students discuss the form in which water moves from one place to another (i.e., solid, liquid, or gas). In most cases water will be moving in its liquid form. However, any time water moves to the clouds, it is in the form of water vapor, with molecules moving rapidly and apart from each other.

5. Tell students that they will

be demonstrating water's movement from one location to another. When they move as liquid water, they will be moving in pairs to represent many water molecules bonded together in a water drop. When they move to the clouds (evaporate), they will separate from their partners and move alone as individual water molecules. When water condenses and rains from the clouds, each student will grab a partner and move to the next location.

6. In this game a roll of the die indicates where the water will go. Students line up behind the dice at the nine different stations. At the cloud station they should be in single file; at all other stations they should line up in pairs. Students roll the dice and go to the location indicated on the label facing up. If they roll "stay," they move to the back of the line.

When students arrive at the next station, they get in line. When they reach the front of the line, they roll again and move to the next station (or proceed to the back of the line if they roll "stay").

In the clouds, students roll the die individually, but if they leave the clouds they grab a partner (the person immediately behind them) and move to the next station; the partner does not roll the die.

7. Students should keep track of their movements. Before beginning the simulation, provide a copy of the **Water Journey Map, Part I**. Ask stu-

dents to draw lines showing their movement from station to station. If students roll "stay," they should record a hatch mark at that station.

Another approach is to place a container with beads of a certain color at each station. For example, offer blue beads at the ocean station, brown beads at the soil station, white beads at the glacier, and so forth. Provide lengths of twine on which to string the beads. As students move from station to station, have them keep track of their movements by picking up beads and stringing them on the twine.

8. Tell students the game will begin and end with the sound of a bell. Play the game!

Part II

1. Ask students to describe how they think water moves in systems that have been constructed by humans. Remind them that in the constructed system, water is processed for human use. That is, water is treated to be suitable for drinking and wastewater is treated to be released into the natural system or to be reused in the constructed system (for irrigation, industry, and even drinking).

2. Have students brainstorm how water is used in constructed systems. It may be easier for them to think of different water users (urban dwellers, farmers, ranchers, industrialists, recreationists, etc.).

3. Have students distinguish between the ways urban and rural dwellers generally receive their water. Discuss the difference between public water supply systems (water treatment and wastewater treatment) and private wells and septic systems.

4. Expand the playing field to include stations and dice for both the natural and constructed systems. It will be necessary to change one to three sides of the following dice to simulate the natural and constructed cycle: river, clouds, ocean, lake, and ground water. New dice will have to be made for the constructed system. (See the Water Cycle Tables.) Provide students with the **Water Journey Map, Part II**, and tell them to record their journey just as they did in the natural system.

5. Remind students to move in pairs to represent water in the form of liquid and ice and to move as single players when they are representing water in the gaseous state. (With smaller classes and the increased number of stations, it may be necessary to explain the changes in state, but not to simulate it. In this situation, students would move singularly from station to station, regardless of the form of water at that station.)

6. Tell students that play will begin and end with the sound of a whistle or bell. Go!

Wrap Up

Have students study their **Water Journey Maps**, Part I and Part II. Ask them what conclusions they can draw about the natural water cycle based on their journey. Could they have predicted the exact pattern of water's movement through the natural system?

Have students compare their journeys from Part I and Part II. Were there stations that could have been predicted as part of water's journey through the constructed system? (For example, water must pass through water treatment for urban users and through wastewater treatment before it enters the natural system.) Discuss water treatment and wastewater treatment with students. Have students describe how these technologies in many ways imitate the cleaning of water in the natural system.

Ask students how many of them are on urban systems? Are they aware of whether or not reclaimed water is being used in their community for irrigation, industry, or drinking water? How do (or would) they feel about drinking reclaimed water?

Have students compare water movement through rural and urban systems. How many of them depend on a well for their home water use? Who is responsible for ensuring the quality of drinking water and the treatment of wastewater in rural households that depend on a residential well? (The family who depends on the well.) How can homeowners help to maintain the quality of water that is returned to the natural system? (They can closely monitor their septic system.) Why is it important that wells are not drilled too closely together? (One well can affect the supply of another. Also, the natural system in a small or confined area may not be able to finish the cleaning process if there are too many septic systems too close together.)

In addition to rural and urban water users, were students (based on their family's work) able to identify with other water users? Ask students to discuss their recreational use of water. Although students were able to play the game without the constructed system, would it be possible to demonstrate water's movement on the planet without the natural system?

How does an understanding of how water moves on the planet contribute to our reasons to conserve water? Do students believe that water is without cost? (Treatment for drinking water and wastewater costs money. It requires workers, facilities, pipes, and materials to clean or treat water. The more water we use, the more water must be

treated or cleaned, and that costs money.)

Ask students to turn over the papers on which they first drew how they thought water moved on the planet. Now that they have run the simulation in Parts I and II of the activity, ask them to illustrate or create a model of how they think water moves on the planet through natural and constructed systems. Ask students to compare and contrast their original and final impressions of the water cycle.

Assessment

Have students:
· role-play water as it moves through the natural system. (**Part I**, step 8).
· identify the states of water as it moves through the natural system (**Part I**, step 4).
· identify the steps in water treatment and wastewater treatment and relate them to natural systems (**Part II**, step 1).
· role-play water as it moves through and connects natural and constructed systems (**Part II**, step 7).
· compare and contrast the movement of water through natural and constructed systems (*Warm Up*).
· draw a picture or create a model of how water moves on the planet through natural and constructed systems. (*Wrap Up*).
· identify how an understanding of the water cycle in natural and constructed sys-

tems supports water conservation measures (*Wrap Up*).

Extensions

Have students compare the movement of water during different seasons and at different locations around the globe. They can adapt the game (change the faces of the dice, add alternative stations, etc.) to represent these different conditions or locations.

Have students investigate how water becomes polluted and is cleaned as it moves through the water cycle. For instance, it might pick up contaminants as it travels through the soil that are then left behind as water evaporates at the surface. Challenge students to adapt the activity to include these processes in both the natural and constructed systems. For example, rolled-up pieces of masking tape representing pollutants can be stuck to students as they travel to the soil station. Some materials will be filtered out as the water moves to the lakes. Have students show this by rubbing their arms to slough off some tape. If they roll clouds, they remove all the tape; when water evaporates it leaves pollutants behind.

Resources
Alexander, Gretchen. 1989. *Water Cycle Teacher's Guide*. Hudson, N.H.: Delta Education, Inc.

Allen, Leslie Frye, Valerie Johnson, Georgann Penson, and Diane Sterling. 1996. *WaterWays: Exploring Northwest Florida's Water Resources*. Havana, Fl.: Northwest Florida Water Management District.

Anderson, Terry L., and Pamela Snyder. 1997. *Water Markets, Priming the Invisible Pump*. Washington, D.C.: Cato Institute.

Gleick, Peter H. 1998. *The World's Water*. Washington, D.C.: Island Press.

Van der Leeden, Frits. 1991. *The Water Encyclopedia*. Chelsea, Mich.: Lewis Publishers, Inc.

Water Cycle Tables
Natural Cycle Part I

Station	Die Side Labels	Explanation
Soil	one side *plant*	Water is absorbed by plant roots.
	one side *river*	The soil is saturated, so water runs off into a river.
	one side *ground water*	Water is pulled by gravity; it filters into the soil.
	two sides *clouds*	Heat energy is added to the water, so the water evaporates and goes to the clouds.
	one side *stay*	Water remains on the surface (perhaps in a puddle or adhering to a soil particle).
Plant	four sides *clouds*	Water leaves the plant through the process of transpiration.
	two sides *stay*	Water is used by the plant and stays in the cells.
River	one side *lake*	Water flows into a lake.
	one side *ground water*	Water is pulled by gravity; it filters into the soil.
	one side *ocean*	Water flows into the ocean.
	one side *animal*	An animal drinks water.
	one side *clouds*	Heat energy is added to the water, so the water evaporates and goes to the clouds.
	one side *stay*	Water remains in the current of the river.
Clouds	one side *soil*	Water condenses and falls on soil.
	one side *glacier*	Water condenses and falls as snow onto a glacier.
	one side *lake*	Water condenses and falls into a lake.
	two sides *ocean*	Water condenses and falls into the ocean.
	one side *stay*	Water remains as a water droplet clinging to a dust particle in the cloud.

© The Watercourse

Natural Cycle Part I, continued

Station	Die Side Labels	Explanation
Ocean	two sides *clouds*	Heat energy is added to the water, so the water evaporates and goes to the clouds.
	four sides *stay*	Water remains in the ocean.
Lake	one side *ground water*	Water is pulled by gravity; it filters into the soil.
	one side *animal*	An animal drinks water.
	one side *river*	Water flows into a river.
	one side *clouds*	Heat energy is added to the water, so the water evaporates and goes to the clouds.
	two sides *stay*	Water remains within the lake or estuary.
Animal	two sides *soil*	Water is excreted through feces and urine.
	three sides *clouds*	Water is respired or evaporated from the body.
	one side *stay*	Water is incorporated into the body.
Ground Water	one side *river*	Water filters into a river.
	two sides *lake*	Water filters into a lake.
	three sides *stay*	Water stays underground.
Glacier	one side *ground water*	Ice melts and water filters into the ground.
	one side *clouds*	Ice evaporates and water goes to the clouds (sublimation).
	one side *river*	Ice melts and water flows into a river.
	three sides *stay*	Ice stays frozen in the glacier.

Natural Cycle Part II

Station	Die Side Labels	Explanation
Soil	One side *plant*	Plant roots absorb water.
	One side *river*	The soil is saturated, so water runs off into a river.
	One side *ground water*	Water is pulled by gravity; it filters into the soil.
	Two sides *clouds*	Heat energy is added to the water, so the water evaporates and goes to the clouds.
	One side *stay*	Water remains on the surface (perhaps in a puddle or adhering to a soil particle).
Plant	Four sides *clouds*	Water leaves the plant through the process of transpiration.
	Two sides *stay*	Water is used by the plant and stays in the cells.
River	One side *water treatment*	Water is withdrawn from the river for treatment.
	One side *irrigation*	Water is removed from the river for irrigation.
	One side *ocean*	Water flows into the ocean.
	One side *animal*	An animal drinks water.
	One side *clouds*	Heat energy is added to the water, so the water evaporates and goes to the clouds.
	One side *stay*	Water remains in the current of the river.
Clouds	One side *soil*	Water condenses and falls on soil.
	One side *glacier*	Water condenses and falls as snow onto a glacier.
	One side *lake*	Water condenses and falls into a lake.
	One side *ocean*	Water condenses and falls into the ocean.
	One side *stay*	Water remains as a water droplet clinging to a dust particle in the cloud.
	One side *recreation*	Water condenses and falls to the earth for various forms of recreation.

Natural Cycle Part II, continued

Station	Die Side Labels	Explanation
Ocean	Two sides *clouds*	Heat energy is added to the water, so the water evaporates and goes to the clouds.
	Two sides *stay*	Water remains in the ocean.
	One side *desalinization*	Water is removed from the ocean for desalinization.
	One side *industry*	Ocean water is used for ballast in seagoing vessels for transporting goods.
Lake	One side *ground water*	Water is pulled by gravity; it filters into the soil.
	One side *irrigation*	Water is removed from the lake for irrigation.
	One side *ground water*	Water flows into a river.
	One side *clouds*	Heat energy is added to the water, so the water evaporates and goes to the clouds.
	One side *stay*	Water remains within the lake or estuary.
	One side *industry*	Water is used for power plants and manufacturing products.
Animal	Two sides *soil*	Water is excreted through feces and urine.
	Three sides *clouds*	Water is respired or evaporated from the body.
	One side *stay*	Water is incorporated into the body.
Ground Water	One side *river*	Water filters into a river.
	One side *lake*	Water filters into a lake.
	One side *stay*	Water stays underground.
	One side *well*	Water is pumped for domestic uses.
	One side *water treatment*	Water is removed and treated for drinking water.
	One side *irrigation*	Water is removed for irrigation.
Glacier	One side *ground water*	Ice melts and water filters into the ground.
	One side *clouds*	Ice evaporates and water goes to the clouds (sublimation).
	One side *river*	Ice melts and water flows into a river.
	Three sides *stay*	Ice stays frozen in the glacier.

Constructed Cycle Part II

Station	Die Side Labels	Explanation
Wastewater	One side *river*	After treatment, water is returned to the river.
	One side *urban*	Water is used to irrigate lawns and parks.
	One side *irrigation*	Water is used to irrigate animal feed crops, cotton, citrus, and other crops.
	One side *industry*	Water is used in processing and cooling (for example, in the steel industry).
	One side *ground water*	Treated water is injected into wells to replenish ground water.
	One side *clouds*	Water evaporates from treatment plant settling ponds.
Recreation	One side *plants*	Water is taken up by plant roots in parks and athletic fields.
	Two sides *river*	People enjoy water through canoeing, rafting, and birding.
	One side *lake*	People enjoy water through boating and skiing.
	One side *animals*	Anglers enjoy water through fishing.
	One side *ocean*	People enjoy beaches, swimming, and snorkeling.
Water Treatment	Two sides *urban*	Water is used for domestic purposes like drinking, bathing, cooking, and fire fighting, and city cleaning.
	One side *industry*	Water is used for the production of goods.
	One side *ground water*	Water is lost during transport through leaky, underground pipes.
	Two sides *stay*	Water remains in the supply facility (tanks, water tower).
Well	Two sides *rural*	Many people living in rural areas pump their water from wells for drinking, bathing, cooking, etc.
	One side *irrigation*	Well water is used to irrigate crops.
	One side *animals*	Well water is used for livestock watering.
	One side *industry*	Well water is used for producing goods.
	One side *stay*	Water remains in the well.

Constructed Cycle Part II, continued

Station	Die Side Labels	Explanation
Desalinization	Two sides *urban*	Water is used for drinking, bathing, cleaning, etc.
	One side *irrigation*	Water is used for watering crops, trees, etc.
	One side *industry*	Water is utilized in the production of goods.
	One side *stay*	Water remains in storage tanks after treatment.
	One side *clouds*	Water evaporates during treatment.
Urban	Two sides *wastewater*	After use, water moves through pipes to the wastewater treatment facility.
	One side *plant*	Plants absorb water through their roots during irrigation of lawns and gardens.
	One side *soil*	Water soaks into soil with watering.
	One side *clouds*	Water evaporates into the clouds with the watering of lawns.
	One side *river*	Water flows from the lawn into storm drains that may connect with the river.
Irrigation	One side *soil*	Water moves into the soil.
	Two sides *plants*	Water is absorbed by plant roots.
	One side *clouds*	Water evaporates into the clouds.
	One side *river*	Water runs off the fields and into the river.
	One side *animals*	Water is used for livestock, waterfowl, and wildlife.
Rural	Three sides *septic system*	Water moves into the septic system for cleaning after use in homes.
	One side *irrigation*	Well water is used for lawns and gardens.
	One side *animals*	Well water is used for livestock and pets.
	One side *clouds*	Evaporation occurs when applying water to lawns and gardens.
Septic System	Two sides *stay*	Water remains in the septic tank of the system.
	Four sides *soil*	After cleaning, water moves into the soil layer.
Industry	Two sides *stay*	Industry recycles water.
	Two sides *wastewater*	After use, water is treated.
	Two sides *clouds*	Water evaporates as steam in industrial applications.

Natural Cycle Box Sides

Directions: Replicate these pages, enlarging them to fit the sides of your boxes, as necessary. Cut the panels apart and glue or paste the artwork onto the six sides of each box. Or, have students create their own illustrations for the boxes.

RIVER

SOIL

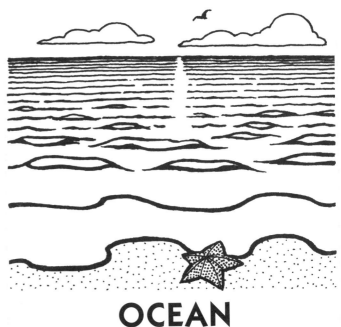

OCEAN

Natural Cycle Box Sides, continued

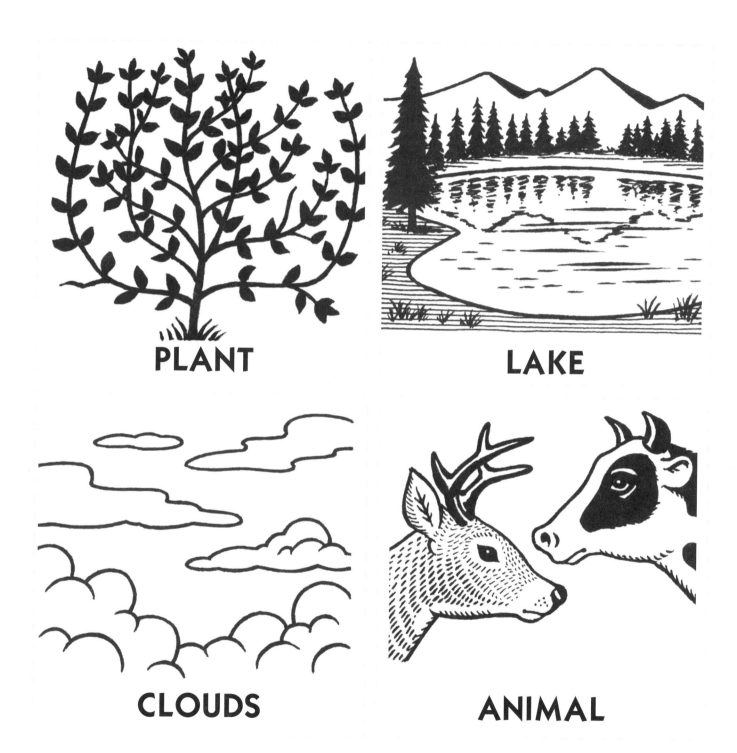

PLANT

LAKE

CLOUDS

ANIMAL

Natural Cycle and Natural Cycle Part II Box Sides

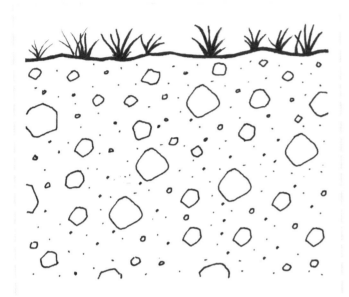

GROUND WATER

GLACIER

RECREATION

WASTEWATER

Natural Cycle Part II and Constructed Cycle Part II Box Sides

WATER TREATMENT

URBAN

IRRIGATION

RURAL

Constructed Cycle Part II Box Sides, continued

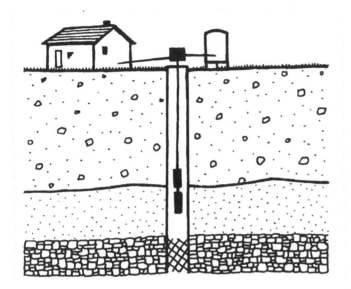

WELL

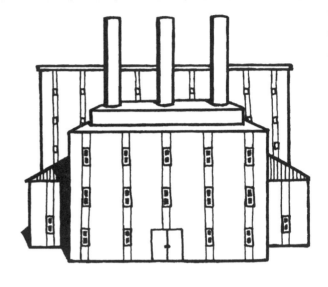

INDUSTRY

DESALINIZATION

SEPTIC SYSTEM

Water Journey Map

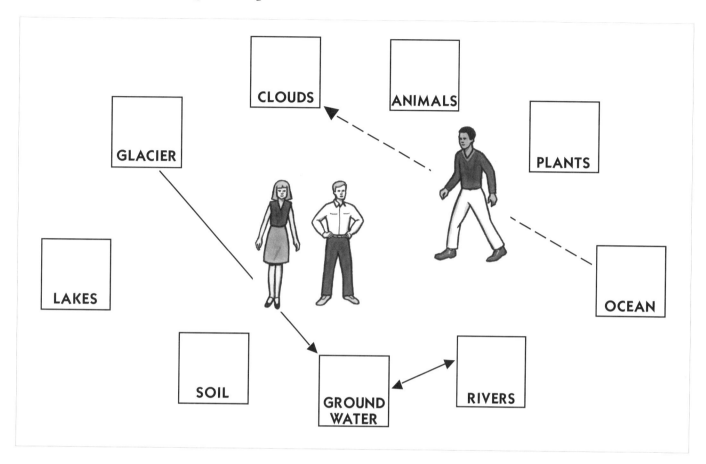

CLOUDS

ANIMALS

GLACIER

PLANTS

LAKES

OCEAN

SOIL

GROUND WATER

RIVERS

KEY

———— STUDENTS MOVING IN PAIRS

– – – STUDENTS MOVING SINGULARLY

Water Journey Map, Part I

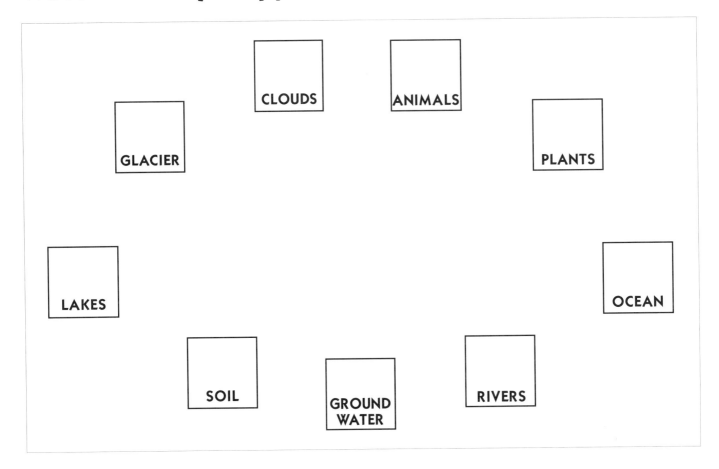

Water Journey Map, Part II

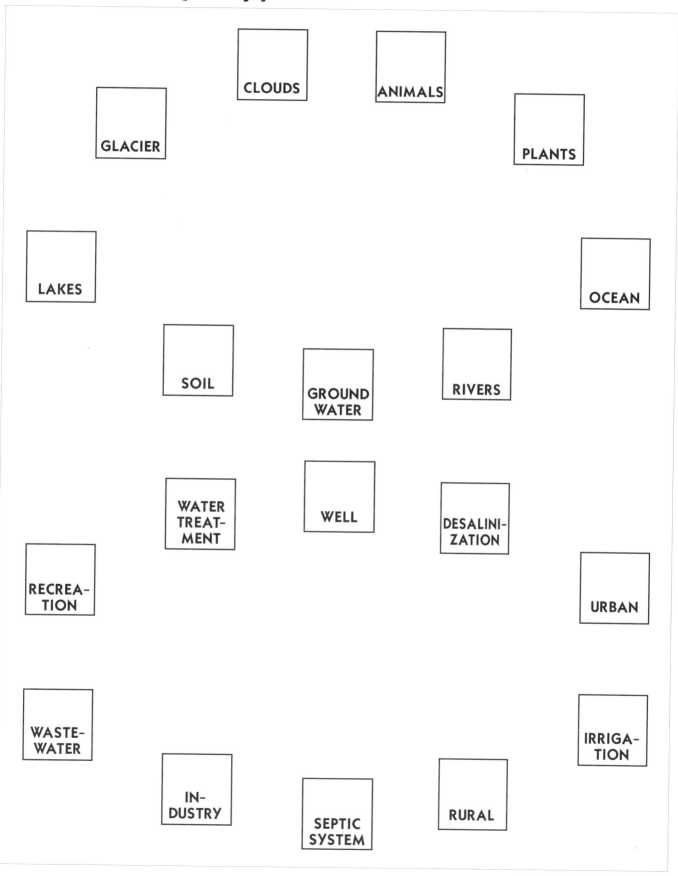

CLOUDS

ANIMALS

GLACIER

PLANTS

LAKES

OCEAN

SOIL

GROUND WATER

RIVERS

WATER TREAT-MENT

WELL

DESALINI-ZATION

RECREA-TION

URBAN

WASTE-WATER

IRRIGA-TION

IN-DUSTRY

SEPTIC SYSTEM

RURAL

Get the Ground Water Picture

Summary
Students will "get the ground water picture," learning about basic ground water principles as they create their own geologic cross section or earth window.

Objectives
Students will:
· identify the parts of a ground water system.
· compare movement of water through diverse substrates.
· relate different types of land uses to potential ground water contamination.

Materials
· 3 clear, 12-ounce plastic soda bottles (with top cut off and holes punched in bottom) or the same number of plastic cups (holes punched in bottom)
· gravel
· sand
· clay (If unable to obtain clay locally, place unscented, nonclumping kitty litter in a blender and grind until fine. Mix with enough water to moisten.)
· hand-held magnifying lens
· 25 1"x12" strips of white paper (Numbered 1 through 25 on one side.)
· blue crayon or colored pencil
· copies of *Well Log Data Chart* Student Copy Page
· copies of *Ground Water* Student Copy Page

Background
Ground water is one of Earth's most valuable natural resources. The water stored in the pores, cracks, and openings of subsurface rock material is ground water. People have used wells dug by hand or machine to retrieve water from the ground throughout history. Scientists use the word aquifer to describe an underground formation that is capable of storing and transmitting water. (See Well Log Ground Water Chart [Cross Section] for identification and definition of the parts of a ground water system.)

Aquifers come in all shapes and sizes. Some aquifers cover hundreds of square miles and are hundreds of feet thick, while others may only cover a few square miles and be a few feet thick. Water quality and quantity vary from aquifer to aquifer; sometimes they vary within the same system. Some aquifers can yield millions of gallons of water per day and maintain water levels, while others may only be able to produce small amounts of water each day. In some areas wells might have to be drilled thousands of feet deep to reach usable water, while in other areas water can be located only a few feet underground. One site might contain several aquifers located at different depths, and another site might yield little or no ground water.

The age of the ground water varies from aquifer to aquifer. For example, an unconfined surface aquifer might hold water that is only a few days, weeks, or months old. On the other hand, a deep aquifer that is covered by one or more impervious layers may contain water that is hundreds or even thousands of years old.

The rate of ground water movement varies based on the rock material in the formation through which the water is moving. After water percolates down to the water table, it becomes ground water and starts to move slowly down gradient. Water moves in response to differences in energy levels. The energies that cause ground water to flow are expressed as gravitational energy and pressure energy, both forms of mechanical energy. Gravitational energy comes from the difference in elevation between the recharge area (where water enters the ground water system) and discharge area (where water leaves the system). Pressure energy (hydraulic head) comes from the weight of overlying water

and earth materials. Ground water moves toward areas of least resistance. (When ground water encounters semi-impervious material, such as clay, it slows down significantly; when it moves toward an open area, such as a lake, water's rate of movement increases.)

Hydrogeologists, scientists who study ground water, know that the above variables exist and that to really "get the ground water picture," they must drill wells. Wells provide the best method of learning about the physical, hydrologic, and chemical characteristics of an aquifer. As the drill goes deeper into the ground, it passes through different rock formations. The driller records the exact location of the well, records the depth of each formation, and collects samples of the rock material penetrated (sandstone, sand, clay, etc.). This data becomes part of the well's record or well log. The driller's record provides valuable information for determining ground water availability, movement, quantity, and quality. The well driller then caps and seals the well to protect it from contamination.

If hazardous wastes, chemicals, heavy metals, oils, etc., collect on the surface of the ground, rain or runoff percolating into the soil can carry these substances into ground water. When hydrogeologists or water quality specialists analyze

the quality of ground water, they consider land use practices in the watershed and in the vicinity of the well.

Procedure
Warm Up
Tell students they are about to learn how they can "get the ground water picture." Explain that hydrogeologists study wells to learn about the types of rock material located below ground. Ask students to draw pictures representing what they think it looks like underground (texture and color of rock formations) or to write brief descriptions of what happens to water after it seeps into the ground.

The Activity
Part I
Ground Water Demonstration. Have students conduct the following activity to learn how water moves through rock materials such as gravel, sand, and clay.

Place gravel, sand, and clay in separate clear containers. Have students look closely at each container. (A hand-held magnifying glass works well.) To demonstrate that ground water moves through underground rock formations, pour water into each container; observe and discuss the results. Which container emptied the fastest? The slowest? How would the different materials influence water movement in natural systems?

Part II

Ground Water Movement Activity.

(May be appropriate for younger students.)

Conduct the following activity to show how different sizes and kinds of rock material affect water movement. Select three or four students to become molecules of water. The rest of the students will be rock material.

A. **Water Movement Through Gravel:** Students become gravel by raising arms outstretched. Students should be able to rotate and not touch other students. The goal of the students representing water molecules is to move (flow) through students representing gravel to the other side of room. (See illustration A.)

B. **Water Movement Through Sand**: Students become sand by extending arms, bending them at the elbows, and touching waists with fingertips. Students should stand so their elbows are almost touching those of other students. The water molecules will experience some difficulty this time, but should still reach the other side. (See illustration B.)

C. **Water Movement Through Clay**: Students become clay particles by keeping arms at their sides and huddling together. They should be very close together, making it a formidable task for water molecules to move through the clay. Without being rough, the water molecules should slowly push their way through the clay. Some water molecules may be unable to move through the clay at all. (See illustration C.)

A

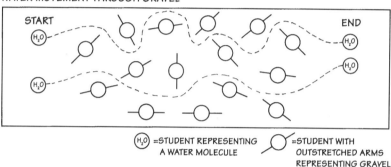

WATER MOVEMENT THROUGH GRAVEL

H_2O =STUDENT REPRESENTING A WATER MOLECULE   =STUDENT WITH OUTSTRETCHED ARMS REPRESENTING GRAVEL

B

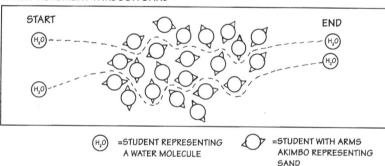

WATER MOVEMENT THROUGH SAND

H_2O =STUDENT REPRESENTING A WATER MOLECULE   =STUDENT WITH ARMS AKIMBO REPRESENTING SAND

C

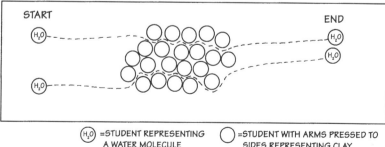

WATER MOVEMENT THROUGH CLAY

H_2O =STUDENT REPRESENTING A WATER MOLECULE   =STUDENT WITH ARMS PRESSED TO SIDES REPRESENTING CLAY

Part III

1.   Hand out the strips of paper numbered 2—24 (students can work individually or in pairs) and copies of the *Well Log Data Chart* to students. The paper strip represents the length of a well that has been dug. Students will receive data about the location and types of rock materials in their well and transfer this information to their strips of paper to make well logs.

2.   Demonstrate how to record the types of rock materials. Divide the strip labeled 1 into 12 1-inch sections. Show students the data for Well #1 on the *Well Log Data Chart.* Mark the level of the water table by drawing a double line at the point on the paper strip that corresponds with the number in the first column of the chart (i.e., draw it 2" from the top). In the second column, find the level of fine sand (0–1"). Measuring again from the top of the column, speckle the first inch with dots. From 1" to 2 $\frac{1}{2}$", the formation is composed of medium sand. Coarse sand exists from 2 $\frac{1}{2}$" to 6", and so forth, until the gravel layer, which exists from 8" to 12". Complete the drawing by coloring (light blue) the area between the water table and the top of the clay layer. Also color the gravel layer.

3.   Have students use the information in the *Well Log Data Chart* to fill in their logs. The number on their strip of paper should correspond to the well number on the chart. Make sure students note the use being made of the land existing above their well sites.

4.   When they have completed their well logs, ask students to answer these questions.

   a.   The horizontal scale of the cross section is 1 inch=1 mile. The vertical scale is 1 inch=50 feet. How many miles are horizontally represented in the cross section? How many feet are vertically represented in the cross section?

Sample Strip

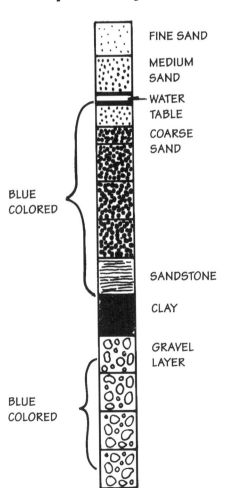

   b.   How many feet below the surface is the water table on their piece of land?

   c.   Ask each student to imagine a drop of water falling on the surface above his or her well. What pollutants might this drop of water pick up as it filters into the ground? (Students can refer to the land use practice above their well, but may conclude they need additional information.)

   d.   Have students describe the drop's movement down the column. Through which layers would it move the fastest? Through which would it move the slowest?

   e.   At which layer might the drop's movement be most restricted? Explain to students that only a slight amount of water would pass through the clay. Have them speculate on the source of the water beneath the clay level (in the gravel layer).

5.   Have students assemble their well logs in number order, and tape them to a wall. Distribute the *Ground Water Student Copy Page* to each student. Compare students' well log cross section to the chart.

   a.   Provide the definitions listed in the box and have students locate these parts of a ground water system on the *Well Log Ground Water Chart (Cross Section).*

   b.   Ask students what direction the ground water is moving in the unconfined aquifer. (It predominantly moves

from left to right.)

c. What are water sources for the unconfined aquifer? (rainfall, wetlands, the river)

d. How long would it take the water in the sandstone formation to move from Well #1 to Well #15? (Assume the water moves at a constant rate of 100 feet per day [1 mile=5280 feet].)

e. Now that students know about the land use above other nearby well sites and the direction water flows, how would they answer question 4c?

f. Have students refer to the Cone of Depression diagram. Explain that the cone of depression results from water being drawn up the well. Ask them to locate the cone of depression on the *Well Log Ground Water Chart (Cross Section)*.

g. Instruct students to refer to the diagram labelled *Ground Water System (Simplified)*. What are possible sources of water in the confined aquifer portion of their well? (Compare answers to 4e.)

Wrap Up

If they had to drill a well, which sites on the *Well Log Ground Water Chart (Cross Section)* would students consider most favorable? Students may be interested in learning about the rock formations beneath their community. The city water department might have a geologic cross section for the city or region. Students could

attempt to interpret the maps.

Assessment

Have students:
· compare the movement of water through diverse substrates (**Part I**).
· construct a well log (**Part III**, steps 2 and 3).
· analyze possible effects on ground water based on interpretations of the well logs (**Part III**, steps 4 and 5).
· identify the parts of a ground water system (**Part III**, step 5).
· determine when additional data are needed to draw valid conclusions (**Part III**, steps 4 and 5).

Extensions

Does your school have its own well? If so, consider visiting the well site and conducting a survey of possible pollution sources in the well's vicinity. What are they and where are they located? Should something be done to remove or mitigate them? What are the options? The water quality of your school's well is public information and would make an interesting study. Has your school experienced water quality problems?

To demonstrate surface water filtration of sediment and other materials carried by water, ask four students to represent water molecules and to lightly attach balloons to themselves with tape. These balloons represent materials picked up by water molecules as they move

across the surface of the ground. Have several students representing soil particles stand elbow to elbow to form Earth's surface. As the "water molecules" pass through the "soil," the balloons will be brushed off because of the proximity of the students. This activity illustrates how soil can filter out sediment and debris carried by water.

Have each of the water molecules rub a little flour on the sides of their arms. The flour represents the small but visible materials that can still be carried by water as it moves downward from the surface to become part of ground water. The students who were soil particles are now rock particles and stand side by side to represent different types of rock material (gravel, sand, and clay). As the water molecules move through the rock material, some of the flour rubs off on the rock material. Although some material is removed by rock filtration, some is still retained by the water molecules.

Water that looks or tastes pure and has no odor is not necessarily potable. Water quality specialists know that water can contain odorless, colorless, and tasteless contaminants. They detect these substances through testing; they collect and analyze a sample of water for specific contaminants (bacteria, nitrates, arsenic, and so forth).

Designate half the students in class as water molecules and the rest as rock particles. Cut small pieces of paper and write the name of one contaminant on each: bacteria, nitrate, arsenic, lead, etc. Secretly distribute these pieces of paper to about half the water molecules and tell students to hide them in their pockets. Have the water molecules move through the students standing side by side who represent rock particles.

After they have all passed through, ask students (except the "contaminated" water molecules), "Do you believe the water that just filtered through the rock particles is clean: that is, would you be willing to drink it?" Students will likely answer yes. Have the contaminated water molecules remove the contaminants from their pockets. Remind students that even though water may "appear" clean, it may still carry contaminants that only testing can detect.

Resources

Ground Water Flow Model: A Plexiglas sand tank model, video, and user's guide that demonstrates basic ground water principles and management concerns. Contact: The Watercourse, 201 Culbertson Hall, Montana State University, Bozeman, MT 59717-0570. Tel. (406) 994-5392. Fax: (406) 994-1919.

Hoff, Mary, and Mary M. Rogers. 1991. *Our Endangered Planet: Ground Water.* Minneapolis: Lerner.

Taylor, Carla, ed. 1985. *Groundwater: A Vital Resource.* Knoxville: Tennessee Valley Authority.

WATER TABLE:
The top of an unconfined aquifer; indicates the level below which soil and rock are saturated with water.

CONFINED AQUIFER:
An aquifer that is bounded above and below by impermeable layers that transmit water significantly more slowly than the aquifer. The water level in a well that taps a confined aquifer will rise above the top of the aquifer because the confined aquifer is under pressure. Also called artesian aquifer.

UNCONFINED AQUIFER:
An aquifer in which the upper boundary is the top of the water table.

PERMEABLE LAYER:
Portion of aquifer that contains porous rock materials that allow water to penetrate freely.

IMPERMEABLE LAYER:
Portion of aquifer that contains rock material or clay layer that does not allow water to penetrate or pass through easily; often forms the base of unconfined aquifers and the boundaries for confined aquifers.

ZONE OF SATURATION:
The part of a water-bearing formation in which all spaces (between soil particles and in rock structures) are filled with water. Water found within the zone of saturation is called ground water.

ZONE OF AERATION:
The unsaturated surface layer of the ground in which some of the spaces between soil particles are filled with air.

Well Log Ground Water Chart (Cross Section)

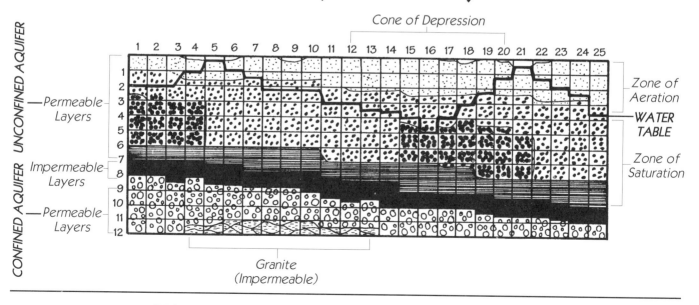

Well Log Data Chart

Well No.	Land Use Type	Water Table	KEY — Fine Sand	Medium Sand	Coarse Sand	Sandstone	Clay Layer	Gravel Layer	Granite
			Note: numbers in vertical columns are in inches						
1	farmland	2	0-1	1-2½	2½-6	6-7	7-8	8-12	
2	farmland	2	0-1	1-3	3-6	6-7	7-8	8-12	
3	farmland	2	0-1½	1½-3	3-6	6-7	7-8½	8½-12	
4	wetland	1	¼-1½	1½-3	3-6	6-7	7-8¼	8¼-11½	11½-12
5	wetland	¼	½-1½	1½-6	——	6-7¼	7¼-8¼	8¼-11½	11½-12
6	wetland	1	¼-1¾	1¾-6	——	6-7¼	7¼-8½	8½-11	11-12
7	farmland	1¾	0-1¾	1¾-6	——	6-7¾	7¾-8¾	8¾-11	11-12
8	farmland	2½	0-1¾	1¾-6	——	6-7¾	7¾-8¾	8¾-11	11-12
9	landfill	2½	¾-1¾	1¾-6	——	6-7¾	7¾-8¾	8¾-11	11-12
10	industry	2½	0-1¾	1¾-6	——	6-7¾	7¾-9	9-11	11-12
11	industry	3	0-2	2-7	——	7-8	8-9¼	9¼-11½	11½-12
12	urban area	3	0-2¼	2¼-7	——	7-8¼	8¼-9½	9½-11½	11½-12
13	urban area	3½	0-2¼	2¼-7	——	7-8¼	8¼-9½	9½-11½	11½-12
14	urban area	3¾	0-2¼	2¼-7	——	7-8½	8½-9¾	9¾-11½	
15	urban area	4	0-2¾	2¾-4½	4½-7	7-9	9-9¾	9¾-12	——
16	urban area	5	0-2¾	2¾-4½	4½-7	7-9	9-9¾	9¾-12	——
17	farmland	4	0-2¾	2¾-4½	4½-7½	7½-9	9-10	10-12	——
18	wastewater treatment plant	3	¼-2½	2½-4	4-7½	7½-9	9-10	10-12	
19	farmland	2½	0-2¼	2¼-4½	4½-8	8-9	9-10¼	10¼-12	——
20	river	1½	¼-2½	2½-4½	4½-8	8-9¼	9¼-10½	10½-12	——
21	river	½	1-2½	2½-5	5-8	8-9¼	9¼-10½	10½-12	——
22	river	1½	¼-3	3-8	——	8-9¼	9¼-10½	10½-12	——
23	national park	2	0-3	3-8	——	8-9½	9½-10¾	10¾-12	——
24	national park	3¼	0-2¾	2¾-8	——	8-9¾	9¾-11	11-12	
25	national park	3¾	0-3	3-8	——	8-10	10-11¼	11¼-12	——

Ground Water Student Page

Name _____   Date _____

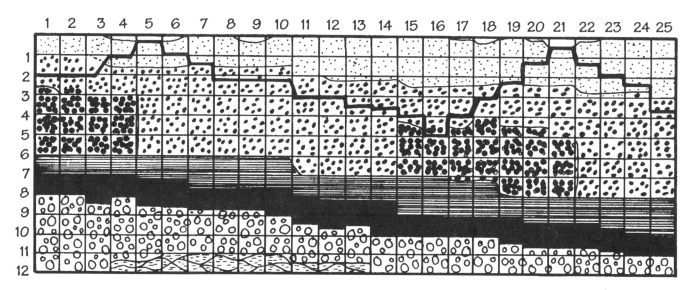

Well Log Ground Water Chart (Cross Section)

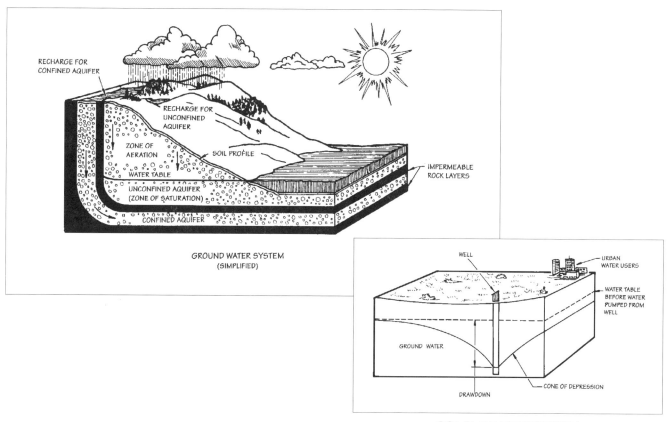

GROUND WATER SYSTEM
(SIMPLIFIED)

CONE OF DEPRESSION

Water Use, Water Users

Water Resources Management is a Conservation Choice

Alligators, Epiphytes, and Water Managers

Conserve Water

Grade Level:
Upper Elementary, Middle School

Subject Areas:
Language Arts, Geography, Life Science, Ecology

Duration:
Preparation time: 30 minutes

Activity time: 50 minutes

Setting:
Classroom

Skills:
Organize (matching), Analyze (identifying components), Interpret (summarizing), Apply

Vocabulary:
adaptations, phreatophyte, xerophyte, epiphyte, radial root system

Summary
Students identify plants, animals, and their water conservation behaviors by analyzing clues that describe water-related adaptations of aquatic and terrestrial organisms.

Objectives
Students will
· recognize water-related adaptations of some plants and animals that apply to water conservation principles.

Materials
· a set of *Water Clue Cards* Student Copy Pages for each group of students (these cards can be mounted on cardboard or laminated for durability)
· a set of *Water Photo Cards* Student Copy Pages for each group of students
· pencil and paper for scorekeeping
· map of the world
· reference materials
· 3"x5" index cards

Background
Although we humans often take credit for behaviors and engineering feats that help us conserve water, other organisms all over the planet have practiced water conservation for thousands of years. In fact, these adaptations to wet or dry environments are embedded in their genetic code and are passed and altered from generation to generation.

Water is one of the more common substances on earth. However, it is not distributed equally across the planet. More than any other single environmental factor, the quantity of available water determines the amount and type of vegetation in an area. Therefore, water "inequality" contributes to the diversity of plant communities and the animals associated with them.

Some animals have amazing relationships with water. Desert nesting sand grouse fly great distances to water sources, sometimes as far as 18 miles. They wet their specialized belly feathers and return to the nest. The chicks suck the water from the parent's feathers.

When a grizzly bear hibernates, it does not take in any water for as long as seven months. However, in preparation for hibernation, bears drink great quantities of water and consume as much as 20,000 calories per day in food. Apparently, the fat that is accumulated serves as the food and water reserve for the hibernating bear.

An Abnaki Indian saying goes: "A bear is wiser than man, because a man does not know

how to live all winter without eating anything." Recent research has revealed that recycling is the key in the unique physiological processes that occur in bears during hibernation. Bears do not urinate during hibernation; under regular conditions this buildup of urea within the system could be toxic. However, in a hibernating bear, urea is reabsorbed through the bladder wall and goes back into the bear's system. Researchers are interested in this process for its potential application to human medicine and human activities such as space travel.

Other animals have adaptations that help them obtain and conserve water. The kangaroo rat seals itself off from the heat in an underground den and recycles the moisture from its own respiration. The animal does this even though it does not exhale much moisture while breathing: special organs in its nose retain water that would otherwise be exhaled. A desert dweller, the kangaroo rat feeds only on dry seeds. The animal metabolizes fat and proteins in a way that provides all the fresh water it needs. The koala—not really a bear—gets all the water it needs from the leaves of the eucalyptus tree, its only source of food.

Even some predators and scavengers such as the turkey vulture get all the moisture they need from their food. However, unlike the kangaroo rat, they will drink if water is available.

Desert animals have diverse mechanisms that allow them to obtain, conserve, recycle, and, like the kangaroo rat, even manufacture water. The typical showpiece for water conservation is the camel. A camel can survive for days or even months on limited water supplies. In fact, it can go for about nine days without a drink of water. The camel retains most of the water that is within its body; it does not sweat much and can tolerate an increase in body temperature of 11 degrees F (6° C). A camel gets moisture from its food and stores water in fat cells throughout its body. However, when they have access to water, camels can drink about 50 gallons at once.

Many animals conserve their resources by avoiding excess heat. Some birds migrate, leaving the desert during the

hottest seasons. Some animals are active only during the cooler periods of the day— at dawn and dusk. Throughout the rest of the day they remain in cool, shady places. Rattlesnakes and Gila monsters generally follow this pattern. Some creatures are nocturnal, moving around only at night. They spend the hot daylight hours in a burrow, a cave, or even the shade provided by a rock. Many snakes, all bats, most rodents, some species of foxes, and skunks are nocturnal animals.

The water-holding frog lives in the hot, dry interior of Australia. It spends most of its time buried underground, sealed in a cocoon made of discarded skin. When it rains—which sometimes doesn't happen for two or three years—the frog leaves its burrow and comes to the surface where it absorbs and stores a lot of water in its bladder. When the rain stops, the frog burrows underground again. Aborigines know how to find these frogs. They sometimes dig them up and squeeze water from them to drink. Apparently this does not physically harm the frog.

Also from Australia, a desert animal with a truly amazing water story is the thorny devil. The lizard's skin is covered with thousands of tiny grooves. When the temperature drops in the desert at night, dew condenses on the thorny devil's

skin. The water flows in the grooves toward the animal's mouth where it is easily sipped.

Some animals manipulate their environment in order to satisfy their water needs. In the Everglades of southern Florida, alligators engineer water holes that retain this precious resource through the dry winter months. Fish, frogs, water snakes, and other creatures retreat to alligator holes as the Everglades dries up. Birds, raccoons, and other predators congregate at these reservoirs because of the concentration of food sources.

The surival of the wood stork, a bird of the Everglades ecosystem, is relevant to the 4 R's of water conservation. The nesting wood stork depends on having the right amount of water at the right time. The wood stork usually nests at the beginning of the dry season. The onset of drying concentrates fish into ponds where they are more easily caught by the adult storks to feed their ravenous nestlings. Drying and the subsequent concentration of food apparently trigger the wood stork's instinct to nest. In recent years when water levels have not reflected natural historic patterns, wood stork nesting has often failed. The population has seriously declined and the wood stork has been listed as an endangered species. Because of its black

head and neck, the bird is locally called "ironhead."

But animals are not the only organisms that conserve water. Several species of plants have adapted to extremes of wet and dry by using both physical and behavioral mechanisms. In the desert, plants called xerophytes have adapted by altering their own physical structures to store and hold water. Cacti are xerophytes.

The water conservation characteristics of cacti include: absence of leaves (which reduces water loss through transpiration); extensive, shallow root systems that can quickly collect large amounts of water when it rains; water storage capability in their stems; spines that provide shade and collect moisture; and a waxy skin that seals in moisture. There are hundreds of varieties of cactus.

Phreatophytes grow extremely long roots to tap limited water supplies. Some species like the creosote bush have a root system that is both radial and deep. This allows the plant to draw upon both surface and ground water resources.

A third group of plants called epiphytes grow on host trees and are common in rainforest areas. Many orchids and ferns are epiphytic. Although they often grow in rainforests, epiphytes have developed mechanisms to counter drought. Nearly all epiphytes have structures that hold water. For example, the leaves of bromeliads form a funnel in which water collects. These small reservoirs also provide moisture for a variety of snakes, snails, lizards, insects, and spiders. Around no more than a cup of water, entire food webs may grow.

So what do alligators, epiphytes, and water managers have in common? Water storage, of course!

Procedure

Warm Up

Discuss the importance of water to all living things. What is the longest time that students have ever gone without water? Have them describe the feeling of thirst. Humans cannot live more than three or four days without water. However, many organisms have physiological mechanisms that allow them to survive for extended periods without water. Ask students if they can list any of these organisms? (hibernating bears, camels, kangaroo rats).

Plants, as well as animals, have evolved mechanisms and structures for the conservation of water. Ask students how having the following characteristics would enable plants to conserve water:
· few or no leaves
· waxy coating on leaves
· extensive root systems that

are radial and deep, shallow, or both
· water-storage capacity

Ask students to explain how evaporation and transpiration may work against organisms that are trying to conserve their water resources.

Have students list different ecosystems and compare water availability in these areas. Are there habitats where mechanisms to conserve water are more prominent in the plants and animals that live there?

The Activity

1. Tell students they are going to play a riddle game in which they must guess an organism's identity using as clues the mechanisms or behaviors it employs to conserve water. Players will also speculate on the habitat of these plants or animals.
2. Distribute a set of *Water Clue Cards* to each group. Caution students not to look through the cards before the game begins.
3. Explain that each card lists characteristics, mechanisms and/or behaviors of a certain organism that may relate to water conservation. Based on the clues, students will try to determine the plant or animal and the habitat in which it is usually found.
4. Each group should select one student to be a "reader." This student will read the clues,

one at a time and in any order, until someone in the group can guess the plant or animal. Answers are listed at the bottom of each card. When students correctly identify the plant or animal, provide them with the organism's picture from the *Water Photo Cards* Student Copy Page and have them place it on the map to show where it lives. (Research books should be available so students can research the organism.)
5. The student who correctly identifies the organism receives points based on the number of clues that were read before he or she was able to name the plant or animal. Assign one student in each group to be scorekeeper and record the scores as follows:
One clue read = four points
Two clues read = three points
Three clues read = two points
Four clues read = one point
6. The student who correctly identifies the organism becomes the new reader and begins reading the clues on the next card. Continue the game until all cards have been read.

Wrap Up

Discuss how adaptations enable organisms to live in their environment. Have students summarize water-related adaptations included in the game. Is it possible for humans to adapt any of these water conservation practices? (For example, could we apply the bear's ability to hibernate and

recycle toxins to the problems of prolonged space travel for humans? Or adapt the thorny devil's water collection system to design water catchment for human structures? Or imitate the engineering of the alligator's water hole to build human reservoirs for water storage during dry periods?)

Remind students that each of the thousands of plants and animals not included in this activity has many adaptations. Have students visit the library and view videos to research other organisms' adaptations for conservation of water resources and make clue cards for their own game. The game can then be played with these new cards, and groups can swap sets for longer games. Encourage students to play this game with family and friends.

Assessment

Have students:
· identify an organism and its habitat from a set of clues describing behaviors that conserve water (steps 4 and 5).
· explain how adaptations enable plants and animals to live in diverse habitats (*Wrap Up*).
· create clue cards for different organisms, listing water-conserving adaptations (*Wrap Up*).

Extensions

Have students identify other behaviors that plants and animals have adopted to conserve water. Then have them research and discover the human analog to these behaviors. Students may begin their research by asking the question: What water conservation efforts undertaken by humans originated from observing and studying plants and animals?

Students can even create a new organism in an environment of the future or in a fictional water environment on a different planet. Have them imagine special features or behaviors the organism would need in order to live in this environment; encourage students to be creative. Students should write a detailed description or draw a picture of the habitat, depicting how the organism blends into the environment and how it obtains, stores, and/or conserves water. Have students evaluate each other's designs and provide suggestions for improvement. The portraits and descriptions can be posted.

Resources

Bailey, Jill. 1992. *Birds*. New York: Dorling Kindersley, Inc.

Brown, Gary. 1993. *Great Bear Almanac*. New York: Lyons and Burford.

The Watercourse. 1996. *Discover a Watershed: The Everglades*. Bozeman, Mont.: The Watercourse.

Internet:
www.panda.org/kids/wildlife/fmthdev.htm
(numerous sites of the World Wide Fund for Nature)

Alligators, Epiphytes & Water Managers
Water Clue Cards

· I may not take in any water or urinate for as long as seven months.
· Urea is reabsorbed through my bladder wall and goes back into my system; if researchers can discover how I recycle this potential toxin, it may benefit space travelers.
· The fat I accumulate serves as my food and water reserve for a period of up to seven months.
· I eat about 20,000 calories a day and drink great quantities of water to prepare for my months of inactivity.

Answer: Hibernating brown bear

· I seal myself in an underground den and recycle the moisture from my own respiration.
· I metabolize fat and protein from dry seeds in a way that provides all the fresh water I need.
· I escape the midday heat in a cool underground den.
· I do not drink water even when it is available.

Answer: Kangaroo rat

· I am able to drink great volumes of water and store it in the fat cells throughout my body.
· I rarely sweat or urinate, and I don't pant or breathe rapidly (in these ways, I reduce evaporation)
· I can travel without drinking water 10 times longer than a human can.
· Fat stored in my hump is broken down for energy, and in the process, water, which I can use, is released.

Answer: Camel—desert

· I have no leaves, which cuts down on water loss through transpiration.
· I have an extensive, shallow root system that can quickly collect large amounts of water when it rains.
· I have a waxy skin that seals in moisture.
· I store water in my stem which expands like an accordion to hold great volumes of water.

Answer: Cactus—desert

Alligators, Epiphytes & Water Managers
Water Clue Cards, continued

· I use my broad snout and powerful jaws and claws as tools in my excavations.
· Many creatures are dependent on the water refuge I maintain, especially during the dry winter months.
· Entire food webs develop around my water hole and I am at the top of my food chain.
· For people around the world I am the symbol of the Everglades, one of my homes.

Answer: American alligator

· I am common in rainforests.
· I usually grow on a host tree.
· Some of my kind store water like a cup.
· Snakes, lizards, insects, and other organisms collect around my small reservoir.

Answer: Epiphytes

· My survival depends on the right amount of water at the right time.
· I am an indicator of the health of the Everglades ecosystem.
· I am an endangered species.
· Black scales cover my head and neck and locally I am known as "ironhead."

Answer: Wood stork

· I have been called Moloch, the devil, because of the large spines that completely cover my fat body and tail.
· I am a lizard that lives in the desert of Australia.
· Although the desert is dry, water condenses on my body at night and flows through the thousands of grooves on my skin to my lips where I sip my fill.
· My favorite food is ants, which I eat one at a time, sometimes consuming thousands in one meal.

Answer: Thorny devil (Molochorridus)

Alligators, Epiphytes & Water Managers
Water Photo Cards

COURTESY OF CINCINNATI ZOO AND BOTANICAL GARDEN

C. ALLAN MORGAN

COURTESY OF CINCINNATI ZOO AND BOTANICAL GARDEN

DON UNSER

Alligators, Epiphytes & Water Managers
Water Photo Cards, continued

COURTESY OF EVERGLADES NATIONAL PARK

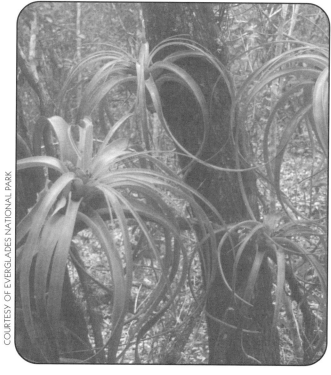

COURTESY OF EVERGLADES NATIONAL PARK

COURTESY OF EVERGLADES NATIONAL PARK

PETER WALTON PHOTOGRAPHY

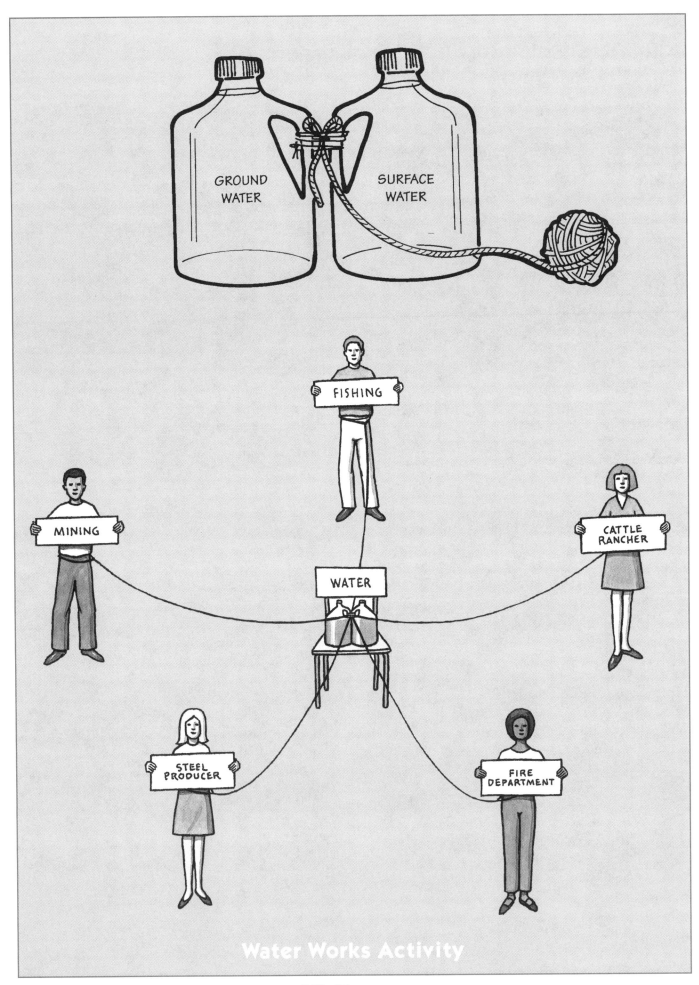

Water Works Activity

© The Watercourse

Water Works

Grade Level:
Upper Elementary, Middle School

Subject Areas:
Government, Environmental Science

Duration:
Preparation time: 30 minutes

Activity time: 50 minutes

Setting:
Classroom

Skills:
Gather information (observing); Analyze (identifying components and relationships); Interpret (inferring)

Vocabulary:
direct water use, indirect water use

Summary
Students create a "water web" to illustrate the interdependence among water producers and users.

Objectives
Students will:
· distinguish between direct and indirect uses of water.
· illustrate the interconnectedness of water users in a community.
· demonstrate the complexity of resolving water shortages among interdependent community water users.

Materials
· copy of *Descriptions of Water Users* Student Copy Pages
· index cards
· marking pens
· tape or string
· 2 plastic milk jugs (Label one jug "surface water" and the other "ground water." Tie the two handles together with string. Fill jugs with water and cap jugs.)
· large ball of string or yarn, or index cards cut into strips

Background
People use water for direct and indirect purposes. Direct uses include bathing, drinking, and cooking. Indirect uses of water include irrigating grains that go into our bread, processing wood for making our paper, and producing steel for building the automobiles we drive, all of which require large quantities of water.

Agriculture, industry, and power production are society's major water users. Sometimes we are critical of the amount of water a manufacturer requires to create a product; however, we are often the major consumers of that product. To resolve this dilemma, many water users are searching for ways to maintain production but reduce water consumption.

Today, many farmers practice more efficient irrigation methods. Manufacturers use less water by incorporating recycled materials into their products or by recycling water within their factories. Producing a ton of recycled paper uses 60,000 gallons (230,000 l) less water than producing a ton of virgin paper. Individuals who conserve water and energy and use recycled products support the efforts of conscientious manufacturers and farmers, ensuring the availability of water for all water users.

Procedure
Warm Up
Have students list the ways they use water. If students do not include indirect uses of water, ask them if they think they use water when they ride in a car or read a newspaper. Explain that producing both cars and paper requires water. Have students suggest other ways they use water indirectly.

Ask students to guess how much water is required to make each of the items listed in the box (right). Do not tell them if their guesses are accurate.

A pair of jeans made from cotton	1,800 gallons (6,840 l)
A 2-pound loaf of bread	1,000 gallons (3,800 l)
A pound of hamburger	4,000 gallons (15,200 l)
A 12-ounce can of soda	16.5 gallons (62.7 l)
The ton of finished steel used to make a car	32,000 gallons (121,600 l)
40 sheets of paper	100 gallons (380 l)

The Activity

1. Instruct each student to select a water user from the *Descriptions of Water Users* Student Copy Pages or from a class-generated list. Make nametags to identify water users. (Students may research how their water user depends on this resource.)

2. Have each student read silently the description of his or her water user. Ask "water users" to consider how they depend on products and services supplied by other users. For example, the steel manufacturer uses water to process steel and wash away waste materials. The production of steel requires not only water, but also energy; therefore, the car manufacturer is dependent on the power plant.

3. Clear an area in the room. Place the two milk jugs, tied together at the handles with string, on a desk or chair in the middle of the cleared area. Tie the loose end of the ball of yarn to the string holding the two jugs together. Explain that the jugs represent sources of water and the ball of yarn symbolizes the water user's need for water.

4. Ask students to stand in a circle around the jugs of water.

5. Select a student to describe the goods or services his or her water user provides and explain how this product or service uses water. Run the ball of yarn to the student (who holds onto a loop in the yarn), back to the jugs and around the string holding the two jugs together. The yarn indicates that this water user consumed water. Repeat the process with each student.

6. Choose one water user (Student 1) and hand him or her the ball of yarn. Ask other students to raise their hands if they use the goods or services offered by Student 1.

7. Tell Student 1 to pass the ball of yarn to one of the students (Student 2) who raised his or her hand. Ask Student 2 to describe how he or she uses the products or services of Student 1.

8. Ask if other students use the products manufactured by Student 2. Have Student 2 pass the ball to another student (Student 3). Have all students repeat the process until connections are made among all or most class members.

9. To emphasize the interdependencies among water users, have one student tug gently on the yarn. Ask those who felt the pull to raise their hands. The tug symbolizes reliance on both water and that student's product.

10. At some time during the activity, the water jugs may shift or be lifted from the chair or table. Explain that this means the supply is overextended. Ask students if they think one water user should leave the circle. What will happen if one student lets go?

NOTE: As an alternative way to make connections among water users, give each student five strips of paper. Have each student write the name of his or her water user on each of the five strips. Students may decorate the "business card" of their water user with illustrations of goods or services provided. One at a time or in small groups, have students distribute their cards to other water users on whom they depend for goods or services. Students should end up holding strips of paper with names of other interdependent water

users. Conclude by having students read aloud their cards and describe the connections they have made.

Wrap Up

Discuss the results of the activity. Have students create a diagram displaying how water users depend on the goods and services provided by other water users.

Inform students of the quantities of water used to produce the materials listed in the *Warm Up*. Do any water users in the activity supply these materials? Do students use any of these materials? If community water supplies are overextended, how would the community decide which manufacturer should reduce water consumption? Students may find it difficult to single out one manufacturer. They may determine that requiring all water users to conserve water is more fair.

Have students contact local manufacturers to ask them how they use water and what conservation measures they practice. Students can create a mural of the waterworks of their community. Include how community members use water, depend upon each other, and, if appropriate, conserve water.

Assessment

Have students:
· describe their direct and indirect uses of water (*Warm Up*).
· draw a diagram showing how water users rely on the goods and services provided by other water users (*Wrap Up*).
· create a mural illustrating the waterworks and interdependencies of their community (*Wrap Up*).

Upon completing the activity, for further assessment, have students:
· conduct a town meeting to discuss proposed solutions to a community water shortage. Highlight the difficulties of identifying one particular water user whose use should be restricted or eliminated to help solve the problem.

Extensions

Tell students a bottle of food coloring represents a source of pollution. Place a drop in one of the jugs. Have students explain how water quality affects the quantity of water available to water users.

Have students form groups of common water users. How do groups relate to other water user groups? Although a common bond is shared in our need for water, discuss how conflicts can arise among water user groups.

Resources

Hammer, Trudy J. 1985. *Water Resources*. New York: Watts.

Miller, G. Tyler, Jr. 1990. *Resource Conservation and Management*. Belmont, Calif.: Wadsworth Publishing Company.

Pringle, Laurence. 1982. *Water: The Next Great Resource Battle*. New York: Macmillan.

Descriptions of Water Users

In addition to the descriptions listed below, students may research a specific water user during the week prior to this activity.

Agriculture: Water is used to produce food and fiber for processing and consumption.

Sugar cane grower: Uses water to irrigate crops and transport chemicals (pesticides and fertilizers) to crops.

Cattle rancher: Uses water to grow food and provide drinking water for cattle.

Fish farmer: Uses water to raise fish to maturity in rearing ponds and to carry waste from the ponds.

Wheat farmer: Uses water to irrigate crops.

Dairy farmer: Uses water to grow food and provide drinking water for cows and to sanitize milking equipment and stalls.

Mining: Water is used in the extraction process of raw materials (coal, iron, gold, copper, sand, and gravel).

Miner: Uses water to carry and wash rock material during the mineral removal processes.

Sand and gravel company: Uses water to wash fine soil and rock material out of sand and gravel formations. Sand and gravel are used in cement and road construction.

Logging: Water is used to grow and harvest trees.

Forest manager: Uses water to support tree growth and control fires.

Logging company: Uses water to float rafts of logs (on rivers and lakes) to collection points.

Transporting/Shipping: Water (rivers, seas, oceans) is used to transport raw materials and finished products to points of distribution (ports).

Slurry pipeline owner: Uses water to transport pulverized coal through pipelines to distant coal-fired power plants.

Ship's crew: Uses water to haul raw materials (e.g., logs, oil, gas, wheat) and finished products (e.g., automobiles, appliances, processed food) to points of transfer.

Business/Industry: Water is used in the processing and manufacturing of goods (cars, food, medical supplies, etc.).

Steel producer: Uses large volumes of water to process iron ore into steel.

Textile manufacturer: Uses water to wash and process raw materials (e.g., wool, cotton, mohair). Dye is mixed with water to color fabric.

Soft drink company: Uses water to produce soft drinks and to sanitize equipment.

Paper mill: Uses water to transport pulp fibers for paper making and to carry away waste.

Chemical manufacturer: Uses water in the production of pesticides and fertilizers.

Descriptions of Water Users, continued

Wildlife: Water provides habitat for countless plant and animal species.

Mammals: Beavers, muskrats, and otters live in and near waterways, and often find their food in water.

Fish: Trout, salmon, and carp live in water and eat organisms that live in water.

Insects: Aquatic insects are a food source for many other organisms, and use water for habitat and reproduction.

Vegetation: Trees and other plants use water in photosynthesis and to transport nutrients.

Recreation: People recreate in and around water for exercise and enjoyment.

Cruise ship: People travel to many parts of the world in cruise ships.

Fishing: People catch fish in rivers, lakes, and oceans.

Water theme park: Uses water to transport people on exciting and fun rides.

Scuba diver: People enjoy exploring underwater environments.

Winter sports: Snow and ice provide fun for skaters, skiers, and sledders.

Power Generation: Water is used to generate electricity.

Hydropower plant: Water flowing in rivers is stored behind dams in reservoirs. As water is released by the dam, it turns turbines that generate electricity.

Nuclear power plant: Uses water in cooling towers to maintain safe operating temperatures.

Coal-fired power plant: Burning coal produces steam heat that turns turbines, creating electricity.

Community: Water is used by community members for domestic, maintenance, and recreational purposes.

Domestic users: Water is used in a multitude of ways in and around the home.

Fire department: Uses water to extinguish fires.

Street cleaner: Uses water to wash oil, litter, and other materials from streets.

Restaurant owner: Uses water to cook meals, clean the kitchen, wash tables and floors, and water lawns.

Park: Uses water in landscaping, in fountains, and in reflecting ponds.

Nothing New Under the Rainbow

The Story of Water in History and Culture

Water Vessels

Summary

Students compete in a water hauling game, create their own vessels to hold and carry water, and write imaginative stories based on the art and history of pottery.

Grade Level:
Middle School

Subject Areas:
Fine Arts, Language Arts, History/Anthropology

Duration:
Preparation time:
  Part I: 15 minutes
  Part II: 15 minutes set up if clay is purchased, or allow students 15 minutes to make the clay
  Part III: none

Activity time:
  Part I: 50 minutes
  Part II: two 50-minute periods
  Part III: three 50-minute periods (research, writing/drawing, presentation)

Setting:
Schoolyard (Part I), Classroom (Parts II and III)

Skills:
Gather information, Organize, Analyze, Apply, Present

Vocabulary:
plasticity, evaporation, porosity, permeability

Objectives

Students will:
· relate how easy access to water can encourage people to use large amounts of water.
· design and construct a water-holding vessel.
· create a vessel in the style of the Pueblo or other cultures.

Materials:

Part I
· 4 1-gallon (3.8 l) buckets
· 2 30-gallon (114 l) garbage cans
· water source or outdoor spigot

Part II
· pottery clay or modeling dough (See *Pueblo Pottery Student Copy Page*)
· paint (optional)
· sand paper (optional)

Part III
· research books on the pottery of diverse cultures
· access to the Internet (optional research tool)

Background

Always we were handicapped by a lack of water. Father's first well, dug nearly eighty feet down, bore nothing but dust. So our thirst sent us

searching for water. At last, we dug a shallow well in a coulee several miles away. We traveled there daily for our water supply, which we carried home in large barrels. We stinted our water carefully for bathing, and washed our clothes in a small washbasin, since we had insufficient water to fill the washtub! (Mary Ellen Wolfe, *A Landowner's Guide to Western Water Rights*)

This is a composite of the memories of families who homesteaded on the North American prairie in the late 1800s. At that time, many people spent hours each week hauling water for their daily needs. People throughout the world of diverse cultures still collect, carry, and store water for domestic use. In fact, some cultures are returning to traditional methods to help solve their water scarcity problems.

Throughout time, cultures used materials from their environment to make containers, many of which were used to carry and store water. Native Americans harvested plant materials such as willow, sedge, cane, birch bark, bracken fern, roots, grasses, and cottonwood to weave beautiful and functional baskets. They often incorporated other materials such as feathers, quills, shells, beads, baleen (from whales), and seal guts into the baskets. In early years, women prepared and

COURTESY OF MUSEUM OF NEW MEXICO, OFFICE OF ARCHAEOLOGICAL STUDIES

Pot from Mogollon area, southwest New Mexico

sized the material for weaving by pulling the plant fibers through their front teeth. Although the process varied from tribe to tribe, most material had to be cured for a year before it could be used to weave a basket.

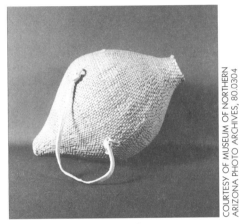

Havasupai or Walapi water basket

All native people constructed baskets. However, the prehistoric people of the southwestern United States have been called the Basket Makers because of the number of baskets uncovered at their burial sites. Some baskets were used as water containers and cooking vessels. The Cliff Dwellers of the Southwest wove their baskets so tightly that they could carry water in them. Later, they smeared clay inside the baskets to make them more waterproof; this practice probably led to pottery making. The Anasazi relied on baskets before they learned how to make pottery. They lined their baskets with pitch to waterproof them and

dropped heated stones into the water for cooking.

Where clay was accessible, people crafted pots, jars, jugs, and other vessels for carrying and storing water. In some cultures, only women worked with clay. The skill was often transmitted from generation to generation within families; a potter might train a relative's daughter or one of her own daughters.

In some areas, potters still dig clay from the earth and dry it. They beat the dried clay and remove stones and other stray materials from it. Then they add water to the clay and mix and beat it until it is the right consistency.

Water is critical in the formation of pottery. Water gives clay its plasticity, allowing it to be malleable and still hold its shape.

The firing temperature and the type of clay (which is produced by the weathering of silicate rocks), water, and filler determine the quality of the end product. When filler (i.e., sand, crushed shells, straw, feathers) is added to the clay, it allows water to evaporate more smoothly and lessens shrinkage, which helps to prevent cracks from forming in the pot or jar.

A person designing a pot to hold water must decide on the

permeability of the material and the color of the vessel. In hot climates, water jar material should be permeable; if the pot is porous, water will seep through from one surface to another. The water that seeps will evaporate and cool the contents. This same concept was used to design the canvas water bag of the 1800s. On hot days, the bag would sweat—water would condense on the outside surface. Air moving over the bag cooled the contents through evaporation. People often draped their bags over automobile headlights or wagon seats to assure the cooling action of moving air. Wrapping a jug in burlap soaked with water performed the same function. Color is also important. A light-colored pottery jar will reflect the sunlight, helping to maintain the temperature of the contents.

On the other hand, if you want to store water over a long period of time or cook with the vessel, you do not want liquids to seep. The heating efficiency of a cooking container that seeped would be reduced; this would extend the cooking time and waste fuel, which is in short supply in some parts of the world.

Whereas women generally make the pots, one of the first tasks of children in many cultures is hauling water. Therefore, any container designed for hauling water must

© The Watercourse

be durable and as lightweight as possible. Water alone weighs about 8 pounds per gallon.

Today, in homes throughout the world, jugs of different kinds are used to hold water; specific uses are determined by the size of the jug. A large, oval jug is usually placed in the home for storing water for drinking or cooking. A medium-sized jug is used for transporting water from the river. The smallest containers are for drinking. In some areas where plastic and metal have replaced clay, the people still use pottery vessels for storing water. They maintain that these containers keep water fresh.

Even canteens have been made from clay. A two-handled flask, round and flat like a modern canteen, was uncovered from an ancient household in Israel, thought to be about 2,700 years old. It could not stand up by itself, so researchers believe it was probably filled with water and carried around.

Over time, clay vessels that held water were constructed in many different shapes and sizes. Some Native American cultures produced beautiful water bottles with long necks, water pitchers, and canteens. Even though most Pueblo pottery is small, the pueblo of Santa Clara also created large *ollas* (containers that held water and food) that were more than two feet tall.

In the southwest, water was transported in tall pottery jars with narrow necks. These large jars were carried in a hammock on the back; extra support was provided by a tumpline around the forehead. There was a great deal of seepage with these large jars which made them impractical for long trips. For carrying water great distances, the people waterproofed small jars with piñon pine pitch.

Many of the vessels crafted by Native Americans were beautifully painted. In the southwestern United States, the designs on Indian pottery were decorative, symbolic or both. The interpretation of a design may vary from tribe to tribe. Rain clouds, snow clouds, rain, snow, and other natural elements and creatures were often carved or painted on the pottery of the dry Southwest. Generally these symbols can be interpreted at face value. Among the Pueblo Indians, snakes and lightning represent rain and therefore fertility.

Throughout the world, explorers, archaeologists, art collectors, and others have recorded seeing or have acquired containers for storing water that native peoples crafted from materials available within their environment. These include: watertight baskets, clay vessels (jugs, pitchers, canteens), buckets crafted from birch bark and other wood, drinking bowls made of coconut shells (collected by explorer James Cook in the South Seas in the late 1700s), hollowed-out gourds, ostrich eggshells, and bags made from the skins of animals and canvas. A saying among Native Americans claims "a piece [of pottery] can speak to you." Surely these vessels would speak of the need for clean and abundant water that sustains the bodies and spirits of people of all cultures.

Pots from Mogollon area, southwest New Mexico

Procedure

Warm Up

Ask students what containers they use to hold water (a glass, mug, paper cup, etc.). What would they use to carry water if they were going on an all-day hike? Some historians claim that the early mountain men did not carry canteens or other water containers; instead, they often followed streams and drank directly from water sources. Why should students carry water and not drink untreated stream water today?

Today most students can turn on the tap to get clean, flowing water. What did people have to do 100 years ago to get their water? Remember that it was usually the children in the family who hauled the water. Ask students to list the chores they are expected to do after school. Do they usually have free time when their work is done? A family of four in the United States currently uses about 175 gallons of water per day. How much free time would they have if they had to haul their family's water each day? If they had to haul their water, would they use less?

The Activity

Part I

1. Tell students they are going to play a water-hauling game.
2. Divide the class into two teams. Each team gets two 1-gallon (3.8 l) buckets. Their task is to haul a single bucket of water from a water source such as a pond, stream, or spigot to a destination (garbage can) about 150 feet (45 m) away.
3. The game is played as a relay race. Team members line up at the water source. One team member from each team fills the bucket then carries it to the destination and pours it into the team's garbage can. He or she returns to the water source and passes the bucket to the next team member, who fills the bucket and relays it. The first team to fill the garbage can wins!
4. Ask students to predict how many trips they think it will take to fill the can. How much time is required? Record their responses for future reference. Ready, set, GO!

Part II

1. Provide students with pottery clay if it is available, or have students make modeling dough. (See the recipe on *Pueblo Pottery* Student Copy Page.)
2. Discuss the various types of vessels produced by native peoples through time for carrying and storing water.
3. You may incorporate a discussion of the role of water in producing clay and introduce or review terms like plasticity, evaporation, porosity, and permeability.
4. Ask students to work with the clay and to experiment in creating a vessel for holding water. What qualities should they be striving for?
5. Discuss what they have made.
6. Distribute the *Pueblo Pottery* Student Copy Pages and have students create a piece of pottery in the style of the Pueblo Indians. How does it compare with their original piece?
7. Introduce the symbols painted on or carved into pottery. They may decorate their pottery with symbols representing their own lives or use those of the Pueblo Indians.

Part III

1. Repeat the Native American saying to students: "A piece [of pottery] can speak to you." Ask students to imagine that they are archeologists and that they have uncovered a water jar or pottery shard (a piece from an original pot) from an ancient culture. They may select the culture (Native Americans of the Southwest, the early people of India or Africa, etc.) or you may choose for them based on curricular needs. Remind students that pottery was not only produced by Native Americans of the Southwest, but also by eastern tribes, tribes of Canada and Alaska, and early native people from the Midwest.
2. Have students conduct research on the culture. Possible key words include: material culture (a culture's products and their uses), pottery, ves-

sels, containers, Pueblo pottery, Hopi, Zuni, Zia, Anasazi culture, Mesa Verde.

3. Using the information they have gathered about the culture, have them write a fictional story that begins with the saying, "A piece can speak to you." Remind them that a common theme should be the culture's need to obtain clean and abundant water. Tell students to describe the environment in which the vessel is used—hot and dry, moist and warm, etc.

4. Have students draw the shard or pot based on their research of the pottery of that culture.

5. Have students share their stories and display their drawings. Discuss how the need for water cuts across all cultural, political, and temporal boundaries.

Wrap Up

Were the students accurate in their predictions of the number of trips and the time it would take to fill the garbage can? Ask students how they felt about hauling water. How might their perceptions change if hauling water was not a game, but a daily task? How would their lives be different today if the task of hauling water for the family was suddenly assigned to them. Would students be inclined to take longer or shorter showers?

Discuss how people's water use habits might change if:
· water was more difficult to obtain.
· water was more expensive.
· water was in short supply.

Compare and contrast the containers that students made out of clay. Have them interpret the symbols they used to decorate their containers. Why are ancient symbols that are associated with rain also associated with prosperity? What are students' feelings about rain? Do they always view rain as positive? Why or why not?

Have students discuss their research procedures. What sources did they use: Internet? Library (books, journals, periodicals)? Encyclopedia? Videos? CD roms? What key words did they use in their search for information? Did they discover stories based on pottery and ancient cultures? Was the information difficult or easy to obtain? Was it interesting to learn about the needs and practices of other cultures? How do the needs of early cultures compare with our needs today?

Assessment

Have students:
· express their feelings about hauling water (*Wrap Up*).
· compare and contrast the pottery containers they created in the style of the Pueblo Indians (**Part II**, step 6, and *Wrap Up*).

· interpret the symbols they inscribed on their pottery (*Wrap Up*).
· write and illustrate a fictional story based on uncovering a clay pot or pottery shard (**Part III**, step 3 and 4, and *Wrap Up*).

Extensions

Remind students that early cultures used material from their environment to produce containers to hold, carry, and store water. Ask students to think about materials within their environment and have them engineer and produce a container to hold, carry, or store water. What qualities would their containers share with ancient vessels? How would the design vary with the use? For example, what kind of container would be appropriate for carrying water on a hike? For keeping water cold?

Have students collect different contemporary water-holding containers. What questions do students think the engineers who design these containers ask themselves? Would these questions relate to container size, durability, volume, stability of the material used to make the container, interaction of the liquid with the material of the container, etc.?

Resources

Arnoldi, Mary Jo, Christraud M. Geary, and Kris L. Hardin. 1996. *African Material Culture*. Indianapolis: Indiana University Press.

Hauser-Schaublin, Brigitta, and Gundolf Kruger, (eds). 1998. *James Cook*. Munich: Prestel.

Hucko, Bruce. 1999. *Southwestern Indian Pottery*. Las Vegas, Nev.: KC Publications, Inc.

The Watercourse. 1993. *The Liquid Treasure Water History Trunk: Learning From the Past*. Bozeman, Mont.: The Watercourse.

Lambert, Joseph B. 1997. *Traces of the Past, Unraveling the Secrets of Archaeology Through Chemistry*. Reading, Mass.: Addison-Wesley.

Orton, Clive, Paul Tyers, and Alan Vince. 1993. *Pottery in Archaeology*. Cambridge: Cambridge University Press.

Wolfe, Mary Ellen. 1996. *A Landowner's Guide to Western Water Rights*. Bozeman, Montana: The Watercourse.

Woods, Ellen. 1997. *American Indian Artifacts*. Washington, D.C.: Seven Locks Press.

Internet sites: The Collector's Guide to the Art of New Mexico http://w.collectorsguide.com/fa/fa008.shtml

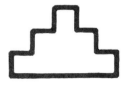

Pueblo Pottery

Undecorated pottery has been discovered in the Rio Grande valley that can be traced back to A.D. 700. This pottery was utilitarian (useful, created to fulfill certain functions). It was used for storing and preparing food, carrying water, and other work. Pottery produced later was often more ornate and is of great interest to collectors. Creating a fine piece of pottery is time consuming, and each pot is unique. Many potters claim that they "talk with the clay." They believe that the clay knows what shape it wants to take and often what designs should be painted or engraved on it. Following are the steps to create a Pueblo pot.

1. **Acquiring and preparing the materials.** The clay is removed from the quarry and dried in the sun for a few days. Then it is soaked in water for two to four days. After being rinsed and mixed several times, the solution is strained through a sieve to remove pebbles, twigs, etc. The thick solution is allowed to "set up" for a few days. Filler is mixed with the clay to help prevent cracking when the pot is fired. Your clay may already be prepared or you may mix the following ingredients to produce your own modeling dough.

Knead together:
1 cup (22.4 g) flour
$^1/_2$ cup (11.2 g) salt
$^3/_4$ cup (180 ml) hot water
1 tablespoon (15 ml) salad oil
1 tablespoon (5 g) alum (optional)
*If consistency is too sticky, add more flour and salt.
This dough cannot be fired, but should be air-dried instead.

2. **Modeling.** Take a lump of clay about the size of your fist and shape it into a cone to form the base of your pot. Pueblo potters use a *kajape* "shaping spoon" to scrape and thin the clay. After the base is ready (that is, you have a "starter bowl") build the vessel by adding rolls or coils of clay. Moisten, rub, and turn the pot to shape it. Your goal is to smooth and thin the walls of the pot and produce a pleasing shape. If you intend to fire it, try to feel for small air pockets or impurities that may cause the pot to crack.

3. **Finishing.** If you are going to carve or press a design into your pot, you must do so before it dries. After decorating the pot, allow it to dry, then sand it.

Pueblo potters allow the pot to dry for two to four days if they are going to paint it. After your pot is dry, sand it with varying grades of paper from coarse to fine. Smooth the pot with a wet cloth. Potters next apply a "slip," a mixture of clay in water that is like thin cream, with a brush or a piece of cloth. After the slip dries, the pot is rubbed with a polishing stone (this is called burnishing).

4. **Decorating.** Before the pot is fired, potters apply traditional, natural paint that comes in three forms: clay, vegetal, and mineral. Although some potters use modern brushes, others still create their designs and patterns with traditional brushes made from yucca plants. Your teacher will supply you with paint. You may decide to use one of the Native American designs on the following pages.

5. **Firing.** If possible, your teacher will fire your pot. For the Pueblo potter, proper firing is essential. If the vessel is not prepared properly, it may explode in the kiln. But this does not usually happen. Some southwestern tribes did not permit talking while pots were in the kiln. They feared that a voice would fill the pot and cause it to explode. Whether your work is fired in the kiln or created with modeling dough, you have produced a beautiful and unique pot by adopting and adapting the style of the Pueblo potter.

Pueblo Pottery Making

**Step 1
Kneading**

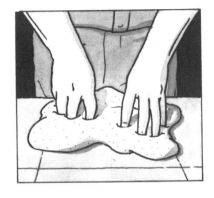

**Step 2
Forming
base**

**Adding
coils**

**Step 3
Finishing**

**Carving
designs**

Burnishing

**Step 4
Painting
designs**

**Step 5
Traditional
firing**

Pueblo Pottery Design Elements

These are replicas of simple, traditional designs made by Pueblo Indians. They represent weather elements and are used to decorate pottery and other art forms.

Lightning (often represented in the form of a snake)

Rain clouds

Snow clouds

Rain

Snow

Border created with elements of snow cloud

Mrs. Alderson, an old woman who homesteaded with her husband in the early 1900s in Montana.

© The Watercourse

Mrs. Alderson
Early Lessons in
Water Conservation

Summary
Students study water artifacts from the early 1900s and impart a message about water conservation through an interactive play.

Grade Level:
Upper Elementary, Middle School

Subject Areas:
Fine Arts, Language Arts, History/Anthropology, Environmental Sciences

Duration:
Preparation time
  Part I: 15 minutes
  Part II: 50 minutes

Activity time
  Part I: 25 minutes
  Part II: 50 minutes

Setting:
Classroom or outdoor theatre

Skills:
Analyze, Interpret, Apply, Present

Vocabulary:
water dowsing, artifact, washboard, ice card, stomper, water bag

Objectives
Students will:
· identify water artifacts from the turn of the twentieth century and relate their functions and connection with water conservation measures.
· demonstrate water use practices from the early 1900s and their relationship to lifestyle and water conservation measures through an interactive play.

Materials
· artifacts such as:
  Sears Roebuck Catalogue
  wooden bucket
  washboard
  dowsing rods
  water bag
  (If items cannot be obtained, students may use pictures from the *Water Artifacts* Student Copy Page.)
· *Water Artifact Photos* Student Copy Page (cut and laminate pictures)
· *Water Artifact Descriptions* Student Copy Page (cut and laminate descriptions)
· costume items (optional)
  old-fashioned dress
  shawl
  wire-rimmed spectacles
  gray wig
  bonnet
  apron
· script cards (cut and laminated)
· letter (written from script)

Background
One of society's concerns of truly fundamental importance is water. This has been the case throughout human history. Early men and women carrying drinking water in skin bags or hollowed-out gourds had the same need to quench their thirst as a modern backpacker with a plastic bottle. Pueblo Indians at the time of Columbus were experimenting with irrigation systems in order to survive the vagaries of weather. Homesteaders who settled the West struggled to grow crops, raise families, and build communities in an often dry land.

We sometimes forget that the past holds the key to the present, and that reflection upon the past helps prepare us for the future. By studying water through history, we can better understand and critique present trends, beliefs, and practices.

Surprising wisdom and important lessons can be found in historical records. Our ancestors used far less water per person than we do. Their technology, although basic and even crude by our standards, was often elegant in its simplicity. The folklore and old practices that deal with water seem quaint and comical to us, until we look closely enough to discover the kernels of truth and understanding that hide within them.

Procedure
Warm Up
Read the following selection to your students:

The atmosphere surrounding the small group of people gathered around a battered wagon on the open plains is strangely reverent. One woman has her hands clasped as if in prayer. A heavy-set man with an air of authority moves apart and, with a curt signal, commands silence. He holds a forked green branch of willow in his beefy hands.

Now he begins to walk, slowly, with the branch outstretched at waist level. The family has recently claimed this homestead on the barren prairie. They stand by in silence, watching attentively, knowing that land is only the first ingredient in their dream of a successful farm. Without water, the land will be useless

and unproductive, their hopes doomed.

The stranger moving about erratically before them has their future in his hands. He has found water on the land of several neighboring families, and he has glib theories to discount his failures on other property.

The stout man stops suddenly. Even at a distance you can see the willow branch quivering, the man's body tensing. The family unconsciously draws closer together while they watch. The figure moves a step to one side, then two or three steps forward.

Then the branch of willow arrows down toward the earth. The large man looks up, finds the family with his gaze and points at his feet. There the well will be dug, and nearby they will build their dwelling and begin the struggle to fulfill the dream that brought them here.

Ask students what event is taking place in this story. Within what time period of American history do they think the story is set? Are students familiar with water dowsing? Tell them that dowsing is a tradition firmly lodged in our history. Some individuals still practice it today, although there are advanced technological methods for locating ground water.

Discuss with students the tools that dowsers used. Forked branches from water-loving willow trees supposedly jerked downward over underground sources of water. Brass rods were also used, one in each hand. When the rods crossed over each other, water presumably lay below.

Ask students if their grandparents have ever mentioned dowsing or dowsing rods. Have students ever discovered other artifacts or antiques in the attics or barns of older relatives or friends? Stories about these items and their uses often reveal a great deal about the water-saving practices of our ancestors. Through a play, students will have the opportunity to learn about artifacts and their connection with the water-saving habits of the past.

The Activity
Part I
1. Organize students into cooperative learning groups. If you have access to the artifacts referenced in the script, give one to each group. If you do not have the actual items, distribute the pictures of the artifacts from the *Water Artifact Photos* Student Copy Pages.
2. Ask students if they have ever used any of these items or observed others using them. Direct students to speculate on how they think the artifacts

© The Watercourse

were used by people in the early 1900s. Have students share, discuss, and record their ideas within their groups.

3. Distribute the descriptions of the artifacts from the *Water Artifact Descriptions* Student Copy Pages and have students compare and contrast this information with their own interpretations. Have each group report to the class on how they thought the item was used and its actual function.

Part II

1. Tell students that they will be acting in a play that is set in the early 1900s in the West.

2. Ask if any student would be willing to play the character of Mrs. Alderson, or have students audition for the part. If no student in the class wishes to play the part, other options include: the teacher, a student from the drama club, or a performer from the community theater playing the role of Mrs. Alderson.

3. Cut out the script and glue it onto index cards so that Mrs. Alderson can actually read from the script. Laminate the cards, hole punch them, and assemble with a ring so that the character can flip the cards from scene to scene.

4. Distribute artifacts and cards so that other players can learn their parts.

5. Outfit Mrs. Alderson with all or any combination of the following items: bonnet, shawl, long old-fashioned looking dress, wire-rimmed spectacles, apron, gray wig. (Halloween is a good time to collect some of these items; second-hand stores may also carry them.)

6. Other students may contribute to the performance by painting background scenes or assembling appropriate props.

7. As students watch the performance, ask them to record the water-saving habits of early homesteaders.

Wrap Up

Ask students to review the list they compiled of water conservation habits that early homesteaders practiced. Do students think any of these practices would work today? Would students be willing to observe any of these measures?

Do students believe that there are people in the world who still observe these same practices? Is this because of the availability or quality of water or their level of technology? How do a culture's attitudes and lifestyle affect water conservation practices?

What other art forms could students develop to deliver a message about conservation of water resources? Could they write historical or international vignettes or develop plays that communicate people's need for water of good quality and sufficient quantity?

Assessment

Have students:

· speculate on the uses of early-1900s water artifacts (**Part I**, step 2).

· compare and contrast their ideas with the descriptions of the 1900s water artifacts (**Part I**, step 3).

· record the water conservation practices of their ancestors while taking part in an interactive play (**Part II**, step 7).

· relate how water availability, technology, and/or a culture's attitudes and lifestyle correlate with water conservation practices (*Wrap Up*).

Extensions

Students may elect to adapt the script to reflect the settlement patterns and water history of their own state or region. *Mrs. Alderson* or the adapted script could be performed for other classes or the community. The character of Mrs. Alderson and/or the performance could be part of a community Water Conservation Celebration.

Students may want to assemble a Water History Conservation Scrapbook. They could collect old photographs, documents, stories, letters, and pictures that represent water use in the past. The 1897 Sears, Roebuck Catalogue is an excellent resource (for information, call The Watercourse, 406/994-5392).

Some students may elect to build a water history house. Using the layout of a late-nineteenth-century house, students can study the 1897 Sears, Roebuck Catalogue to select items to furnish the house. As they locate water-related items, they should cut them out and glue them in place. Students could even determine the amount of water used by appliances from 1897 and compare them with present-day averages. Class members will be better able to understand, discuss, and appreciate the lifestyles of their ancestors and to compare past and present-day needs.

Another option is to have students select an artifact or photograph and write a short fictional story focusing on a scene that the artifact/picture suggests. To lend historical accuracy to the stories, encourage library research. (The selection from the *Warm Up* is an example.) Students' stories could be collected into a small book of water history and conservation fiction.

Resources

Alderson, T. Nannie, and Helena Huntington Smith. 1942. *A Bride Goes West*. Lincoln: University of Nebraska Press.

The Watercourse. 1993. *The Liquid Treasure Water History Trunk: Learning From the Past.* Bozeman, Mont.: The Watercourse.

WATER ARTIFACTS PHOTOGRAPHY BY SHELL BECK

Water Artifact Photos

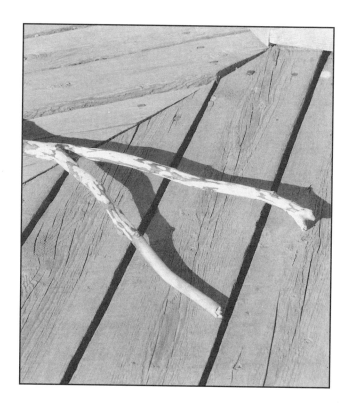

Water Artifact Photos, continued

Water Artifact Descriptions

Sears Roebuck and Company Catalogue

When outdoor privies or outhouses were the norm, catalogue pages and fruit wrapping paper were the most common toilet paper. They represent a time when water treatment and disposal technology were quite primitive and prone to cause problems. In some towns hundreds of well/outhouse combinations created serious water contamination. In modern times water treatment and waste water treatment plants have mitigated most of these difficulties.

Pages of the catalog are also full of historic items of interest, providing a view of the different life-styles illustrated by the products advertised at the time. Many products in the catalogue pages reflect water use and showcase human concerns of historic significance.

Water Bag

All people have needed containers to carry and store water. The traditional canvas water bag not only held water but also cooled it at the same time. On hot days water would condense or "sweat" on the outside surface. Air moving over the bag cooled the contents through evaporation, the same way that a breeze against sweaty skin feels chilly. People often draped their bags over automobile headlights or wagon seats to assure the cooling action of moving air. A jug wrapped in burlap and soaked with water performed the same function.

Washboard

A standard wash-day device and a great improvement over beating clothes against rocks. Most boards were constructed of tin, brass or glass and held in wooden frames. Some well-used boards will show the worn-down faces produced by many hours of tiresome rubbing. Washboards made entirely out of wood are a rare and exciting find. Wooden boards were made when conserving metal was necessary for wars or other national efforts. The wood faces show wear more readily than other materials.

Forked Willow Branch/Brass Rods:

These were the main props used by "dowsers" in their attempts to unlock the mysterious whereabouts of ground water. Using their tools, dowsers claimed the power to discern the location of accessible ground water, and they often were called upon to help families locate the all-important household well.

Forked branches from water-loving willow trees supposedly would jerk downward over underground sources of water. Brass rods also were used, one in each hand. When the rods crossed over each other, water presumably lay below.

Water Artifact Descriptions, continued

Other Water-related Items (not in the script)

Bucket

Before modern plumbing, families hauled water to their homes in buckets or cream containers and set the drinking supply in a handy spot. Ladles were used to dip up water and sometimes were referred to as the "community cup," since any thirsty member of the household might use it. In cool parts of the country, dippers often were scarred with chips and cracks from users breaking a skim of ice on the water bucket.

Stomper/Clothes Agitator

The hand-held, hand-operated stomper was used to wash and rinse clothes in much the same manner as the agitator mechanism in automatic washing machines. The user stood over a bucket or tub and worked the stomper up and down. The appliance was named for this stomping action.

Ice Tongs

Before electricity and modern refrigerators were common place, most rural families had a set of tongs with which to carry blocks of ice harvested during winter months from the icehouse to the icebox. In towns, ice companies used tongs to ferry blocks from their wagons into homes.

Ice Card

The standard ice card was placed in the window of a home to notify the local ice company that a delivery was needed. Some cards indicated the number of pounds or blocks of ice required.

SCRIPT: Mrs. Alderson

Before the play, choose a narrator. The narrator will inform the assembled group that they are not just members of the audience, but players. The players with their props may be scattered through the audience. Mrs. Alderson will perform on a stage or at the front or in the center of the classroom. Players should stand when they speak their lines.

The narrator will introduce Mrs. Alderson, an old woman who homesteaded with her husband in the early 1900s in Montana.

ENTER MRS. ALDERSON:

MRS. ALDERSON: Well, I see you young'uns been rummaging around in my old trunk. Folks don't see much in there they recognize anymore. **[Old woman wanders over to someone holding an artifact, and takes it in her hands.]** But these old things are as dear to me as people I've known and loved. Maybe that's because each one has a story. I look at that Sears catalogue and I want to laugh till the tears run down my cheeks, or I look at Mr. Alderson's water bag and tears want to drip again—but not from happiness.

PLAYER HOLDING SEARS CATALOGUE: But, Mrs. Alderson, what's an old Sears catalogue got to do with life on the frontier?

MRS. ALDERSON: I grew up in West Virginia and led a life of mahogany furniture and fine silver. Mr. Alderson had run away from home as a boy and returned to West Virginia as a young man when his father fell ill.

He had worked as a cowboy in Texas and was determined to go to Montana and run a ranch. Much to my mother's dismay, I agreed to marry him and become his partner on the ranch.

We traveled by train to Montana but the days of the journey were an agony for me.

PLAYER HOLDING SEARS CATALOGUE: Were you worried about wild animals or living in an isolated cabin?

MRS. ALDERSON: Heavens no. You see I had been raised very modestly and I was afraid to ask my new husband if he had properly outfitted our ranch for a lady—that is, had he built me a proper outhouse? When we were only a few miles away from our valley, I finally screwed up the courage to ask him. Why Mr. Alderson burst out laughing and he said, "I knew all the time you were worrying about that. I just wouldn't help you out." Fortunately, as the years passed, Mr. Alderson got smarter.

PLAYER HOLDING SEARS CATALOGUE: Well, had he built you a proper outhouse?

Mrs. Alderson, continued

MRS. ALDERSON: Oh, it was lovely. It was just a one-seater with walls all the way around, and it was open to the stars. Back then they just dug a pit and placed the outhouse over it. When the smell was so bad you could see and nearly taste it, you just dug a new pit and moved the outhouse. Didn't waste no water. But you didn't want your outhouse too close to the garden or your water supply.

PLAYER HOLDING PIECE OF WOOD: Did this piece of wood come from your out-house?

MRS. ALDERSON: No, no, that came from our first little cabin. Deciding where to build your house was awful important. I remember I was so upset when I saw where Mr. Alderson had built our little cabin. Our cabin was on high ground above the river. To me the river bottom with the beautiful willow trees looked so appealing. But a year later I was thankful for Mr. Alderson's wisdom. Terrible black thunderheads were building up over the mountains. One of our ranch cowboys said, "I shouldn't wonder if we have a cloudburst tomorrow." No sooner were the words out of his mouth when a wall of water came rushing down that river bottom—why it carried trees right along with it and I shall never forget the stench of mud and decay.

I heard of one tenderfoot who built his house too near an undercut bank. First good rain, the whole dern thing slipped right into the river.

PLAYER WITH BUCKET: Mrs. Alderson, so what about this bucket?

MRS. ALDERSON: Child, as rough as things were on the ranch we always had running water.

PLAYER WITH BUCKET: How could you have had running water such a long time ago?

MRS. ALDERSON: You come on up here with me and I'll prove it to ya. Now you take this bucket in hand and run down yonder, and when you get it full you run on back here. Yep, that's what we call "running water"—running with a bucketful of water.

We sure did spend a lot of time "running" water—particularly on washday.

PLAYER WITH WASHBOARD: I imagine this came in handy on washday.

Mrs. Alderson, continued

MRS. ALDERSON: It was the worst day of the week—the dreaded washday. I never met a woman on the prairie who had a good thing to say about it. Neighbor of mine used to say after washday she felt worse than a stewed witch.

In her own words she wrote it down. Who'd do an old lady a favor and read this washing recipe for her? **[Remove from pocket and ask a member of the audience to read.]**

Bild fire in back yard to het kettle of rain water.
Set tubs so smoke won't blow in eyes if wind is peart.
Shave 1 hole cake lie sope in bilin water.
Sort things. make 3 piles. 1 pile white, 1 pile colors, 1 pile work briches and rags.
Stur flour in cold water to smooth then thin down with bilin water (for starch).
Rub dirty spots on board. Scrub hard. Then bile. Rub colors but don't bile just rench and starch.
Take white things out of kettle with broom stick handel then rench, blew and starch.
Pore rench water in flower bed.
Scrub porch with hot soppy water.
Turn tubs upside down.
Go put on a cleen dress, smooth hair with side combs, brew cup of tea, set and rest and rock a spell and count blessings.

MRS. ALDERSON: Yes, we should always count our blessings—specially when we're imagining we have none. This morning I found this apron in an old trunk, and when I reached my hand into the pocket, I found a letter from an old friend of mine. She and her husband also homesteaded in Montana, and this is what she wrote a long time ago. **[Remove from pocket and ask a member of the audience to read.]**

"The greatest hardship of all is the scarcity of water. At first we were filled with dismay to find no water anywhere. Sometimes we had none even to drink until Alec brought a barrel which he fills with water each day when in town and brings home on top of his load of lumber. We have to wash a few pieces of laundry at a time in the washbasin, because there is no water to fill the tub!"

Why I remember my friend telling how they licked the dew from the grass and washed their hands and faces with it.

I remember when I got this letter. It was a good kick in the pants to me. Instead of complaining, I should count my blessings that at least I had water so that I could do the dreaded washday!

Mrs. Alderson, continued

MRS. ALDERSON: But talk about counting your blessings—that was the Saturday night bath. I still remember Mr. Alderson taking the tin bathtub down from the back porch wall and putting it on the hooked rug right in front of the open oven door.

We'd be hauling and heating water—we might have had "running water," but it was mighty cold. I went first, then the young children, the older boys, and, being the dirtiest, Mr. Alderson always went last. Course we never wasted a drop—sometimes black as coal it went into the slop buckets for the animals. Now I know you young'uns will be wrinkling your noses, but we never changed the water in between bathers. We just kept adding hot water to keep it steamy.

We didn't waste anything back then—we didn't have it to waste. And water, my it was precious. We spent many an hour hauling it.

MRS. ALDERSON: You know, with all the work, I seldom heard a plains woman complain. Most of them held true to what an army wife once said to me: "I never said I was hungry unless there was food to eat and I never said I was thirsty unless there was water to drink."

PLAYER WITH DOWSING RODS: You know I figured out the use of most of the things in the trunk except for these. What did you do with these—use them as antennae for your T.V. along with your running water?

MRS. ALDERSON: Friend, those are dowsing rods. They belonged to my uncle. He helped people all over the country find water, so they would know where to dig their wells. Why he could hardly keep a hold on those rods once they found a wet spot. Come on up here with those rods! **[Demonstrate how dowsing was done.]**

PLAYER WITH DOWSING RODS: That was just a lot of hocus pocus wasn't it?

Mrs. Alderson, continued

MRS. ALDERSON: Maybe, but there were lots of folks that believed in it and some still do. Just like weather signs—there's a lot of old timers that still swear by them to-day. I bet you know some of them from your own grandparents. Here I got a few of 'em written down.

See if you can figure this one: If a dog eats grass, it is a sign it will_____. (rain)

An early heavy coat on farm animals means _____. (a long cold winter is ahead)

When cattle bunch, it's a sure sign of _____. (rain)

Students acting up in school indicate _____. (a change in the weather)

PLAYER WITH WATER BAG: Mrs. Alderson, what did you use this for?

MRS. ALDERSON: That was Mr. Alderson's water bag. He used to hang it over the horn of his saddle. That bag sweats like a person and when the cool air moves over it, the water inside the bag is cooled.

Well, young'uns I've got to move on. But I've enjoyed visiting with ya. You come any time. I love company. Always lots of company on the ranch.

PLAYER WITH WATER BAG: But, Mrs. Alderson, what was it about the water bag that made you sad?

MRS. ALDERSON: (thoughtful pause) Mr. Alderson's water bag? You know most sto-ries live in our brains, and that's right close to our tongues, so we tell those stories. But some stories live in our hearts, and those we keep deep down inside ourselves.

Well, children you come and visit anytime. But next time why don't you make it washday? I might even let you haul a bucket of water or two.

EXIT MRS. ALDERSON

The End

Meeting the Challenges

Water Conservation Dilemmas and Choices

Conservation Choices

Grade Level:
Middle School, High School

Subject Areas:
Government, Environmental Science

Duration:
Preparation time: 10 minutes

Activity time: 50 minutes

Setting:
Classroom

Skills:
Analyze, Interpret, Evaluate, Present

Vocabulary:
dilemma, values, Xeriscape

Summary
Students confront a variety of water conservation dilemmas and choose courses of action to deal with them. In the process they face ethical, financial, and practical issues.

Objectives
Students will:
· evaluate the merits of various responses to water conservation dilemmas.
· discuss and examine their own values/priorities when it comes to water conservation

Materials
· *Conservation Choice Cards* Student Copy Pages, 1 set of cards per group

Background
A dilemma is a problematic situation that requires a person to choose from two or more alternatives, each of which can produce desirable or undesirable effects. Making water conservation choices can create dilemmas, with conflicts developing between what one wants to do versus what one believes should be done. For example, taking a long, hot shower is relaxing, but a short, warm shower—though less comforting—conserves resources. Not voting on a ballot issue that would allocate tax money for water supply projects requires less effort than researching the potential impacts of the projects and casting a vote.

People use various strategies to determine a course of action when confronted with a dilemma. These range from flipping a coin to conducting extensive research and attending meetings where decision makers wrestle with the options. One method of decision-making consists of listing the alternatives, identifying the pros and cons for each, and projecting possible outcomes. Factors to consider include costs (monetary and environmental), time, energy, citizens who will be directly affected, personal values, etc. Emotions and instincts also influence which alternative is chosen.

In confronting dilemmas, considering options, and finally selecting a course of action, individuals within the group may come into conflict. Why? Finding, proposing, and implementing alternatives requires an understanding of values. When this understanding is lacking, attempts to resolve the dilemma often meet with resistance.

How do individuals develop different value systems? Often taking years to develop, values are influenced by culture, family, and the social and physical environment. Values usually form an integral part of an individual's pattern of living. When a group examines options to resolve a dilemma, the process can generally be made less stressful, and often less emotional, if individuals acknowledge their own values and show respect by thoughtfully listening to and considering the values of other participants.

In the final analysis, water conservation comes down to making choices. Many decisions (taking shorter showers, planting a drought-tolerant shrub) seem small and mundane, but, taken together, their cumulative impact is enormous. The choices we make reinforce our values, establish habits, and in turn, create an ethic that informs our attitudes and daily lives.

Procedure
Warm Up
Ask students if they know what a dilemma is? If they are willing to share some examples, use these to illustrate the inherent conflict of dilemmas and the extent to which our lives are not made up of black-and-white decisions, but of choices among grays.

If no one can come up with a good example, describe the following scenario. You and your friends are playing baseball one afternoon. One of you hits a long fly ball that breaks a garage window in a nearby

home. Most of the group wants to run home and escape the consequences of the act, but several of you think it would be best to confess and deal with the results.

This is a dilemma, full of conflict between the "right" thing to do and the easy, convenient, and least-stressful thing to do. Life is full of these choices, in every area. The activity that follows concentrates on dilemmas associated with the conservation of water.

The Activity
1.   Split the class into small groups of four to six students and hand out one set of *Conservation Choice Cards* to each group. Pile the cards facedown in the middle of the table.
2.   One at a time, students pick a card. They should read the dilemma silently and take a minute to think through the situation and their response. Tell them to be realistic about what they would do, even if they know it might not be the most admirable response.
3.   When the time is up, students should read the dilemma and the list of choices out loud, then explain which choice they made, briefly defending their course of action.
4.   The other students in the group should score the individual responses on a scale of 1—10, with one being complete agreement with the response

and ten being complete disagreement. Total the group scores for each situation. The lower the total, the greater the level of group consensus on the chosen course of action.
5.   Continue until all students have had a turn.

Wrap Up
Have each group decide which dilemma was their most difficult or controversial one. Read it aloud to the class and allow a brief discussion of the choices and the problems they bring up.

Ask students if the exercise has heightened their awareness of the conservation dilemmas that face us in everyday life. Do they think they'll approach these choices differently as a result of this exercise?

Assessment
Have students:
· choose between water conservation actions and defend their choices (steps 2 and 3).
· evaluate their own and other group members' choices (step 4).
· discuss the merits and difficulties inherent in a variety of conservation scenarios (*Wrap Up*).
· confront the impacts of specific water conservation decisions (*Wrap Up*).

Extensions
Have student groups make up

new sets of *Conservation Choice Cards*, swap them, and repeat the exercise.

Encourage students to take some of the most interesting dilemmas home to share with their families and then report the results back to the class.

Resources

Miller, G. Tyler, Jr. 1991. *Environmental Science: Sustaining the Earth*, 3rd ed. Belmont, Calif.:Wadsworth Publishing Company.

Polesetsky, Matthew, ed. 1991. *Global Resources: Opposing Viewpoints*. San Diego, Calif.:Greenhaven Press, Inc.

Conservation Choice Cards

1. *A group of your friends have invited you to join them on a shopping trip. You want to wear your favorite pants, but they are dirty. You have time to wash and dry them, but there is no other dirty laundry to make up a load.*

You could:
a. Throw them in alone and wash them on the small load setting.
b. See if you can scrounge up sheets, towels, or other dirty laundry to make at least a small load.
c. Decide you can do without your favorite pants, even if you won't fit in with the group.
d. Decline the invitation.
e. Put your pants on dirty and wear them anyway.
f. Other

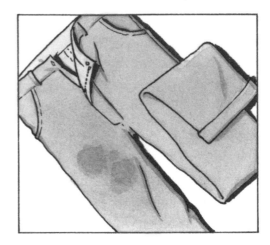

2. *An older friend of yours drives a really nice car and sometimes invites you along for a ride. He is a fanatic about keeping the car spotlessly clean and washes it at least once a week. Every time he washes the car, he leaves the hose running throughout the entire process.*

You could:
a. Point out the wastefulness of his habit and hope he takes the hint.
b. Do some simple math to illustrate how much water he wastes every month and share the results.
c. Figure it's his business and leave it at that.
d. Bring up the point that he'll save money on the water bill by shutting off the hose.
e. Decide that you don't want to risk losing his friendship (and the rides) and keep quiet.
f. Other

Conservation Choice Cards, continued

3. *Your family has just bought a home in a subdivision. Part of the yard is not landscaped, and the developer has suggested putting in sod and grass to extend the lawn. Your family is discussing options at dinner one night.*

Which option would you advocate?
a. Go with the developer's suggestion, despite the need for maintenance and extra watering.
b. Investigate more adaptable grasses that might be more expensive initially, but wouldn't need much water.
c. Choose to use ground cover instead of grass, though, by doing so, you remove that part of the property from being a good play/activity area.
d. Organize a neighborhood educational campaign to raise consciousness about landscaping and water use.
e. Stay out of the discussion because it's your parents' decision.
f. Other

4. *Your family has inherited a farm from an uncle. It has several fields that grow alfalfa and wheat under flood irrigation. Before he died, your uncle was considering investing capital to install a more efficient irrigation system. The funds to make that transition are part of his estate, but now you have to decide whether to go through with the plan or not.*

You could:
a. Take the money and invest it in a college fund for the kids.
b. Go ahead with your uncle's plans to develop more efficient irrigation.
c. Stop irrigating altogether and let the farm return to a more natural, wild state.
d. Keep using flood irrigation and save the money for a rainy day.
e. Sell the farm with the stipulation that the new owners install more efficient irrigation systems.
f. Other

Conservation Choice Cards, continued

5. *On your way home from school on a hot June afternoon, you come across a group of kids playing in water spurting from a fire hydrant that they found a way to turn on. You know that this wastes a tremendous amount of water and that the city water supply has been taxed in recent years, but it is awfully hot and the kids are having a great time.*

You could:
a. Keep walking home and forget about it.
b. Go home and report the incident to the fire department.
c. Join in the fun.
d. Try to talk to the kids and convince them to turn the water off again.
e. Other

6. *In your family's new apartment, you notice that the shower runs out of hot water after one long shower or two short ones. You are often the third person to take a shower and you're getting tired of the cold water treatment.*

You could:
a. Report this fact to the landlord and ask if the hot water heater is adequate.
b. Lobby for a strict three-minute limit on showers.
c. Investigate the type of showerhead fixture you have and see if a low-flow model would help solve the problem.
d. Figure cold water showers are good for you and get used to it.
e. Other

Conservation Choice Cards, continued

7. *You are helping your older brother change the oil in his car. Suddenly he hands you the pan of dirty oil and tells you to dump it down the storm drain. You hesitate, but he tells you to hurry up because the two of you are going to a new movie that you have been looking forward to all week.*

You could:

a. Dump the oil down the storm drain because you don't want to argue with your brother.

b. Quickly explain to your brother that everything from the storm drain flows into the nearby river. You tell him that you will take responsibility for the oil by pouring it into a can, closing it with a lid, and taking it to a proper disposal center.

c. Sneak around the side of the house and hide the open pan of oil in the bushes. "Out of sight, out of mind," you always say.

d. Pour the oil down the drain of the utility sink in your mom's laundry room.

e. Show your brother the fish stenciled by the storm drain and tell him that you and your ecology club stencil storm drains. The fish is a reminder that everything that goes down the storm drain flows into the local river. You ask him if he still thinks you should dump the oil.

f. Other

8. *During a severe regional drought, you go to a restaurant and are served a glass of water, even though you didn't ask for it.*

You could:

a. Make a point of explaining to the waitress the importance of conserving water.

b. Complain to the manager.

c. Leave the glass untouched as a subtle symbol of your disappointment.

d. Figure one glass of water isn't a big deal and ignore it.

e. Leave a note on the table.

f. Design a brochure or flyer to distribute to restaurants about not providing water unless patrons ask for it.

g. Other

Conservation Choice Cards, continued

9. *A drought has plagued your region for months, and your town is facing severe restrictions.*

You would advocate:
a. Restricting each household to 50 gallons/person/day.
b. Banning water use for swimming pools, lawn sprinklers, and car washes.
c. Instituting strict guidelines for yard sprinkling, restaurants, industry, golf courses, and other major water users.
d. Calling for a long-term water use plan, that would address everything from landscaping practices to agricultural irrigation.
e. Other

10. *Your school has announced a contest for the most practical water conservation idea, with a $50 prize.*

You would advocate:
a. Replacing sprinklers with drip irrigation systems.
b. Installing low-volume flush toilets in place of high-volume models.
c. Having all faucets spring loaded so they'll turn themselves off.
d. Banning water fountains.
e. Conducting a school-wide audit to identify and fix water leaks.
f. Other

Pass the Jug

Grade Level:
Middle School

Subject Areas:
Social Studies, Environmental Science, History, Government

Duration:
Preparation time
   Part I: 15 minutes
   Part II: 15 minutes

Activity time
   Part I: 30 minutes
   Part II: 30 minutes

Setting:
Classroom

Skills:
Organize, Analyze, Apply

Vocabulary:
riparian areas, water rights, water allocation, consumptive use, nonconsumptive use, snowpack, streamflow

Summary
Students simulate and analyze different water rights policies to learn how water availability and people's proximity to the resource influence how water is allocated.

Objectives
Students will:
· describe historical and current aspects of water rights.
· illustrate how water rights are used to allocate water.
· evaluate water rights allocation systems.

Materials
· large quantity of candy, popcorn, pencils, stickers, or other appropriate items for distribution
· 1 copy of *Water Rights Q & A* Student Copy Pages for each student
· paper cups or glasses (1 per student plus extras)
· water jug (e.g., apple cider or gallon milk container)
· *Water Users (Descriptions)* Student Copy Page (cut into strips)
· funnel

Background
Water rights provide an organized and systematic manner for allocating water. A water right allows a person, business, community, or other group to use a specified amount of water. People receive only the right to use the water; they do not own the water.

The history of water rights is related closely to the history of settlement and land ownership. Settlers in the East adapted a water rights policy similar to what the populace used in England. The Riparian Rights or Common-Law Doctrine gives people who own land bordering a water source the right to use that water however they choose. A more recent version of the doctrine requires people to justify their uses as reasonable. They must also ensure that landowners downstream have their fair share of water.

East of the Mississippi, average annual rainfall is more plentiful than in the West. This is apparent from a geographical view. From about the 100th meridian of longitude west to the Pacific Coast, average annual rainfall dips significantly below the 20 inches that normally sustain nonirrigated crops in the East.

Scarcity generates Westerners' preoccupation with water and water rights. Western water rights were developed for the needs of nineteenth century settlers. They evolved from the customs and practices of miners from about 1848 who developed systems for protecting their claims to land and minerals. More than 100 years later, after investing billions of dollars to build water diversion and storage projects such as ditches, dams, and reservoirs, Westerners remain strongly committed to ensuring a continued supply of water for their irrigation and mining needs.

In many parts of the West, the Prior Appropriation Doctrine regulates water rights. The doctrine maintains "first come, first served," or "first in time is first in right." In other words, whoever uses the water first has the "prior" or first right to the supply of available water. If all the water in a stream is allocated, no new users are allowed.

Exceptions to the state-based Prior Appropriation Doctrine are federal and tribal reserved water rights. Reserved water rights were created to provide adequate water for lands owned by the federal government and Native American nations. Unlike state rights allocated under the Prior Appropriation Doctrine, reserved rights on federal and tribal lands do not have to remain used to be valid.

In the last 20 years, many changes have added new dimensions to water rights and water allocation programs. Irrigated agriculture is a large consumer of water. Individuals and corporations invest millions of dollars in irrigation systems to grow crops for

people and livestock. Cities also need water to meet the needs of residents, businesses, and industries. Water for recreation and for fish and wildlife is receiving growing attention. Many communities depend on water resources for energy production methods such as hydroelectric and thermoelectric generation plants. The challenge of meeting today's growing demand for water will involve nontraditional allocation strategies. Several methods, such as water rights transfers, water rights changes, water marketing, and water leasing, have evolved as considerations to satisfy twentieth-century needs.

Procedure

Warm Up

Present students with a large quantity of candy, popcorn, pencils, stickers, or whatever is appropriate for distribution. Ask them how you should distribute the items to the students in the class. Should you give everyone an equal amount? Should you give a

larger quantity to the first person who asks or to the student who arrived first at school that day?

After students discuss various methods for sharing the candy or stickers, tell them that you are going to be discussing how people in the East and West share water. Distribute one copy of *Water Rights Q & A* Student Copy Pages to each student. Use these questions and answers to guide your initial discussion of water rights with students.

The Activity
Part I

1. Arrange students' seats in a row or around a table and give each student a cup. Starting at one end, have the first student pour out as much water from the water jug as he or she needs and pass the jug to the next student in line. Because of the limited amount of water in the jug, there might not be enough to go around.

2. Ask students (those who received water and those who

did not) to express how they feel. Tell them that sometimes there is not enough water available to meet everyone's needs.

3. Ask students what they could do to make sure they all get water. Have them repeat the activity and put their plan into action.

4. Provide students with a brief description of riparian rights. Ask them to explain how passing the jug relates to riparian rights.

Part II

1. After students have emptied their cups, inform them that they will now simulate the allocation of water rights in many places in the West. Explain how the Prior Appropriation Doctrine gives people who originally moved into an area and started using water the right to use water first, whether or not their land borders the water source.

2. Have each student write down his or her birth month and day on a piece of paper and display it so everyone can see. Then distribute *Water Users (Descriptions)* Student Copy Page by handing the strips out in the order of students' birthdays (from January 1 to December 31). This process represents the concept of first in time, first in right.

3. Explain that the descriptions are numbered. The student with description number one is the first person

who moved into the area ("first in time"). Along with the right to use the water, each description also states how the water is used and how much is needed.

Note: An alternative is for students to make up their own water use and the quantities needed.

4. Pass around the jug of water in the order of the numbered cards. Have students read aloud how they use water. Each student must take the amount of water indicated on his or her card. Some water users, such as fisheries and hydroelectric power plants, utilize water without reducing water quantity; water managers call these users nonconsumptive. (However, reservoirs associated with hydroelectric power plants do lose some water to evaporation.) Students who represent these water users should pour water into their cups and then funnel it back into the jug.

5. When water runs out, have students express their opinions about this system. What are the benefits of this system? (It protects the investments — money, time, and energy—and the rights of first water users.) What are some shortcomings? (It restricts new or different water users' access to water.) How or why would students change the system?

Wrap Up

Have students summarize the two general approaches to al-

locating water rights and how each evolved. Encourage students to investigate options for individuals or groups of people who do not have enough water. For example, they could promote conservation, invest in engineering projects that collect or divert water supplies, etc.

Have students research water allocation in their community. (They should contact a city or state water manager or the public health department.) Suggest that they create a display for the school outlining their community's and/or state's water rights system (e.g., "Our Water Rights Made Simple").

Assessment

Have students:

· develop a strategy to distribute a limited resource (e.g., a bag of candy, an hour of television time, a five-dollar bill) among students in the class (*Warm Up* and **Part I**, step 3).

· compare and evaluate different approaches to allocating water rights (**Part II**, step 5, and *Wrap Up*).

· summarize how water rights practices evolved (*Wrap Up*).

Extensions

To simulate annual fluctuations in streamflow, change the amount of water in the jug and repeat the activity. Some years have heavy streamflow; in other years, the river runs dry.

Simulate a drought by asking students not to drink water one hour prior to the activity. You might even take a short hike to generate thirst.

To demonstrate how pollution affects water users, have students add a drop of food coloring or dunk a tea bag in their cups—simulating their "use" of the water. Students will return some of this used water to the jug (demonstrating runoff and discharge). Add a sugar lump to symbolize invisible chemicals that are carried in water. Have students list ways in which water quality can affect water quantity.

To simulate snowpack, freeze colored water in layers in a plastic liter bottle. The layers represent the amount of water that is frozen or "held" in snowpack over the winter. The first layer, colored green, represents November, the second,

colored red, symbolizes December, and so on through to the top clear layer, March. (The colored layers will remain distinct as long as each freezes solid before the next layer is added. The four colors in a box of food coloring plus one clear layer will make up the five layers.)

Arrange students in a circle. Distribute cups and tell them that you will "pass the jug" once again. Hand the first student the frozen bottle of water and suggest that he or she pour into the cup whatever is needed. When students express confusion, ask them what must happen before they can share this water. Inform them that in some parts of the country snow accumulates in the mountains through the winter months (November through March) and results in "snowpack." In spring, warmer temperatures melt this snow and the water is released. Streams are often swollen (sometimes overflowing their banks) during the spring thaw. This water is critical for irrigating crops, for providing lush vegetation for grazing wildlife and livestock, and for filling reservoirs that may have been drawn down over the winter months.

Remind students that snowpack is often referred to as a "water bank." That is, water is "saved" until the rise in temperature (above 32 degrees F

[0 degrees C]) "opens the bank." Ask students to speculate on what conditions might exist in the spring if there was very little precipitation during the winter and a reduced snowpack.

Have students adapt "Pass the Jug" to demonstrate how federal reserved water rights could affect water allocation. These rights are designed to ensure that public lands (e.g., parks) and Native Americans receive the water they need. Their demands can sometimes supersede other water rights systems (e.g., riparian, prior appropriation).

Demonstrate needs of instream flows for fish and wildlife by placing a fish bowl at the end of the line of students. Explain that at least one cup of water must be poured into the fish bowl to meet this requirement. How do your students adjust to meet this new need?

Resources

Getches, David. 1990. *Water Rights in a Nutshell*. St. Paul, Minn.: West Publishing Co.

Marstib, Betsy. 1987. *Western Water Made Simple*. Washington, D.C.: Island Press.

Wolfe, Mary Ellen. 1994. *A Landowner's Guide to Western Water Rights*. Bozeman, Mont.: The Watercourse.

Water Rights Q & A

Questions	Answers
1. Study the 100th meridian map below. How much rain falls east of the 100th meridian as compared to west of it? Would the scarcity of water in the West have anything to do with the fact that people in the West are very concerned about water and their right to use water?	1. East of the Mississippi, average annual rainfall is more plentiful than in the West. From about the 100th meridian of longitude west to the Pacific Coast, average annual rainfall dips significantly below the 20 inches that is normally needed to sustain crops that are not irrigated in the East.

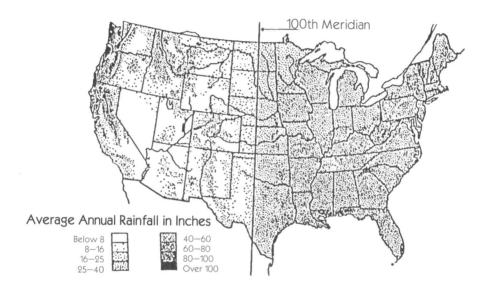

100th Meridian

Average Annual Rainfall in Inches

Below 8
8—16
16—25
25—40

40—60
60—80
80—100
Over 100

Questions	Answers
2. What is a water right?	2. A water right is a right to use a public resource for a beneficial or useful purpose. Water rights are considered property rights, but people do not actually own the water; they own the **right** or privilege to **use** the water.
3. Who needs a water right?	3. Anyone who is diverting water (capturing water before it is put to some other use) or controlling water in a western state needs or should already have a water right. Farmers or ranchers who irrigate crops may hold water rights; people who supply water to cities or towns may hold water rights; industries that need water to manufacture their products may hold a water right.

Water Rights Q & A, continued

Questions	Answers
4. Does my family need a water right if we live in a western city and get our water from the city?	4. No, the water right is usually held by the agency that supplies the water to the city.
5. What is a consumptive use of water?	5. Consumptive water use means that some part of the water diverted is consumed, making at least a portion unavailable for use by others. Irrigation, private domestic wells, fish raceways and ponds, and stock water ponds (where cattle, sheep, etc. get their water) are all examples of diversionary, consumptive uses of water.
6. What is an instream (or nonconsumptive) use of water?	6. Instream water may include water for hydropower production, fisheries and wildlife habitat, water quality protection, and stream channel protection. Some states have adopted laws and regulations that provide protection for these nonconsumptive uses. In effect, these laws "speak for the fish!"
7. What is the prior appropriation system?	7. The prior appropriation system is a widely used method to distribute water in the West for many uses and needs. It rests on the idea of "priority," sometimes referred to as, "first in time, first in right."

What does that mean? Whoever began using water first (the senior user) has the right of first use. Also, the senior user is entitled to his full amount of water before those who received a later water right (the junior users) get their share. |

Water Rights Q & A, continued

Questions	Answers
8. Are there any other kinds of water rights besides the prior appropriation system?	8. There are federal and tribal reserved water rights. Reserved water rights were established to provide water for lands owned by the federal government and Native American nations. Water rights evolved with settlement patterns and land ownership. People who first settled in the eastern United States, where precipitation can be abundant, adopted a water rights policy that was similar to what they had known in England. The Riparian Rights or Common-Law Doctrine gives people who own land bordering a water source the right to make reasonable use of the water on that land if the use does not interfere with the reasonable uses of other riparian landowners.
9. Can a person lose a water right?	9. Yes, water rights under the prior appropriation system can be lost if they are not used, often within particular time periods. In some states, new laws are being considered that would allow the owner of a water right to sell his excess water. This may help to prevent water waste.
10. So, is this all there is to know about water rights?	10. No! Although this is a good introduction, water rights are very complicated, and the laws are different from state to state and change over time. If you or your parents would like to learn more about western water rights, you can read the book from which this material was adapted: *A Landowner's Guide to Western Water Rights* by Mary Ellen Wolfe, produced by The Watercourse and published by Roberts Rinehart Publishers, 1996. Copies are available by calling The Watercourse at (406) 994-5392.

Water Users (Descriptions)

Number 1	You are a descendant of the first homesteader that moved into the area. You own a goat dairy farm and grow alfalfa and corn.	use 2 cups
Number 2	Your ancestor was heading toward California during the great gold rush, but got distracted by the flowers. While picking daisies, he found a huge deposit of copper and started a copper mining company. Your family runs this small, but lucrative, operation.	use 2 cups
Number 3	Your great-great-grandmother came out to teach the children of the copper miners. You still live on the property she bought and need water for personal use and crop irrigation.	use 1 cup
Number 4	You represent a small community of families who work in the mine. You use water for daily domestic and irrigation purposes. Your water needs may increase as the town grows.	use 2 cups
Number 5	Your grandparents left their farm in Iowa to start a farm here. You help meet the needs of the growing community. Your grandfather is still alive and resists using modern farming practices.	use 5 cups
Number 6	To avoid competition in the big city, your father moved his coat hanger factory to this growing community. The industry provides a means of income for community members.	use 2 cups
Number 7	You represent a hydroelectric company with a dam upstream of the town. The water you use passes through the dam to generate electricity. Show this by pouring three cups of water back into the jug.	use 4 cups
Number 8	You represent a town that grew as more people escaping the city moved to the countryside. Consequently, your town has become a city. You use water for domestic and irrigation purposes.	use 3 cups
Number 9	You are a high-tech farmer that has moved here to supply food to the growing communities.	use 2 cups
Number 10	You have decided to start an industry that you think meets a growing need: shoulder pad storage racks.	use 1 cup

The rest of the user cards can be copied and numbered in any order. If the community is allocated only one jug of water, there will probably be no water left by this time.

	Small farmer	1 cup
	Industry	1 cup
	Small town	1 cup
	Rancher	1 cup

Irrigation Innovation

Grade Level:
Middle School

Subject Areas:
History/Anthropology, Earth Science, Environmental Science

Duration:
Preparation time
 Part I: 20 minutes
 Part II: 30 minutes
 Part III: 5 minutes

Activity time
 Part I: 50 minutes
 Part II: one 50-minute period for construction; observation/recording for six weeks
 Part III: 20 minutes

Setting:
Classroom

Skills:
Analyze, Interpret, Apply, Evaluate

Vocabulary:
waterlogging, salinization, water-stress, micro-irrigation, subirrigation, sprinkler irrigation, surface irrigation, furrow irrigation, perennial, irrigation, topography, tailwater

Summary
Students apply their knowledge of irrigation systems to determine the appropriate method of water application for diverse crops and topography through a simple card game; simulate the four methods of irrigation; and solve an irrigation mystery from the past.

Objectives
Students will:
· define irrigation.
· describe different irrigation systems and evaluate the advantages and disadvantages of each.
· simulate irrigation systems and manage for maximum productivity while conserving water.
· discuss salinization and waterlogging in the context of ancient cultures.

Materials
· *Irrigation Innovation Card Game* Student Copy Pages, 1 set of cards for each group
· trays or nursery flats
· clay
· sand
· potting soil
· vegetable seeds
· sprinkling can
· small funnels
· paper cups
· plastic straws, some with flexible sections
· modeling clay or wood glue
· *Irrigation Innovation Mini-*

Mystery Student Copy Page, 1 per student

Background
People have been growing crops for a long time. In fact, some 10,000 to 12,000 years ago, a cultural shift known as the agricultural revolution began in several regions of the world. This food-production revolution involved a gradual move from a lifestyle based on nomadic hunting and gathering to one of settled agricultural communities; people learned how to domesticate wild animals and cultivate wild plants. Early growers practiced subsistence farming; that is, they grew only enough for themselves.

About 7,000 years ago, the invention of the plow allowed farmers to cultivate larger areas. In some arid regions, early farmers increased crop output by diverting water from nearby streams into ditches and canals, dug by hand, to irrigate crops. This gradual shift from hunting and gathering to farming had significant effects. Population increases, better living standards, and longer life spans resulted from greater food supplies. People built increasingly larger irrigation systems, cleared additional acreage, and organized villages.

Today, in the United States, because of dry conditions west

of the 100th meridian, irrigated agriculture is largely a western phenomenon. According to *Water in the West: Challenge for the Next Century* (pp. 2—24),"The 17 western states, together with Arkansas, Florida and Louisiana, account for 91 percent of all U.S. irrigated acreage and 82 percent of all irrigated farms. Four-fifths of all irrigators are located in the West."

Irrigation is defined as the "managed application of water to soil for the purpose of increasing crop production." The ability to irrigate crops, in addition to other technological improvements, has increased the farmer's productivity.

Throughout the world, the largest single use of water is agricultural. Many farmers and ranchers are in fact "water managers." They are concerned about the importance of quality water of the right amount, at the right time, and at the right cost. Several factors are encouraging them to also be water conservationists: the unavailability and expense of labor; high energy costs (the costs of power to pump water); limited water availability; and environmental concerns (*Water in the West*). In some areas, farmers are feeling the pressure from cities and other economic sectors that are competing for rural water.

On the other hand, even though farmers and ranchers may want to conserve water, they are restricted by several factors. They may be operating with limited capital to invest in new and more water-efficient irrigation systems, which are very costly. In some cases, the technology is not available to them, and the water rights laws under which they function do not support them in their efforts. Although the laws are changing, in some states if you do not use the full extent of your water right (even if you don't necessarily need all of the water), you may lose your right to the water. Although "water transfers" are currently limited and often controversial, some farmers are being allowed to sell their excess water.

However, many farmers are finding it economically feasible to adopt more efficient water and energy practices. Positive effects include: reduced energy costs, less erosion and sedimentation, reduced salinity, improved water quality, and greater crop production (*Water in the West*).

There are four main types of irrigation systems: **surface**, **sprinkler**, **micro** (drip/trickle), and **subirrigation**. Some irrigators use a combination of two or more of these. These combinations are called hybrid systems. (*Irrigation of Agricultural Crops*)

In **surface irrigation**, water is applied at the top end of a field and flows by gravity across the soil surface. **Furrow irrigation** is a type of surface irrigation that is often used for annual row crops and sometimes for trees and vine crops. In furrow irrigation, crops are planted in rows and water is distributed via furrows or troughs between the rows, and flows by gravity through the field.

The characteristics of surface irrigation include:
· All crops may be irrigated by some type of surface irrigation system.
· This type of irrigation is best suited to fine- to medium-textured soils. Water percolates very quickly through coarse soils; therefore, the water would be absorbed and would not flow across the field.
· The topography of the field must be prepared so that the water will spread uniformly across the field.
· In order to adequately irrigate the bottom part of the field, additional water must be supplied that results in some runoff. Unless this water is recaptured through a tailwater recycling system, this application of water may be inefficient.
· In the western United States, surface irrigation systems are often supplied by gravity flow through canals from streams or storage facilities.

In **sprinkler irrigation**, water is

applied to the soil with a mechanism that directs an airborne stream of water. The water flows through a pressurized pipe to the sprinkler device. This method is designed to mimic rainfall. If sprinkler irrigation is applied correctly, less water evaporates than in surface irrigation.

· Sprinkler systems are designed to be set (they are stationary and intended to water only one portion of the field at a time) or they are mobile (like the center-pivot, in which the pipeline rotates about a stationary end through which the water flows).

· This type of system can be used to cool crops and also to protect plants from frost. (How? When water freezes into a solid state, heat is released. The heat created provides enough of a temperature increase to protect the sensitive parts of the plants.)

· When these systems are well designed and managed, they are capable of delivering water in an efficient and uniform way under diverse conditions.

· This system can be used on land that you would not want to level, because there is too much slope or because the soil is so shallow that leveling would remove the productive material.

· Sprinkler irrigation can be used on most any soil, especially shallow soils, with minimal runoff and erosion.

· The center-pivot sprinkler irrigation system requires less

attention and less labor than surface irrigation. Consequently, more center-pivots are being used.

· This system is at a disadvantage in a windy environment or with plants that are prone to developing disease when their leaves are wet.

· Other disadvantages of sprinkler irrigation include: capitol investment is higher than in surface irrigation; maintenance costs may be higher; and power costs are higher than for surface watering.

Microirrigation is delivered through several methods (drip/trickle, subsurface, bubbler, spray). According to the National Handbook of Recommended Methods for Water Data Acquisition website, microirrigation is described as "the frequent application of small quantities of water as drops, tiny streams, or miniature spray through emitters or applicators placed along a water delivery line." The drip/trickle method was actually invented in Israel because water was scarce and saline (salty). Today, over half of Israel's land is watered by drip irrigation, and in California, more and more systems are being converted to drip irrigation.

· Microirrigation is a good choice under the following conditions: when labor is costly; when water is scarce, expensive, and often saline; when adopting other methods

would be hard (e.g. on rough terrain such as an orchard on the side of a hill); or when you are irrigating for greenhouse or landscape purposes.

· One of the main disadvantages of this system is the high cost of installation. In general, it is economically feasible only for high-profit crops such as avocados, grapes, citrus, cotton, strawberries, and vegetables.

· This system works well on all soil types, but especially sandy soils.

· Microirrigation can be adapted for steep slopes and is not usually affected by weather such as wind because water is applied close to the soil surface.

· This system can contribute to water conservation through improved irrigation efficiency, but it requires capitol and a fairly high degree of education and training.

In **subirrigation**, the water table level is monitored and managed for the watering of crops. In some areas, the water table is so high that farmers do not have to irrigate. However, they sometimes construct systems of open ditches to affect the water table.

· This system is used mainly for perennial crops.

· The field must be fairly level so the water table is consistent throughout the area.

· This system is often used in areas of high rainfall (over 50 inches of rain per year) where droughts may occur periodically.

For the most part, any of the main irrigation methods can be adopted for use on any crop requiring watering. However, the **shape of the land**, the **type of soil**, and the **crop** often have an impact on the choice of a system.

After a farmer or rancher selects and installs an irrigation system, he or she must decide when to water and how much to water. What factors will affect this decision?
· Weather: Is rain expected or did it just rain yesterday?
· Soil type and characteristics include: The soil's ability to allow water to soak in or infiltrate. The water-holding capacity is the soil's ability to retain most of the infiltrating water so that it is available to the plant roots. Soil with good water-holding capacity is like a sponge, and plants can draw upon this water between rains or irrigation. Another characteristic is evaporative water loss from the soil surface.
· Moisture: How wet is the soil at the level of the roots?
· Crop requirements: Drought-resistant and saline-tolerant crops are being developed throughout the world.
· Soil salt concentration: Moisture is measured to determine if there is adequate drainage.
· Crop condition: The farmer monitors this with instruments or by visual examination. Expe-

rienced farmers can tell when a plant is becoming water-stressed by studying the leaves. Young leaves in particular begin to curl. However, the crop should be irrigated before this stage is reached.
· Evapotranspiration: If a plant is water-stressed, it will close its stomata to conserve moisture. The plant receives carbon dioxide through its stomata. If the plant is not taking in carbon dioxide, photosynthesis is limited and plant growth slows, lessening productivity.

Other factors may complicate an irrigation schedule:
· Water is unavailable when the farmer determines that the crop needs it.
· There is pressure to take too much water because of a "take it or lose it" water rights situation.
· A farmer may be trying to manage water for a number of different crops with different watering needs.

Two conditions a farmer definitely does not want are salinization and waterlogging. Both occur because irrigation water may contain salts. In dry climates, much of the water from a saline irrigation solution evaporates, leaving the salts behind in the topsoil. Plants are also taking up the water and leaving the salt behind. The accumulation of these salts, called salinization, stunts crop growth, lowers yields, eventually kills crop plants, and can ruin the land.

Waterlogging is also a problem. Farmers often apply extra irrigation water to wash salts deeper into the soil and away from the root zone. Without adequate drainage, water collects underground, gradually raising the water table. Saline water eventually surrounds the roots of plants and kills them. Too much water can strip nutrients from the soil (leaching) and reduce oxygen in the soil. The roots of most plants need oxygen for survival. (Although plants produce oxygen through photosynthesis in leaves and stems, there is no way to pass this oxygen to plant roots.) Soil aeration is the passing of oxygen into the soil and the release of carbon dioxide from it.

A look at the past reveals evidence of cultures devastated by the salinization of their soil. The Hohokams lived in the Gila and Salt River valleys (in the American Southwest) in A.D. 1300. The Salt River was named Rio Salado by the early Spanish and Jesuit explorers. Because it passes through a heavy salt formation about 100 miles (160 km) north of Phoenix, the river has a high salt content.

The Hohokams lived in this location for more than 1,000 years. They built complex cities and had an advanced irrigation system consisting of ditches running from the Salt River to their crops.

The Hohokams suddenly disappeared from the area around A.D. 1400. Some scientists think a widespread epidemic might have occurred. The people could have become frightened and fled, but no evidence supports this hypothesis. Other scientists think the area was hit by a severe drought. Perhaps the mountains received little or no rain for many years and the rivers dried up, eliminating the Hohokams' water source. Evidence exists of a drought from A.D. 1277 to A.D. 1299. Tree ring studies from both river valleys indicate little growth during these years. This may be an indication of limited rainfall. However, scientists have found that only people from the villages near the small canals moved at that time; the people living on the rivers, streams, and large canals remained.

Some scientists believe Hohokam irrigation practices may have severely damaged the land. After years of irrigation, the soil became less absorbent, and the water did not run off as quickly. The soil became waterlogged at the surface. The high salt content of the Gila and Salt Rivers killed the roots of plants. Finally, the salt content of the soil was so high, plants could not grow.

Irrigated lands in some areas of the world are prone to salinization problems today. In areas where these problems exist, landowners can reduce

salinization by flushing fields or leaving fields fallow for a few years.

Procedure
Warm Up
Ask students what it means to irrigate. Why do they think irrigation is necessary? Why is the greatest percentage of irrigation done west of the 100th meridian? Ask them if they believe irrigation is a new idea or if it has been practiced for a long time. Are they aware of irrigation methods from the past?

The Activity
Part 1
1. Divide the class into groups of four to five students. Distribute the *Irrigation Systems* Student Copy Pages. Discuss the four main types of irrigation with students. Remind students that farmers consider many factors before they select a particular irrigation system. Have students list those factors. How many of the following factors were they able to come up with on their own?
· the distance from the field to a water source
· the water requirements of the crop
· the quality of irrigation water
· the cost of water
· the shape of the land
· the type and characteristics of the soil
· the annual rain and snow fall
· the cost of irrigation systems

· the labor to set up and maintain the system
· the tendency of the crop to get diseases from water falling and standing on their leaves
· drainage of excess irrigation water
2. Provide each group of students with a set of *Irrigation Innovation Card Game* playing cards and the following playing directions:
   a. Have one player shuffle the cards and deal one card to each player until all the cards have been distributed.
   b. Players should look at the cards in their hands and determine if they have any cards that match. What would constitute a match? Either:
· the player matches an irrigation system with a characteristic (or characteristics) of that system, or
· the player matches an irrigation system with the topography and crop that require that system
   c. Players may place piles of matching cards facedown in front of them.
   d. The dealer then turns to the player to her right and selects a card from his hand. (Cards should not be shown.)
   e. Play continues around the circle. Whenever a selected card creates a match in a player's hand, that match should be put down on the table.
   f. Play continues until all possible matches have been made.

g. Who wins? Players must check their matches against the answer grid. Each card that is correctly matched to another card is worth two points (+2). Each card left remaining in a player's hand without a match is worth minus one (-1). Incorrect matches also count against a player, (-1) per card. Therefore an incorrect match of two cards equals (-2).

h. The player left holding the Bad Luck card loses half of his or her total points. This represents things a farmer or rancher cannot control, such as severe weather, pests, equipment failure, or a drop in market prices.

i. Players tally their points. The player with the most points wins!

Part II

1. Assign each of the groups from **Part I** an irrigation system: surface, sprinkler, or drip. Have them simulate the system in nursery flats or a metal tray. If necessary, share with them the design for the drip irrigation system.

2. Discuss the factors a farmer or rancher must consider when maintaining an irrigation schedule.

3. Have them plant vegetable seeds in each flat. Based on the type of soil and the requirements of the vegetable, have them determine a schedule for watering. Remind them about adequate drainage.

4. Have each group keep records of the amount and frequency of watering. Challenge them to manage for maximum productivity with the least amount of water. Have them practice a visual examination of their plants to determine if the crop becomes water-stressed.

5. Based on their simulations, were they able to confirm any of the advantages or disadvantages associated with the different systems? Were they able to draw any conclusions about the different systems and water conservation?

Part III

1. Read or have students read the mini-mystery, "Lost Homeland." Allow them to ask 20 questions to find the answer. They may only ask questions that can be answered with a "yes," "no," or "not relevant."

2. If students are not close to the answer after 15 questions, provide additional information about the location and the water source of these people (the Salt River).

3. After students have guessed or been told the solution, ask them if they think modern cultures could have these same problems. Discuss the benefits and problems of current irrigation practices.

4. To demonstrate how salt collects in soil, have students do the following: Saturate some water with salt, carefully measuring the amount of salt added to the water. Poke a number of small holes in the bottom of a paper cup and fill the cup two-thirds full of soil.

Pour the salt solution through the soil. Collect the water that runs through the soil; then allow it to evaporate. Compare the amount of salt left after evaporation to the measured amount added to the water. Dry the soil and look for evidence of salt among the soil particles.

Wrap up

Review the four irrigation systems with students. Repeat the following quotation: "The most modern, best-designed surface irrigation system, or any irrigation method, can apply water efficiently only if the system is properly managed." Ask students how this relates to irrigation and water conservation.

Discuss the card game with students. Ask them about the significance of the Bad Luck card. (Even if a farmer or rancher is an excellent manager and applies water efficiently, there are elements such as severe weather, pests, equipment failure and a drop in market prices that are beyond his or her control and have an effect on the success of the crop.) Ask students how they felt when they were left holding the Bad Luck card. How do they think farmers and ranchers feel when crops that have been carefully tended are affected or destroyed by elements beyond their control?

Before participating in this activity, were students aware of how complex farming and ranching were? Did they have an idea of the degree of chemistry, biology, and earth science a farmer or rancher must know in order to maintain crop productivity and a healthy landscape?

Assessment

Have students:
· outline the factors a farmer must consider before selecting an irrigation system (**Part I**, step 1).
· match irrigation systems with corresponding types of topography and crop (**Part I**, step 2).
· construct one of four water irrigation systems in a tray or nursery flat (**Part II**, step 1).
· analyze the disappearance of an early culture (**Part III**, steps 1 and 3).

Extensions

If possible, plan a field trip so that students can spend a day with a farmer or rancher. Or have students share books and stories about farm and ranch life. Have students talk with parents or grandparents; many of them may have at one time lived an agrarian lifestyle. Plan a garden with students and discuss how they will efficiently irrigate it, or plant a classroom garden.

Resources

1998. *Water in the West: Challenge for the Next Century.* Springfield, Va.: National Technical Information Service.

The Watercourse. 1999. *Project WET Curriculum and Activity Guide.* Bozeman, Mont.: The Watercourse.

Gleick, Peter H. 1998. *The World's Water.* Washington, D.C.: Island Press.

Niebel, Bernard J., and Richard T. Wright. 1996. *Environmental Science, The Way the World Works.* Upper Saddle River, New Jersey: Prentice Hall.

Stewart, B. A., and Dr. R. Nielsen, eds. 1990. *Irrigation of Agricultural Crops.* Madison: American Society of Agronomy, Inc.

WEB site: Water Share by the Department of the Interior, Bureau of Reclamation http://209.21.0.235/waterlearn/teachers_room/agriwater/junior_lesson_plan.htm

Design a Drip Irrigation System

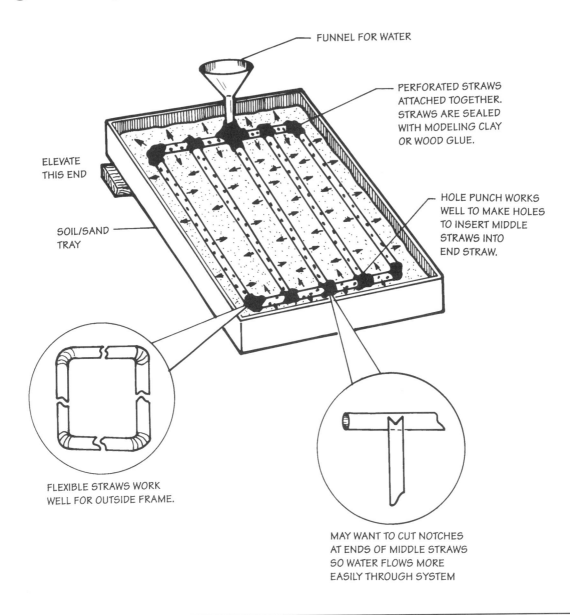

FUNNEL FOR WATER

PERFORATED STRAWS ATTACHED TOGETHER. STRAWS ARE SEALED WITH MODELING CLAY OR WOOD GLUE.

ELEVATE THIS END

SOIL/SAND TRAY

HOLE PUNCH WORKS WELL TO MAKE HOLES TO INSERT MIDDLE STRAWS INTO END STRAW.

FLEXIBLE STRAWS WORK WELL FOR OUTSIDE FRAME.

MAY WANT TO CUT NOTCHES AT ENDS OF MIDDLE STRAWS SO WATER FLOWS MORE EASILY THROUGH SYSTEM

Irrigation Innovation Card Game Answer Key

1. Sprinkler

2. Sprinkler

3. Subirrigation

4. Microirrigation

5. Microirrigation

6. Microirrigation

7. Surface Irrigation

8. Sprinkler Irrigation

9. No irrigation

10. Sprinkler Irrigation

11. Microirrigation

12. Microirrigation

13. Surface Irrigation

Irrigation Systems

Sprinkler Irrigation

In sprinkler irrigation, water is applied to the soil with a mechanism that directs an airborne stream of water. The water flows through a pressurized pipe to the sprinkler device. This method is designed to mimic rainfall. If sprinkler irrigation is applied correctly, less water evaporates than in surface irrigation.

· Sprinkler systems are designed to be *set* (they are stationary and intended to water only one portion of the field at a time) or they are *mobile* (like the center-pivot, in which the pipeline rotates about a stationary end through which the water flows).

· This type of system can be used to cool crops and also to protect plants from frost. (How? When water freezes into a solid state, heat is released. The heat created provides enough of a temperature increase to protect the sensitive parts of the plants.)

· When these systems are well designed and managed, they are capable of delivering water in an efficient and uniform way under diverse conditions.

· This system can be used on land that you would not want to level, because there is too much slope or because the soil is so shallow that leveling would remove the productive material.

· This can be used on most any soil, especially shallow soils, with minimal runoff and erosion.

· The center-pivot sprinkler irrigation system requires less attention and less labor than surface irrigation. Consequently, more center pivots are being used.

· This system is at a disadvantage in a windy environment or with plants that are prone to developing disease when their leaves are wet.

· Other disadvantages of sprinkler irrigation include: capitol investment is higher than in surface irrigation; maintenance costs may be higher; and power costs are higher than for surface watering.

Subirrigation

In subirrigation, the water table level is monitored and managed for the watering of crops. In some areas, the water table is so high that farmers do not have to irrigate. However, they sometimes construct systems of open ditches to affect the water table.

· This system is used mainly for perennial crops.

· The field must be fairly level so the water table is consistent throughout the area.

· This system is often used in areas of high rainfall (over 50 inches of rain per year) where droughts may occur periodically.

Irrigation Systems, continued

Microirrigation

Microirrigation is delivered through several methods (drip/trickle, subsurface, bubbler, spray). Microirrigation is described as "the frequent application of small quantities of water, as drops, tiny streams, or miniature spray through emitters or applicators placed along a water delivery line." The drip/trickle method was actually invented in Israel because water was scarce and saline (salty). Today, over half of Israel's land is watered by drip irrigation. In California, more and more systems are being converted to drip irrigation.

· Microirrigation is a good choice under the following conditions: when labor is costly; when water is scarce, expensive, and often saline; when adopting other methods would be hard (e.g. on rough terrain such as an orchard on the side of a hill); or when you are irrigating for greenhouse or landscape purposes.

· One of the main disadvantages of this system is the high cost of installation. In general, it is economically feasible only for high-profit crops such as avocados, grapes, citrus, cotton, strawberries, and vegetables.

· This system works well on all soil types, but especially sandy soils.

· It can be adapted for steep slopes and is not usually affected by weather such as wind.

· This system can contribute to water conservation through improved irrigation efficiency, but it requires capitol and a fairly high degree of education and training.

Surface Irrigation

In surface irrigation, water is applied at the top end of a field and flows by gravity across the soil surface. The characteristics of surface irrigation include:

· All crops may be irrigated by some type of surface irrigation system.

· This type of irrigation is best suited to fine- to medium-textured soils. Water percolates very quickly through coarse soils; therefore, the water would be absorbed and would not flow across the field.

· The topography of the field must be prepared so that the water will spread uniformly across the field.

· In order to adequately irrigate the bottom part of the field, additional water must be supplied that results in some runoff. Unless this water is recaptured through a tailwater recycling system, this application of water may be inefficient.

· In the western United States, surface irrigation systems are often supplied by gravity flow through canals from streams or storage facilities.

Irrigation Innovation Card Game

Scoring:

Correct Match, each card = 2 points

Incorrect Match, each card = -1 point

No Match, each card = -1 point
(If you have cards remaining in your hand without matches, each card is worth -1 point)

BAD LUCK Card = lose one-half of total points
(If you are left holding the BAD LUCK card at the end of the game, you lose one-half of your total points)

Surface Irrigation

Surface Irrigation

Sprinkler Irrigation

Sprinkler Irrigation

Irrigation Innovation Card Game, continued

| Sprinkler Irrigation | Sprinkler Irrigation | Microirrigation |

| Microirrigation | Microirrigation | Microirrigation |

Conserve Water! Educators' Guide © The Watercourse

Irrigation Innovation Card Game, continued

Microirrigation	Subirrigation	No irrigation required
Occasionally, you use this method to cool crops or protect them from frost.	The land to be irrigated has too much slope to level and the soil is shallow.	The field is level and your annual rainfall is plentiful (more than 50 inches per year), but you sometimes experience drought.
I	2	3

Irrigation Innovation Card Game, continued

Labor, land, and water are expensive. You are raising avocados. 4	You have a greenhouse. 5	You have an orchard on the side of a hill. 6
Most all crops can be irrigated with this method. 7	You have forage grass on uneven ground. The type of irrigation for this grass can be used on most any soil, especially shallow soils, with minimal runoff and erosion. 8	The climate here is humid and damp. You are raising field rhubarb, a deep-rooted perennial. 9

Irrigation Innovation Card Game, continued

This system does not work optimally in a windy environment or if crops are prone to develop diseases when their leaves are wet. 10	This system uses water very efficiently, but it is expensive to install and requires training to manage it. 11	You raise strawberries in an area where water is expensive and the supply is limited, the salt concentration is high in the soil, and drainage is poor. 12
You raise sorghum. To irrigate your crop, you apply water only at one end of the field. Tailwater runoff and rain supply water to the rest of the field. This system minimizes loss of irrigation water attributed to runoff. 13	**BONUS CARD!** This card can be matched to any other card.	**BAD LUCK CARD** • Severe weather • Pests • Equipment failure • Low market value for product Don't be left holding this card at the end of the game. If you are, you lose half your total points!

Irrigation Innovation Mini-Mystery

Lost Homeland

By A.D. 1300 a certain culture of the Southwest had lived in the area for more than 1,000 years.

The people had developed a huge irrigation system. They used sharp sticks to dig long, deep canals. These canals carried water across the desert. Some of the canals ran up to 12 miles (19 km) from the river; one of them was 30 feet (9 m) deep. By A.D. 1300, the canals covered approximately 150 miles (240 km).

The people also built dams across the river that were made of brush cut in the nearby mountains. These dams backed up the water and made it easier to send it into the canals. The dams also held back water to be stored for times of the year when no rain fell in the mountains.

The people grew cotton, corn, beans, squash, and pumpkins on their irrigated land. They hunted deer in the mountains. They trapped rabbits and other small game in the desert.

This was an advanced and creative culture. They made beautiful objects, like pottery. They built sturdy houses; walls and roofs were made of poles, brush, and mud plaster. At first the houses had only one story. By A.D. 1300, however, these people were building houses of several floors. They even had four-story buildings.

Sometime around A.D. 1400 these people seem to have disappeared from the area.

What was the cause of their sudden departure?

Examples of pots from the arid Southwest

PHOTOGRAPHS COURTESY OF MUSEUM OF NEW MEXICO, OFFICE OF ARCHAEOLOGICAL STUDIES

Water Audit

Grade Level:
Middle School

Subject Areas:
Math, Health, Environmental Science

Duration:
Preparation time: 10 minutes

Activity time: two 50 minute periods

Setting:
Classroom and Home

Skills:
Gather, Organize, Analyze, Interpret, Evaluate

Vocabulary:
audit, desalinization, water diversion, retrofitting, potable

Summary

Students conduct a home water audit and compare and contrast results with and without the implementation of water conservation practices.

Objectives

Students will:
· provide a rationale for implementing home water conservation measures.
· describe the benefits of at least five home water conservation practices.
· recommend water conservation strategies to be implemented within their own homes.

Materials

· *Conserve Water!* Student Copy Page
· *Water Audit Data Sheet I* Student Copy Page (one copy per student)
· *Water Audit Data Sheet II* Student Copy Page (one copy per student)

Background

Earth is often referred to as the blue planet or the water planet. Photographs of Earth taken from space are predominantly colored in shades of blue. This is not surprising since water circulating in oceans or frozen in ice fields covers about 71 percent of the planet. In fact, scientists estimate that there is enough water on Earth to cover the whole United States with water 93 miles deep! Nature uses and moves more water through the water cycle than any other thing. For example, each day the sun evaporates 1,000,000,000,000 (a trillion) tons of water.

Switching from the global to the personal perspective, the human body has nearly the same percentage of water as the planet—about 65—70 percent. The brain is almost all water (95 percent) and sayings that allude to "dry bones" are misleading—the human skeleton is 25 percent water.

So, if we are such watery creatures living in a watery world, why do we need to use water wisely? It boils down to a simple formula: the right amount of water, in the right place, of the right quality, at the best price. Water that is good enough to drink, that can be used by agriculture or industry and shared with wildlife, is a precious resource.

All of the water on the planet is not available for use by plants or animals. About 97 percent of the water on Earth is found in oceans. Only about 3 percent is fresh. Of this fresh water, a large percentage is frozen in icecaps and glaciers or is unavailable because it is too far underground, polluted, or trapped in soil. Stated simply, if a full bathtub holding 30

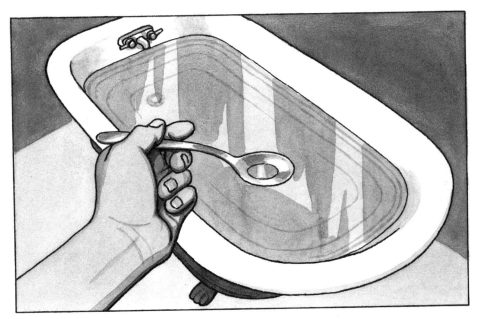

gallons represented all the water in the world, about one-half teaspoon of water would symbolize the amount of potable, available fresh water.

On a global scale, only a small percentage of water is available, but this percentage represents a large amount per individual. The irony is that for some people water may appear plentiful while for others it is a scarce commodity. Water is not equally distributed on the planet, and its availability depends on geography, climate, and weather.

For example, in the western United States, the climate is predominantly dry. In many areas, people rely on systems of dams and diversions to deliver fresh water, often from distant places. The water that runs from a tap in Los Angeles, California has likely traveled

hundreds of miles from the Rocky Mountains down the Colorado River and across the Mojave Desert. This delivery system is not only extensive, it is expensive!

Even if you live in a water-rich area, water treatment costs money. Water flows from its source—such as a river or well—through pipes to water treatment plants where it is cleaned. From the water treatment plant, it moves through pipes to our residences and industries. After use, water must be treated before it is released into a river or other water source.

Communities can suffer water shortages because of drought or sudden increases in population growth. Building larger water treatment plants (or in some areas, dams), desalinization facilities, or water diversion projects can increase

a community's water supplies. However, these options are expensive and some communities cannot afford them. What can citizens do?

Wherever a community is located, citizens can use less water by implementing water conservation practices. However, before a water conservation program is put into practice, a water audit can provide excellent baseline data from which to measure the progress of the program.

An audit is one of the first steps to take along the path to water conservation knowledge and action. Just as a financial audit informs a person about the way he or she truly makes and spends money, a water audit quantifies the actual use of water in an informative way. Before we can take steps to solve problems, we need documented benchmarks to start from, and to measure our progress against.

Water audits are becoming a standard feature of long-range planning for industries, communities, and individuals. The findings are, without exception, illuminating; and they are often surprising. As the costs of providing water escalate, the importance of benchmark data and conservation strategies based on reliable figures also rises. Several of the case studies (the bathroom retrofitting program in New York City,

the measures taken by the water authority in Boston, and others) depended on water audits as a critical part of the decision-making process.

Procedure
Warm Up
The *Conserve Water!* assessment is designed to determine if students understand the availability of fresh, potable water; the distribution of water on the planet; the cost of water (water and wastewater treatment); and the potential of water conservation measures to offset a community's increased water demands.

Distribute the assessment and allow students a few minutes to complete the form. Then, go through each question with students, discussing their responses and introducing information and concepts important for understanding the rationale for conducting a home or school water audit.

The Activity
1. Organize students into cooperative learning groups.
2. Have each group list all the ways they use water in a 24-hour period inside and outside their homes.
3. Record their ideas on the board.
4. Hand out the *Water Audit Data Sheet I* Student Copy Page to each student.
5. Ask students to review the sheet.
6. Ask them to record on the

sheet in column A by each water use the number of times they believe they conduct that activity in a 24- hour period.
7. Instruct them to record the number of times they actually conduct each water use activity over the next 24 hours in column B of *Water Audit Data Sheet I.*
8. Have students compare the number of gallons they predicted with their actual use. Did they use more water than they guessed? Less? Were students surprised by the amount of water they used?
9. Ask students if they know of any ways to reduce the number of gallons of water they use. Do their parents frequently ask them to turn off the shower? Why? Is water free, just because it flows freely from the faucet?
10. Do students believe that using water resources wisely makes sense?
11. Ask students to suggest some water conservation practices.
12. Hand out *Water Audit Data Sheet II* Student Copy Page. Ask students to again record the amount of water they use in a 24-hour period, but this time they will implement as many water conservation practices as they can.
13. Ask students to calculate the total amount of water they used in a 24-hour period when they were practicing water conservation measures. Direct students to compare the total number of gallons on *Data*

Sheet I to the total on *Data Sheet II.*

Wrap Up
Have students respond to the following questions related to water conservation practices:
· How did their water consumption change after implementing water conservation measures? How many gallons of water did they save? Were they more careful about their use of water after they realized how much they used?
· Which conservation measures were the easiest to institute?
· Which practices were the most difficult? Why?
· If you were only allowed 30 gallons of water per day, to what water uses would you give the highest priority?
· Select three of the water conservation practices that you found fairly easy to use. If you were to apply these three practices routinely, how many gallons of water would you save each month? If every member of your family consistently employed these practices, how many gallons would be saved per month within your own household?
· Is it a good idea for a school, business, or hospital to conduct a water audit? Why would a water audit be beneficial for these institutions?

Have students write a set of at least five recommendations or suggestions for their family based on their home water audit. These suggestions should include short- and long-term actions. For example, for long-term actions, students may suggest that low-flow showerheads be installed or water-saving appliances purchased when the current ones no longer function. Have students share their recommendations with the class.

Assessment

Have students:
· indicate their responses on the *Conserve Water!* assessment form (*Warm Up*).
· complete *Water Audit Data Sheet I* in order to calculate how much water they use in a 24-hour period (steps 6, 7, and 8).
· complete *Water Audit Data Sheet II* in order to compute how much water they use in a 24-hour period when they are implementing water conservation practices (steps 12 and 13).
· formulate a list of at least five recommendations for their family based on their home water audit (*Wrap Up*).

Extension

Although it is certainly more complicated, students may conduct a water audit of their school. Engage in this activity only after securing full permission from school administrators. The forms for a school water audit are included with this activity.

Break the class into three audit teams, as follows:
· Research and information team
· Indoor water use team
· Outdoor water use team

Hand out copies of the *Team Worksheets* Student Copy Pages and explain each team's job description (also explained on the worksheets) as follows:
· Research and information: To track down billing records; identify historic and yearly water use patterns; and conduct interviews with appropriate officials to pinpoint water use hot spots.
· Indoor water use: To document major indoor uses of water, pinpoint problem areas (leaks), and gather as much specific information as possible.
· Outdoor water use: To document outdoor uses of water, pinpoint problem areas, and gather as much specific information as possible.

Set a deadline for when teams should have results (one week should be sufficient) and tell them when they will report their findings to the class.

Allow the class time to organize their approach to the tasks.

Be available to provide suggestions, assistance, or information during the audit process.

After the allotted audit time, regroup and ask one person from each team to present their findings to the class. Ask them to summarize their data, highlight the most obvious areas of concern, and list their conclusions pertaining to the school's use of water.

Once all the teams have reported, reconfigure the groups. Each of the new teams should have representatives from all three original teams.

Tell students that the point of all their initial work was to provide foundation information on which future policy and action can be based. The second phase of their work together is to formulate a set of strategic suggestions to present to school officials; their job is to aid in developing a comprehensive, schoolwide water conservation program.

Give the new teams a class period (30-50 minutes) to work through the *Strategy Sheet* Student Copy Page, pooling their collective information.

When the groups finish, ask for a spokesperson from each to present the basic elements of their strategic suggestions.

Tell students that they've now gone through the essential steps of a basic audit, and they've come to some conclu-

sions as a result. The next phase is to organize their data and suggestions in a concise, factual, and persuasive statement.

As a class, fill out a single, final *Strategy Sheet*, combining the best and most practical information from their audit process, along with a summary of the best strategy suggestions.

If it can be arranged, invite school officials to hear the class's final report and summary in a formal presentation. Alternatively, the class could send a delegation to meet with school officials and make a presentation.

Resources

The Watercourse. 1999. *Conserve Water* Student Booklet. Bozeman, Mont.: The Watercourse.

The Watercourse. 1999. *Project WET Curriculum and Activity Guide*. Bozeman, Mont.: The Watercourse.

Angelo, Thomas A., and K. Patricia Cross. 1993. *Classroom Assessment Techniques*. San Francisco: Jossey-Bass Publishers.

Johnson, Cynthia. *Water Ways*. 1997. Florida: Office of Public Instruction, St. Johns River Water Management District.

Conserve Water!

This is not a test, so it is okay to answer "I don't know." After you complete these questions, you and other students will have a discussion with your teacher guided by your responses. This is a tool to help you learn more about water conservation.

1. Where does the water come from that flows out of your faucet at home?
    a. Home well
    b. Flows through pipes from the city water treatment facility
    c. Directly from the river or ocean
    d. I don't know

2. Is water that flows out of your faucet at home free of charge?
    a. Yes
    b. No
    c. I don't know

3. Where does water go after it is flushed down the toilet or swirls down the drain in your home?
    a. To the city wastewater treatment plant
    b. Directly to the river
    c. Through the home septic system
    d. I don't know

4. If a bathtub full of water represents all the water in the world, what measurement below shows the amount of water in the world that is fresh, usable water?
    a. One cup of water
    b. One bathtub full of water
    c. One teaspoon of water
    d. One bucket of water

5. What percentage of the human body do you believe is made up of water?
    a. 50%
    b. 10%
    c. 70%
    d. 5%

6. Why are some places in the world dry and others very wet? That is, why is water distributed un-evenly throughout the world?
    a. Some places just waste a lot of water so it is dry
    b. Because of differences in weather, climate, and geography
    c. In some places, the sun never sets, so it is always hot and dry
    d. I don't know

7. Do you believe it is possible for individuals to change their habits and use less water? Do you think that individuals choosing to use less water can have a positive impact on the water supplies of their community? (Write 2 to 3 sentences to answer this question.)

Water Audit Data Sheet I
Home Water Audit

Water use	Column A Predicted # of water uses per day	Column B Actual # of water uses per day	Column C # of gal. per use	Column D Actual # of gal. used per day (B x C = D)
Brush teeth for two minutes, water running			6 gallons	
One toilet flush			5 to 7 gallons	
Wash dishes by hand, rinse in running water			20 gallons	
Shower			5 gallons/minute	
One dishwasher cycle			12 to 15 gallons	
Bath			30 gallons	
Wash hands, water running			3 gallons	
One clothes-washing cycle			50 gallons	
Get a drink with water running			1/4 gallon	
Water lawn, 10 minutes			75 gallons	
Wash car with hose running			10 gallons/minute	
				TOTAL:

1. Write down any other water uses that are not listed. Research to find out how many gallons of water that use requires.
2. Think of how often you directly use water every day. Write down how many times you think you conduct a particular activity each day in column A.
3. Throughout the following day (as soon as you get up in the morning) record how many times you actually use water.
4. Multiply the number of times you use water by how many gallons each use generally requires.
5. Add all the numbers in column D.
6. Write your answer in the last box in Column D. This is the estimated number of gallons of water you use every day.

Water Audit Data Sheet II
Home Water Audit

Water use	Column A Water Conservation Action (suggested or your own action)	Column B # of water uses per day	Column C Estimated # of gal. per use		Column D Actual # of gal. used per day B x C = D
			without conservation action	with conservation action	
Brushing teeth for two minutes, water running	Brush and rinse, water not running		6 gal.	$1/_2$ gal.	
One toilet flush	Low-flush toilet		5-7 gal.	3 gal.	
Wash dishes by hand, rinse in running water	Wash dishes and dip in pan of water to rinse		20 gal.	5 gal.	
Shower, water running	5 minutes with low-flow showerhead		*5 gal./min.	12 gal.	
One dishwasher cycle			12-15 gal.		
Bath			30 gal.		
Wash hands with water running	Turning off water between wash and rinse		3 gal.	$1/_2$ gal.	
One clothes-washing cycle	Adjusted water level		50 gal.	25 gal.	
Get a drink with water running	Pour glass from water pitcher in 'fridge		$1/_4$ gal.	$1/_{16}$ gal.	
Water lawn, 10 minutes			75 gal.		
Wash car with hose running	Use bucket, sponge, and controlled-flow nozzle		**10 gal./min.	5 gal. total	
					TOTAL:

*5 gal. x length of shower in minutes = total water use
**10 gal. x number of minutes hose is running = total

1. Write down any water uses that are not listed.
2. Conduct your daily water activities, but think of ways in which you could conserve water. Several suggestions are listed in the chart, but you may contribute any ideas you have and estimate your water savings.
3. Add up the total number of gallons in Column D.
4. Compare the total number of gallons in Column D with the number of gallons you used on *Water Audit Data Sheet I.*
5. How many gallons did you save in one day by practicing a few simple water conservation actions?
6. How many gallons would your family save in one day if everyone participated in these water conservation actions?
7. How many gallons would your family save in one month?

Team Worksheet—Research and Information

Your role in the audit is to conduct research and interviews to document your school's water use figures and establish general water use patterns.

1. Identify the offices and individuals responsible for handling water at your school (fiscal manager, accountant, maintenance department, building manager). Contact these offices for an interview appointment with the people who have direct knowledge about or information on the school's water use.

2. See if you can obtain copies of water bills and meter readings over the past year (longer if possible). Analyze them for times of peak and low use and any other obvious patterns.

3. Through meter readings and interviews, try to identify the major water users at the school (pool, sprinkler system, gym showers, bathrooms) and the times of peak demand.

4. Find out if school officials have a way of itemizing water use for different parts of the school (separate meters are the most reliable way to do this).

5. Either from actual figures or interview information list your school's top five uses of water.

_____

_____

_____

_____

_____

6. In your interview (especially when you talk with people involved in the day-to-day use of water—pool maintenance, lawn watering, etc.) ask specific questions like:
· What are the top water consumption activities at the school? On what information do you base that conclusion?
· In what areas is water used most inefficiently?
· Have you noticed specific water fixtures that leak persistently?
· In your opinion, what measures could be taken to conserve water most effectively at school?
· How could you more precisely document the school's water use?

7. Compare information from the various interviews to find common ground, and summarize your findings on a separate piece of paper.

Team Worksheet—Indoor Water Use

Your role is to survey the school building and document the major users of water. You will also search out leaks and other obvious problem areas.

1. Begin by touring the school buildings to take an inventory of water consuming fixtures/installations. As much as possible, document how much water each fixture uses. Cover at least the following:

Fixture/Installation Total #	Water Consumed/Used	
Indoor swimming pool		
Toilets/urinals		
Showers		
Drinking fountains		
Hot water heating pipes/AC		
Boiler		
Utility closets		
Bathroom sinks		
Indoor sprinkler system		

2. If you come across any leaky fixtures as you conduct the survey, do your best to measure the wasted water. Put a cup or jug under the leak and time it for one minute. Measure the amount of water, then multiply by 60 to get the amount lost every hour; multiply again by 24 to arrive at the daily total.

3. Identify fixtures that could be replaced with more efficient models (aerated faucets, low-flow showerheads, low-flow toilets) and multiply by the total number of fixtures.

4. Calculate several examples of the yearly savings that would result from some basic renovations. For example, how much water would be saved every year if the school fixed the leaks you found? If the school installed more efficient showerheads or low-flow toilets, how many gallons would be saved every 100 flushes or every 100 showers?

5. Are there too many water fixtures in some areas (drinking fountains, bathrooms)? Could the school reasonably do without some of these? Are the fixtures located in the best spots?

6. In general, what are the most intensive indoor uses of water at your school?

7. Are there other comments you would add after your tour? Other areas of concern you think would be worth investigating?

Team Worksheet—Outdoor Water Use

Your role is to survey the school grounds and document the major uses of water. You will also search out leaks and other obvious problem areas. (During winter months in some climates students will have a hard time documenting some aspects of outdoor water use. They can still take their tour and make observations, but they will probably want to supplement their research with interviews with groundskeepers, maintenance staff, and so on.)

1. Start with a tour of the school grounds. Inventory all the obvious water-consuming devices. If possible, document how much water is used in each application. Likely outdoor water fixtures include:
    * sprinkler systems
    * outdoor pool
    * fountains or ponds
    * outside faucets

2. If possible, measure any leaks you find along the way by collecting water for one minute, multiplying by 60, and then again by 24 to arrive at the water lost every day.

3. Identify fixtures that could be made more efficient (drip irrigation, timers on sprinklers, covers for outdoor pools to reduce evaporation) and try to estimate the savings that might be achieved.

4. Consider other avenues of outdoor water conservation. For example, designing a water conservative landscape; a watering regime tied to times of day and climate conditions that would minimize evaporative loss; adjusting sprinkler heads so that water is not wasted by watering asphalt; the possibility of recirculating/reusing water for some applications. Write up a summary of your suggestions.

5. After your tour, list the top outdoor uses of water at the school and brainstorm suggestions to make conservation improvements in those areas.

6. Did you come up with other observations or insights you'd like to comment on? If so, address these on a separate sheet of paper.

Strategy Sheet

Now that you've gathered a quantity of raw data, you can draw some conclusions and make informed suggestions to your school. Pool the information collected by the three teams and use this form to summarize and direct your findings.

1. List the major uses of water at your school (the most dramatic and easily achieved results usually come from targeting the biggest water users).

Top Indoor Consumers	Top Outdoor Consumers

2. Briefly describe the leaks found by teams and list the three that are most serious.

_____

_____

_____

3. How much water could your school save every year if they fixed every leak found by your group?

4. Based on your study of water bills, how much money would the school save by fixing all the leaks?

Strategy Sheet, continued

5. What measures can you suggest that will have the most dramatic impact on water savings for your school?

Indoor:

Outdoor:

6. Come up with three to five concrete examples of water savings your school could achieve through simple measures or changes in practice (e.g., the installation of low-flow toilets or toilet dams would save the school 3 gallons/flush). If possible, give one or two examples of the potential financial savings that would accrue through lower water bills as a result of conservation. (For instance, if low-flow toilets saved 50,000 gallons/month, the school would pay X dollars less on the monthly water bill.)

a. Water conservation measures

b. Financial savings that would result

Hydrograph for the Year 2000

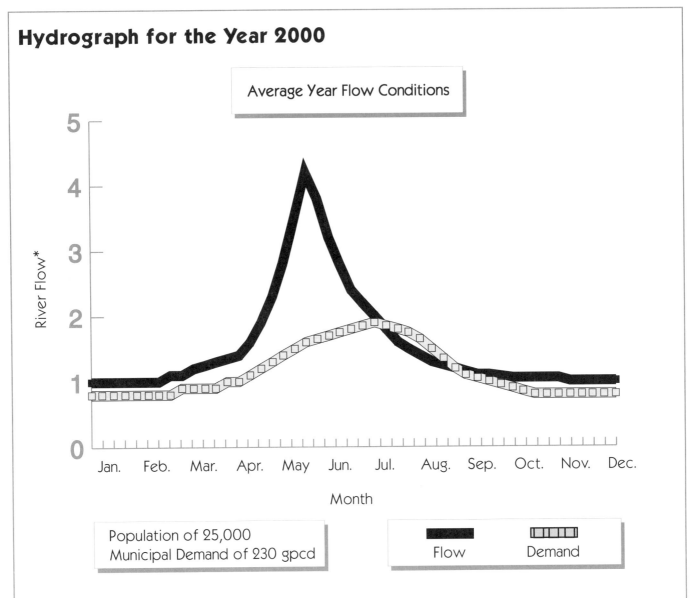

Average Year Flow Conditions

River Flow*

5
4
3
2
1
0

Jan. Feb. Mar. Apr. May Jun. Jul. Aug. Sep. Oct. Nov. Dec.

Month

Population of 25,000
Municipal Demand of 230 gpcd

Flow   Demand

*Number 1 represents the base flow of the river and ascending numbers are proportional to the base flow.

Your Hydrologic Deck

Conserve Water

Grade Level:
Middle School and High School

Subject Areas:
Government, Environmental Science, Mathematics

Duration:
Preparation time
Part I: 10 minutes
Part II: 10 minutes

Activity time
Part I: 50 minutes
Part II: two 50-minute periods

Setting:
Classroom

Skills:
Gather, Organize, Analyze, Interpret, Apply, Evaluate, Present

Vocabulary:
hydrology, hydrograph, per capita use rate, instream flow, drought, watershed, instream water use, diversionary water use, wastewater treatment, reservoir

Summary
Analyzing and applying data, students work as members of decision making teams to manage the water resources of a community over a period of 25 years.

Objectives
Students will:
· analyze hydrographs and other resource data to make water management decisions.
· recognize and relate the diverse elements that a water manager must balance in supplying the water needs of the community.

Materials
· copies of *Hydrograph for the Year 2000* Student Copy Page, 1 copy per group
· copies of *Your Hydrologic Deck* Student Copy Pages, 1 copy per group

Background
We all live in and depend on watersheds. These are places where water connects with the land and flows across and beneath earth's surface on an incredible journey through the water cycle. During its course toward the oceans water can be stored temporarily in lakes and rivers, seep underground, evaporate or move into another watershed.

Towns and cities, farms, ranches, and industries divert water for various consumptive uses. What remains in the channel is used for nonconsumptive instream purposes such as navigation, fish and wildlife habitat, hydroelectric production, and recreation. Both instream and diversionary water users depend on an adequate supply of plentiful, clean water.

Without ample municipal water supplies we could not meet our **domestic** needs—water for drinking, cooking, washing, sewage removal, watering lawns, and irrigating gardens. Other water uses include **public uses** such as fire fighting, street cleaning, and irrigating parks and athletic fields. **Industry** requires water for producing food products such as chocolate, flour, canned fruits and vegetables and soft drinks. Water for industry also produces textile products such as cotton for clothing, lumber and wood products, paper, and chemicals. **Commercial use** includes water for motels, restaurants, office buildings, other commercial facilities, and civilian and military institutions.

Nearly 75 percent of American cities rely on ground water, at least in part, to fulfill water requirements. Whatever the mix of surface and ground water resources, municipal supplies are often retained in storage reservoirs to ensure adequate supplies year round.

Water is rarely used without prior treatment; some urban supplies require much more treatment than others do. After water is used, waste from homes and factories is delivered in pipes leading to a sewage main which transports it to a wastewater treatment facility. Sewage water is then treated through primary treatment (settling and chlorinating) and secondary treatment (biologic processing using microbes). A final tertiary treatment is sometimes considered, which involves oxidation and the spraying of effluent on croplands. Some homes have their own treatment systems called septic systems.

A per capita use rate for a city is the total amount of water used by a city divided by the population of that city. This may be expressed as gallons per capita day (gpcd). This figure is based on the level of several daily activities, and varies from city to city depending on water use practices. Some arid cities, for example, might use more water for irrigating lawns and fire protection.

If the per capita use rate stays the same, but the population grows, the water demand will increase and may lead proportionately to shortages. Therefore, conservation measures often are set in place to better utilize supplies. Many daily practices can be modified significantly: number of

car washes, laundry loads and showers, and methods of landscape watering. Water supply, system leakage, and the level of industrial development may also be modified.

Procedure
Warm Up
Water resource managers are charged with the responsibility of planning adequate water supplies for many water uses including domestic, commercial, industrial, and public use. In order to plan for the water needs of their communities, these managers must compile specific information about their watersheds. They must be aware of: total and seasonal water availability, the needs of diverse water users, the reservoir size that will guarantee a certain supply during dry months, the minimum flow required to protect the fishery, the accessibility of ground water, the existing level of water conservation education and practice, the condition of the city's water delivery system, the potential for the city's growth, and many other factors.

Water managers use many tools to help them in the decision-making process. One of these tools is a hydrograph, a type of graph that shows variations of discharge, velocity, or other properties of water over time. The information that is plotted on hydrographs is collected at streamflow gauging stations. In

fact, the United States Geological Survey (USGS) works with hundreds of local, state, and other federal agencies to coordinate a streamflow gauging station network that collects information about the country's water resources. Over half of the more than 7,000 stations provide "real-time" information via satellite. Data from these stations is transmitted every 3 or 4 hours by an earth-satellite-based communications system. Through the Internet individuals may access this information for streams within their respective states. (See the National Atlas of the United States on the World Wide Web.)

A hydrograph is expressed in terms of flow (y-axis) per unit of time (x-axis). Make copies of the Hydrograph for the Year 2000 (opposite the title page to this activity) and distribute the copies to groups of four to five students. Have students look at the hydrograph. Ask them how they know this is an annual hydrograph (the months of January through December are recorded on the x-axis). The river flow is recorded on the y-axis. Ask students what conclusions they can draw from reviewing the hydrograph. For example, in what month did the peak runoff occur? (Peak runoff occurred in June and returned close to base flow in July.) In what months did the demand peak? (Peak demand occurred

in July and August). Why did demand peak in these two summer months? (lawn irrigation, increased car washing, etc.) Ask students to look at the relationship of the two lines on the graph. When did the demand exceed the natural flow? (In July and August, the demand exceeded the natural flow and the city was dependent on water stored in the reservoir.)

Tell students that they will be participating in a simulation in which they will work with hydrographs. They will review one hydrograph in each five-year period. For the purposes of this simulation, this hydrograph represents the most critical year within the five years. Throughout the activity ask them to observe how the shape and magnitude of the hydrographs vary from year to year. What do they believe is the main reason for this variation? (This fluctuation is a function of seasonal and climatic variations in rain and snow. To a lesser extent, it is also related to the permeability of aquifers, which can store ground water and supply streams during times of shortage.)

The Activity

1. Organize students into cooperative learning groups. Each group represents a decision-making team responsible for the management of water resources within their community.

2. Have the teams decide upon a decision-making strategy: majority vote, consensus (work toward all team members agreeing on a solution), and so forth.

3. Have the entire class consider and discuss the following questions that will be pertinent to their work as water managers:

· What may affect the amount of available water? (This includes weather such as rain, snow or drought; population increases or decreases; water storage (reservoirs, water tanks); and water conservation strategies.

· What things can water managers control? (If funding is available, storage tanks and reservoirs can be constructed. Other water resources can be explored such as drilling additional wells for ground water. Water conservation strategies can be implemented.)

· What things are beyond the control of water managers? (weather, drought, flood)

· How is a water manager's success or failure in providing adequate water resources for the community affected by the *hydrological deck of cards that the manager is dealt?*

· Who must share the water within a watershed? (All water users! For the purpose of this simulation, they include domestic, public, industrial, and commercial users.)

· How is water shared with wildlife? (Streamflow is the amount of water remaining in a stream after all uses, which is required to maintain a particular aquatic environment or accommodate other purposes such as hydroelectric production, navigation, and recreation.)

· If water managers determine that they must increase water supply and recommend enlarging the community's reservoir or the drilling of additional wells, who will pay for this? (The community's citizens will pay increased taxes.)

· Would different communities have different concerns regarding customer needs, taxation, growth, or maintaining sufficient streamflow to meet recreation and fish and wildlife needs? (Yes. Some communities may be mainly concerned with keeping taxes low. Others may be interested in growth and desire water managers to plan for it by increasing water supplies. There are endless variations on these four concerns.)

· What are some examples of water conservation practices that communities can implement? (Communities can replace or repair leaky water mains. They can educate citizens about the value of water conservation through school education programs, public service announcements, inserts in utility bills, and so forth. Communities can provide rebates on efficient appliances and fixtures and landscape conservation programs. Water charges can also be increased to encourage people to conserve.

4. Distribute: *Your Hydrologic Deck*, Student Copy Pages. Review the following with students:

· Directions
· Scenario
· Study generated by consultant group
· Four areas of community concern
· Water Department Annual Report (Hydrograph for Year 2000)

5. Distribute: *Your Hydrologic Deck* Student Copy Pages. You may wish to work through the first set of charts with students (Year 2001: Your recommendations for the next 5 years; Water Usage Report 2005; Year 2005 Evaluation).

6. In their cooperative groups, have students work on their own for the remaining 20 years of the simulation.

Wrap Up

Ask groups with high scores to discuss the strategies they used to make decisions. What are the advantages and disadvantages of making decisions based on the input of a team of people? What were students' feelings during the simulation? Do students believe it would be a demanding job to be part of such a team? A rewarding job?

Have students discuss alternatives for increasing water supply such as constructing dams and reservoirs, building water tanks, tapping ground water or other water resources. Are these alternatives always available to communities? Can all communities afford these alternatives?

Ask students to discuss water conservation practices for reducing the demand on water introduced through the simulation. Do they believe that water conservation can affect water availability? How may the successful implementation of water conservation practices affect the water treatment and wastewater treatment facilities of a community?

Do students believe that in the face of continued growth, it is possible to improve water use efficiency by 10% indefinitely? Are there limits to the use of water conservation strategies? Is there a limit to how much citizens are willing to conserve? How much would students be willing to conserve? With continued growth, without increasing water supplies, is there a limit to the effectiveness of water conservation practices?

Ask students to summarize in one paragraph the balance that they believe a water manager must achieve in observing the priority concerns of a community and accommodating growth by increasing a community's water resources supply, and/or reducing de-

mand for water resources through conservation practices. Does the manager's lack of control over the weather, drought, or flood affect this balance? How does a manager's knowledge of historical patterns (often revealed through hydrographs) affect this balance? Is a manager's success based in part on the *hydrological hand of cards he is dealt*?

Assessment

Have students:
· interpret a hydrograph (*Warm Up*)
· determine a decision-making strategy for their team (Step 2)
· discuss the parameters within which a water manager must work (Step 3)
· complete the 25 year simulation and evaluate their scores (Step 6)
· write a paragraph describing the balance a water manager must achieve in providing a sufficient water supply for all water users within the community (*Wrap Up*)

Extensions

Have students investigate how the water needs of their communities are identified and satisfied. Instruct them to determine if their community depends upon: surface water, ground water or both

Ask students if they are aware of a water conservation education plan within their school

or community? Ask students to develop (or review and improve) a water conservation education plan for their home, school, or community. They may want to conduct a survey to determine what people already know and to assess their attitudes about conservation and identify their needs.

Based on an analysis of the survey and their knowledge of water conservation practices, students may develop a water conservation education plan. This plan may include:
· writing and producing a brochure of effective water conservation practices for distribution
· producing radio and television public service announcements
· conducting school programs
· providing publications on water conservation

Resources

Higgins, Susan. 1994. *The Watershed Manager Teacher's Guide*. Bozeman, Mont.: The Watercourse.

Van der Leeden, Frits, Fred L. Troise, and David Keith Todd. 1991. *The Water Encyclopedia*. Michigan: Lewis Publishers, Inc.

National Atlas of the United States on the World Wide Web.

Your Hydrologic Deck

Directions:

Read the information below, then turn to the worksheets and follow the directions. This information may help you to make decisions so that you will be long remembered as an effective water manager for your city. You and your group will provide recommendations every five years, for a period of 25 years. You will score your decisions every five years. At the end of the simulation, you will add up your scores. The higher your score, the more successful you were as a water manager, based on the established priorities of your city (customer need, growth, streamflow, and taxes). You can play this simulation again and again by changing the priorities.

Scenario

You live in an urban area located in a watershed in the western United States. Your city relies on surface water for its water supply. In previous years, a small dam was built to create a storage reservoir that holds about one-eighth of the annual river flow. The current population of the city is about 25,000.

You have just graduated from college and have been hired by the city water department. You work with a team that provides recommendations to the mayor and the city commission regarding water supply for the city. For simplicity, the mayor and commission will accept your recommendations in full for each scenario in this simulation.

Your first job is to review the following *Study Generated by a Consultant Group* and, based on that information, to make recommendations to the mayor for future water supply decisions.

Your Hydrologic Deck, continued

Study Generated by Consultant Group

The study revealed the following:

1. The study projected the population growth for the next 25 years. The consultants based their projections on an estimated growth rate of from 2 to 4 percent per year. They estimated that the population may increase from the current level of 25,000 to 40,000, possibly up to 60,000, by the year 2025.

2. Based on the current amount of storage, the city may experience water shortages within the next 25 years if population increases at the 2 percent level. If the population increases at a higher rate, the probability of water shortages also increases.

3. The study also determined the current level of use by different water user groups and provided the graph that follows. Water use is currently at the level of 230 gallons per person per day. There is great potential for conserving water.

Four Areas of Community Concern

Throughout your employment as a water manager, you will need to address four areas of concern related to your city. Other areas of concern exist, but in order to simplify matters for this simulation, you need only consider these four:

· Customer Needs
· Streamflow
· Taxes
· Growth

In the year 2000,
· customer needs were fully met.
· there was no increase in taxes (the current dam has already been paid for).
· the low taxes and sufficient water supply encouraged growth.
· regarding streamflow, there was ample water in the stream to meet recreation and fish and wildlife needs.

[SEE THE PRIORITIES WORKSHEET]

Worksheet Priorities

Community Concerns	Sample Priorities	Your Priorities
Customer Needs	2	
Streamflow	2	
Taxes	2	
Growth	1	
Total	7	7

*You will retain these priorities throughout the simulation.

Your Hydrologic Deck, continued

Priorities Worksheet

1. You and your group must establish the priorities on which you will base your management decisions.

2. On the *Priorities Worksheet,* enter a number in the column marked Your Priorities across from each concern. The higher the number, the more important that concern is to you and your city in making decisions. You must place a number by each concern, and all of the numbers must add up to seven. You will only determine your priorities once and you will retain them throughout the simulation.

[SEE THE YEAR 2001: YOUR RECOMMENDATIONS FOR THE NEXT FIVE YEARS]

Your Recommendations

1. You have decisions to make in three areas: whether to increase the city's supply of surface water or ground water; whether to reduce water demand through various conservation measures; or you may choose to take no action.

Increase Supply

· Reservoir Size: Decide whether you will keep your water storage capacity the same (one-eighth of annual river flow) or increase your reservoir capacity. If you increase, it will cost money. You must record that cost in the column marked Your Choices.

· Develop Ground Water: You may increase your water supply by tapping not only surface water now stored in the reservoir, but also ground water if you decide to drill wells. However, drilling wells costs money that the taxpayers must provide. If you drill additional wells, indicate the cost in the column marked Your Choices.

Reduce Demand

You can select from four options to reduce demand through conservation measures. You may select no options, or any combination of the four. Place the costs in the column marked Your Choices.

No Action Required

You may choose to take no action, thus requiring $0 from taxpayers.

Total the Your Choices column. The result is the total tax you must levy to put your recommendations into action.

[SEE THE WATER USAGE REPORT 2005]

Water Usage Report

You may use the *Water Usage Report* to figure out how much water you used in relation to conservation actions that you may or may not have recommended. The types of water use are listed in columns across the top of the chart: domestic, commercial, industrial, and public. The number under each use shows how much of the total water use (230 gallons per capita day) is required in each category. For example, of the 230 gpcd, 130 gpcd are needed for domestic use and 35 gpcd for public use.

1. If you made conservation recommendation #1 to replace or repair leaky water mains and replace worn water meters, public use of surface water was reduced by 10 percent (.10).

· Public Use
35 gpcd (public use) x .10 = 3.5
Round up to 4.0 gpcd
Write 4 in the column under Public Use.

2. If you made conservation recommendation #2 to provide conservation education, you will see reductions in domestic use (2 percent), commercial use (3 percent), and industrial use (2 percent).

· Domestic Use
130 gpcd x .02 = 2.6 gpcd
Write 3 in the column under Domestic Use.

· Commercial Use
40 gpcd x .03 = 1.2
Round down to 1 gpcd
Write 1 in the column under Commercial Use.

· Industrial Use
25 gpcd x .02 = 0.5
Round up to 1 gpcd
Write 1 in the column under Industrial Use.

Your Hydrologic Deck, continued

3. If you made Conservation Recommendation #3 to offer rebates, you will see reductions in domestic use (4 percent), commercial use (4 percent), industrial use (4 percent), and public use (2 percent).

· Domestic Use
  130 gpcd x .04 = 5.2
  Round down to 5 gpcd
· Commercial Use
  40 gpcd x .04 = 1.6
  Round up to 2 gpcd
· Industrial Use
  25 gpcd x .04 = 1 gpcd
· Public Use
  35 gpcd x .02 = 0.7
  Round up to 1 gpcd

Record each number in the appropriate square.

4. If you made conservation recommendation #4 to increase water charges, you will see reductions in domestic use (5 percent), commercial use (5 percent), and industrial use (8 percent).

· Domestic Use
  130 gpcd x .05 = 6.5
  Round up to 7 gpcd
· Commercial Use
  40 gpcd x .05 = 2 gpcd
· Industrial Use
  25 gpcd x .08 = 2 gpcd

Record each number in the appropriate square.

5. To determine TOTAL WATER USAGE per day:

If you opted for all the conservation recommendation, you would perform the following operations.

· Domestic Use
  3 + 5 + 7 = 15 gpcd conserved
  130 − 15 = 115 gpcd
· Commercial Use
  1 + 2 + 2 = 5 gpcd conserved
  40 − 5 = 35 gpcd
· Industrial Use
  1 + 1 + 2 = 4 pgcd conserved
  25 − 4 = 21 gpcd

· Public Use
  4 + 1 = 5 gpcd conserved
  35 − 5 = 30 gpcd

To find the total water usage per day, add: 115 + 35 + 21 + 30 = 201 gallons per capita day (gpcd). If all conservation measures had been implemented, use was reduced by 29 gpcd (230-201 = 29 gpcd).

6. To determine the average total water demand per day:

201 gpcd (total water usage per day) x 27,000 (population) = 5,427,000/1,000,000 = 5.427 MGD (million gallons per day)

The designation "million gallons per day" (MGD) is the unit most commonly used by water utilities.

7. Look at your recommendations for ground water development. Circle the number in the SUPPPLY FROM GROUND WATER chart that indicates how many wells you decided to drill.

8. To determine the average demand from surface water (given new wells/ground water supplies):

5.427 MGD (average total water demand per day, see #6 above) − 2.0 MGD (supply from ground water if you drilled 5 wells, see SUPPLY FROM GROUND WATER chart) = 3.427 MGD (average water demand from surface water)

Explanation: Once you have determined the water demands of your population (including any water savings related to recommended conservation practices), you must determine how much is supplied from surface water and how much you may have decided to supply from ground water. In order to score your recommendations, you will need to know how much water the population required and how much you supplied through surface and possibly ground water.

[SEE THE CHART LABELED YEAR 2005 EVALUATION]

Your Hydrologic Deck, continued

Your Evaluation

Now it is time to score your recommendations. Imagine that five years have passed in your community. Notice that the Year 2005 Evaluation returns to the four concerns that you initially prioritized. In the column marked Priority, record how you first rated the concerns (customer needs; streamflow; taxes; growth). Remember, you must stay with your original figures and they must add up to seven.

Customer Needs
· Based on what happened in your community in the last five years, if you recommended increasing the dam size to one-fourth of the annual river flow or more, you were able to fully meet customer needs. In the Points column, circle the number "4."
· If the reservoir retained less than one-fourth of the river flow, circle the "3."
· If the reservoir retained less than one-fourth of the river flow, but the surface water demand was less than 5 MGD, circle the "4."

Streamflow
· If the dam retains one-fourth of the annual river flow or more, you were able to provide ample flow for fish and recreation. Circle the "3."
· If the reservoir holds one-fourth of the river flow or more, and the surface water demand was less than 5 MGD, circle the "4."
· If the reservoir holds less than one-fourth of the river flow, circle the "1."
· If the reservoir holds less than one-fourth of the river flow, but the surface water demand is less than 5 MGD, circle the "3."

Taxes
· If the taxes are less than $6, circle the "4."
· If the taxes are less than $16, circle the "3."
· If the taxes are less than $30, circle the "2."
· If the taxes are less than $50, circle the "1."
· If the taxes are $50 or more, circle the "0."

Growth
· Add the points you have already accumulated for customer needs, streamflow, and taxes.

· If 10 or more points, circle the "4."
· If 8 or more points, circle the "3."
· If 6 or more points, circle the "2."
· If 4 or more points, circle the "1."
· If less than 4 points, circle the "0."

1. Go to the column marked Score. For customer needs, multiply the number of points you circled by the number in the Priority column. Write the answer in the Score column. Perform the same calculation for streamflow, taxes, and growth.

2. Add up all the numbers in the Score column. Write your total score in the last box under the Score column.

Your Recommendations

You are now ready to consider your recommendations for the next five years and to repeat the process of:
· Determining your recommendations and recording the costs of your choices.
· Calculating the total water usage based on the implementation of conservation choices, the amount of surface water needed, and the amount of ground water tapped to supplement the surface supply. **On each successive water usage report, you must look at the figures from the report of five years before. For example, to fill in the blanks at the top of the form for 2010 under domestic use, commercial use, industrial use, and public use, you must use the totals from 2005.**
· Scoring your recommendations on the Evaluation form.

Your Final Score

In the year 2025, after 25 years of service as a water manager for your community, you will retire. To determine your final score, record your scores for each five-year interval and total.

Discuss your group's score with other groups. How do groups with the highest scores explain

Your Hydrologic Deck, continued

their success? Change your priorities and play the simulation again. How did your results differ from the previous game?

Your Hydrologic Deck, continued

YEAR 2001: YOUR RECOMMENDATIONS FOR THE NEXT FIVE YEARS			Tax: Cost per person per year (Population: 25,000)	
Increase Supply				Your Choices
Reservoir Size	**Initial Reservoir Capacity** 1/8 of annual river flow (2,000 Acre-Feet)	**Flow Rate*** (1.8 MGD avg.)	$0	
	Increase to 1/4 (4,000 Ac.-Ft.)	(3.6 MGD avg.)	$10	
	Increase to 1/2 (8,000 Ac.-Ft.)	(7.1 MGD avg.)	$25	
	Increase to 1 (16,000 Ac.-Ft.)	(14.3 MGD avg.)	$50	
	Increase to 2 (32,000 Ac.-Ft.)	(28.6 MGD avg.)	$90	
Develop Ground Water	Drill 1 well Drill 5 wells	0.4 MGD 2.0 MGD	$2 $10	
Reduce Demand Increase Delivery System Efficiency	#1 Replace/repair leaky water mains and worn water meters		$8	
Conservation Education	#2 Develop and distribute water conservation information and make public announcements: bill inserts, flyers, billboards, etc.		$2	
Conservation Programs	#3 Rebates on efficient appliances, fixtures, and landscape conservation measures		$4	
	#4 Increase water charges to encourage conservation		$5	
No Action Required for Current Conditions			$0	
Total Tax: Add figures in Your Choices column for total cost per person per year				

*Flow Rate: This is the average amount a reservoir this size could provide over the period of one year.

Your Hydrologic Deck, continued

Hydrograph for the Year 2000

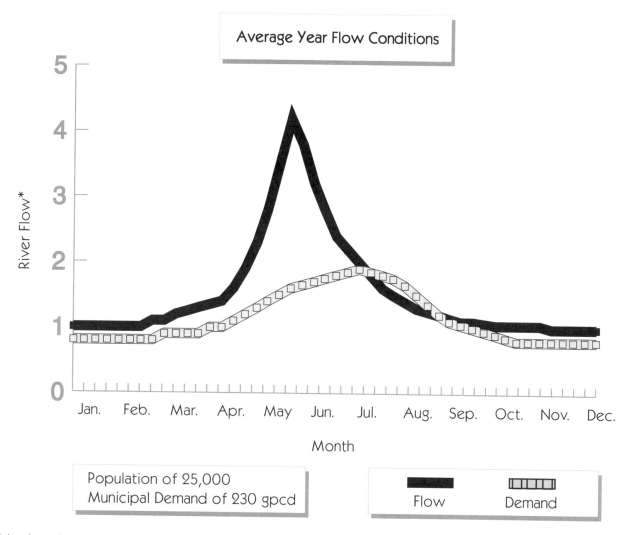

Average Year Flow Conditions

Population of 25,000
Municipal Demand of 230 gpcd

Flow   Demand

*Number 1 represents the base flow of the river and ascending numbers are proportional to the base flow.

Interpretation:
1. The hydrograph indicates that the year 2000 was an average year for flow conditions.
2. Peak runoff occurred in June and returned close to base flow in July.
3. Peak demand occurred in July and August due to lawn irrigation, increased car washing, and so forth.
4. The demand exceeded the natural flow in July and August, when the city was dependent on water stored in the reservoir. There was enough water in the reservoir to supply the city's needs.
5. The supply of water in the reservoir was sufficient to supply minimum levels of streamflow to protect recreational uses and fish and wildlife.

Your Hydrologic Deck, continued

Water Usage Report 2005						Pop. 27,000
Water Use	Domestic Use 130 gpcd		Commercial Use 40 gpcd	Industrial Use 25 gpcd	Public Use 35 gpcd	Total Use 230 gpcd
If Conservation #1 (Repairs)					-10% -4 gpcd	
If Conservation #2 (Education)	-2% -3 gpcd		-3% -1 gpcd	-2% -1 gpcd		
If Conservation #3 (Rebates)	-4% -5 gpcd		-4% -2gpcd	-4% -1 gpcd	-2% -1 gpcd	
If Conservation #4 (Increased charges)	-5% -7 gpcd		-5% -2 gpcd	-8% -2 gpcd		
TOTAL WATER USAGE per day (subtract all conservation reductions from initial use)	Total for Items 1-4					

1. Average Total Water Demand Per Day:

Total Use Per Day _____ gpcd x Population 27,000 = _____ gal. per day/1,000,000 = _____ MGD

2. SUPPPLY FROM GROUND WATER	MGD
Number of Wells 1 well =	0.4 MGD
5 wells =	2.0 MGD

3. Average Daily Demand from Surface Water:

Average Total Water Demand Per Day (1): _____ MGD
Supply from Ground Water (2):   - _____ MGD
Average Daily Demand from Surface Water: _____ MGD

Your Hydrologic Deck, continued

Year 2005 Evaluation	Points	Priority	Score*
<u>Customer Needs</u> ·If the dam size is 1/4 of annual flow or greater, you were able to fully meet customer needs, circle ·If the dam is not greater than 1/4, circle ·If the dam is not greater than 1/4, but surface water demand is less than 5 MGD, circle	4 3 4		
<u>Streamflow</u> ·If dam size is 1/4 of annual flow or greater, you were able to provide ample flow for fish and recreation, circle ·If dam size is 1/4 of annual flow or greater and surface water demand was less than 5 MGD, circle ·If the dam size is less than 1/4, circle ·If the dam size is less than 1/4, but surface water demand is less than 5 MGD, circle	3 4 1 3		
<u>Taxes</u> ·Less than $6, circle ·Less than $16, circle ·Less than $30, circle ·Less than $50, circle ·$50 or greater, circle	4 3 2 1 0		
<u>Growth</u> Total points from <u>Customer Needs</u>, <u>Streamflow</u>, and <u>Taxes</u> = ·If 10 or more points, circle ·If 8 or more points, circle ·If 6 or more points, circle ·If 4 or more points, circle ·If less than 4 points, circle	 4 3 2 1 0		
TOTAL SCORE			

*Points x Priority = Score

Your Hydrologic Deck, continued

YEAR 2006: YOUR RECOMMENDATIONS FOR THE NEXT FIVE YEARS			Tax: Cost per person per year (Population: 27,000)	
Increase Supply				Your Choices
Reservoir Size	**Initial Reservoir Capacity** 1/8 of annual river flow (2,000 Acre-Feet)	**Flow Rate** (1.8 MGD avg.)	$0	
	Increase to 1/4 (4,000 Ac.-Ft.)	(3.6 MGD avg.)	$9	
	Increase to 1/2 (8,000 Ac.-Ft.)	(7.1 MGD avg.)	$22	
	Increase to 1 (16,000 Ac.-Ft.)	(14.3 MGD avg.)	$45	
	Increase to 2 (32,000 Ac.-Ft.)	(28.6 MGD avg.)	$80	
Develop Ground Water	Drill 1 well Drill 5 wells	0.4 MGD 2.0 MGD	$2 $9	
Reduce Demand Increase Delivery System Efficiency	#1) Replace/repair leaky water mains and worn water meters		$7	
Conservation Education	#2) Develop and distribute water conservation information and make public announcements: bill inserts, flyers, billboards, etc.		$2	
Conservation Programs	#3) Rebates on efficient appliances, fixtures, and landscape conservation measures		$4	
	#4) Increase water charges to encourage conservation		$5	
No Action Required for Current Conditions			$0	
Total Tax: Add figures in Your Choices column for total cost per person per year				

Your Hydrologic Deck, continued

Hydrograph for the Year 2005

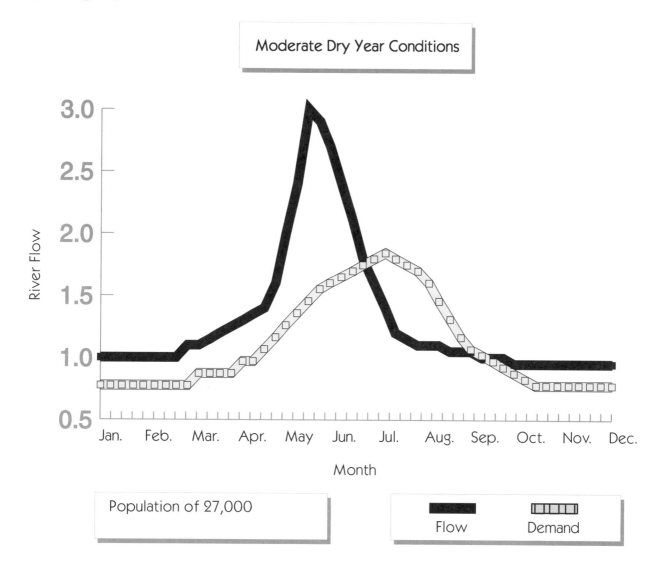

Moderate Dry Year Conditions

Population of 27,000

Flow   Demand

Interpretation:

1. The hydrograph indicates that 2005 was a moderately dry year.
2. Peak runoff occurred toward the end of May and returned close to base flow in July.
3. Peak demand occurred in mid-July through August, likely due to summer activities.
4. The demand substantially exceeded natural flow from mid-July to September.

Your Hydrologic Deck, continued

Water Usage Report 2010					Pop. 35,000
Water Use from 2005 Water Usage Report	Domestic Use* _____ gpcd	Commercial Use* _____ gpcd	Industrial Use* _____ gpcd	Public Use* _____ gpcd	Total Use _____ gpcd
If Conservation #1, reduce use category by:				-9%	
If Conservation #2, reduce use category by:	-2%	-2%	-2%		
If Conservation #3, reduce use category by	-4%	-4%	-4%	-2%	
If Conservation #4, reduce use category by:	-5%	-5%	-6%		
TOTAL WATER USAGE per day (subtract all conservation reductions above from beginning use for each category)					

*Fill in these blanks from the water uses you calculated in the **Water Usage Report 2005**.

1. Average Total Water Demand Per Day:

Total Use Per Day _____ gpcd x Population 35,000 = _____ gal. per day/1,000,000 = _____ MGD

2. SUPPLY FROM GROUND WATER	MGD
Number of Wells 1 well =	0.4 MGD
5 wells =	2.0 MGD

3. Average Daily Demand from Surface Water:

Average Total Water Demand Per Day (1):   _____ MGD
Supply from Ground Water (2):   - _____ MGD
Average Daily Demand from Surface Water: _____ MGD

Your Hydrologic Deck, continued

Year 2010 Evaluation	Points	Priority	Score*
Customer Needs			
·If the dam size is greater than 1/2 the annual flow, circle	3		
·If the dam size is greater than 1/2 the annual flow, but surface water demand is less than 7.5 MGD, circle	4		
·If the dam size is greater than 1/4 the annual flow, circle	2		
·If the dam size is greater than 1/4 the annual flow, but surface water demand is less than 7 MGD, circle	3		
·If the dam size is greater than 1/4 the annual flow, and the surface water demand is less than 6 MGD, circle	4		
·If the dam size is less than 1/4, circle	1		
·If the dam size is less than 1/4, but surface demand is less than 6 MGD, circle	2		
·If the dam size is less than 1/4, and surface demand is less than 5 MGD, circle	3		
Streamflow			
·If the dam size is greater than 1/4 annual flow, circle	3		
·If the dam size is greater than 1/4 annual flow, and surface demand is less than 5 MGD, circle	4		
·If dam size is less than 1/4 annual flow, circle	1		
·If dam size is less than 1/4 annual flow, but surface demand is less than 5 MGD, circle	3		
Penalty: Flooding damages stream banks and fishery. If the dam is smaller than 1/2 annual flow, subtract 1 point.			
Taxes			
·Less than $6, circle	4		
·Less than $16, circle	3		
·Less than $30, circle	2		
·Less than $50, circle	1		
·$50 or greater, circle	0		
Penalty: Flood damage costs city a lot. If the dam is smaller than 1/2 annual flow, subtract 1 point.			
Growth			
Total points from Customer Needs, Streamflow, and Taxes =			
·If 10 or more points, circle	4		
·If 8 or more points, circle	3		
·If 6 or more points, circle	2		
·If 4 or more points, circle	1		
·If less than 4 points, circle	0		
TOTAL SCORE			

*Points x Priority = Score

Your Hydrologic Deck, continued

YEAR 2011: YOUR RECOMMENDATIONS FOR THE NEXT FIVE YEARS			Tax: Cost per person per year (Population: 35,000)	
Increase Supply Reservoir Size	**Initial Reservoir Capacity** 1/8 of annual river flow (2,000 Acre-Feet)	**Flow Rate** (1.8 MGD avg.)	$0	Your Choices
	Increase to 1/4 (4,000 Ac.-Ft.)	(3.6 MGD avg.)	$7	
	Increase to 1/2 (8,000 Ac.-Ft.)	(7.1 MGD avg.)	$18	
	Increase to 1 (16,000 Ac.-Ft.)	(14.3 MGD avg.)	$35	
	Increase to 2 (32,000 Ac.-Ft.)	(28.6 MGD avg.)	$63	
Develop Ground Water	Drill 1 well Drill 5 wells	0.4 MGD 2.0 MGD	$2 $7	
Reduce Demand Increase Delivery System Efficiency	#1) Replace/repair leaky water mains and worn water meters (If you have selected leak repairs for 10 years, reduce tax to **$3**)		$6	
Conservation Education	#2) Develop and distribute water conserva-tion information and make public announce-ments: bill inserts, flyers, billboards, etc.		$2	
Conservation Programs	#3) Rebates on efficient appliances, fixtures, and landscape conservation measures		$4	
	#4) Increase water charges to encourage conservation		$5	
No Action Required for Current Conditions			$0	
Total Tax: Add figures in Your Choices column for total cost per person per year				

Your Hydrologic Deck, continued

Hydrograph for the Year 2010

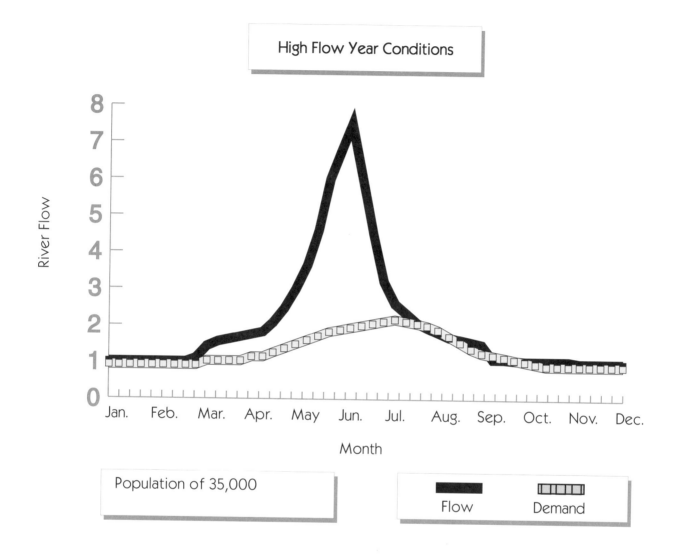

High Flow Year Conditions

Population of 35,000

Flow   Demand

Interpretation:

1. The hydrograph indicates that this was a high flow year.
2. Peak runoff occurred in mid-June and sharply subsided in early July (note the spike and rapid decline). Due to the very high flow conditions, flood waters may have caused damage if there was not sufficient storage capacity in the community's reservoir.
3. Demand did not exceed the natural flow within the year.
4. Because of the high flow, if sufficient storage was not available, flooding would have damaged stream banks and impacted the fishery.

Your Hydrologic Deck, continued

Water Usage Report 2015							Population 45,000
Water Use from 2010 Water Usage Report	Domes. Use ____ gpcd		Comm. Use ____ gpcd		Indust. Use ____ gpcd	Public Use ____ gpcd	Total Use ____ gpcd
If Conservation #1						-8%	
If Conservation #2	-2%		-2%		-2%		
If Conservation #3	-3%		-3%		-3%	-2%	
If Conservation #4	-4%		-4%		-5%		
TOTAL WATER USAGE per day (subtract all con-servation reductions above from beginning use for each category)							

1. Average Total Water Demand Per Day:

Total Use Per Day _____ gpcd x Population 45,000 = _____ gal. per day/1,000,000 = _____ MGD

2. SUPPLY FROM GROUND WATER	MGD
Number of Wells 1 well =	0.4 MGD
5 wells =	2.0 MGD

3. Average Daily Demand from Surface Water:

Average Total Water Demand Per Day (1): _____ MGD
Supply from Ground Water (2): - _____ MGD
Average Daily Demand from Surface Water: _____ MGD

Your Hydrologic Deck, continued

Year 2015 Evaluation	Points	Priority	Score*
Customer Needs			
·If the dam size is greater than 1/2 annual flow, circle	2		
·If the dam size is greater than 1/2 annual flow, but surface water demand is less than 7.5 MGD, circle	3		
·If the dam size is greater than 1/2 annual flow, and surface water demand is less than 6 MGD, circle	4		
·If the dam size is greater than 1/4 annual flow, circle	1		
·If the dam size is greater than 1/4 annual flow, but surface water demand is less than 7 MGD, circle	2		
·If the dam size is greater than 1/4 annual flow, and surface water demand is less than 6 MGD, circle	3		
·If dam size is less than 1/4, circle	0		
·If dam size is less than 1/4, but surface demand is less than 6 MGD, circle	2		
·If dam size is less than 1/4, but surface demand is less than 5 MGD, circle	3		
Streamflow			
·If dam size is greater than 1/4 annual flow, circle	3		
·If dam size is greater than 1/4 annual flow, and surface demand is less than 5.0 MGD, circle	4		
·If dam size is not greater than 1/4 annual flow, circle	1		
·If dam size is not greater than 1/4 annual flow, but surface demand is less than 5.5 MGD, circle	3		
Taxes			
·Less than $6, circle	4		
·Less than $16, circle	3		
·Less than $30, circle	2		
·Less than $50, circle	1		
·$50 or greater, circle	0		
Growth			
Total points from Customer Needs, Streamflow, and Taxes =			
·If 10 or more points, circle	4		
·If 8 or more points, circle	3		
·If 6 or more points, circle	2		
·If 4 or more points, circle	1		
·If less than 4 points, circle	0		
TOTAL SCORE			

*Points x Priority = Score

Your Hydrologic Deck, continued

YEAR 2016: YOUR RECOMMENDATIONS FOR THE NEXT FIVE YEARS			Tax: Cost per person per year (Population: 45,000)	
Increase Supply				Your Choices
Reservoir Size	Initial Reservoir Capacity 1/8 of annual river flow (2,000 Acre-Feet)	Flow Rate (1.8 MGD avg.)	$0	
	Increase to 1/4 (4,000 Ac.-Ft.)	(3.6 MGD avg.)	$6	
	Increase to 1/2 (8,000 Ac.-Ft.)	(7.1 MGD avg.)	$14	
	Increase to 1 (16,000 Ac.-Ft.)	(14.3 MGD avg.)	$28	
	Increase to 2 (32,000 Ac.-Ft.)	(28.6 MGD avg.)	$50	
Develop Ground Water	Drill 1 well	0.4 MGD	$1	
	Drill 5 wells	2.0 MGD	$6	
Reduce Demand				
Increase Delivery System Efficiency	#1) Replace/repair leaky water mains and worn water meters (If you have selected leak repairs for 10 years, reduce tax to **$2**)		$5	
Conservation Education	#2) Develop and distribute water conservation information and make public announcements: bill inserts, flyers, billboards, etc.		$2	
Conservation Programs	#3) Rebates on efficient appliances, fixtures, and landscape conservation measures		$4	
	#4) Increase water charges to encourage conservation		$5	
No Action Required for Current Conditions			$0	
Total Tax: Add figures in Your Choices column for total cost per person per year				

Your Hydrologic Deck, continued

Hydrograph for the Year 2015

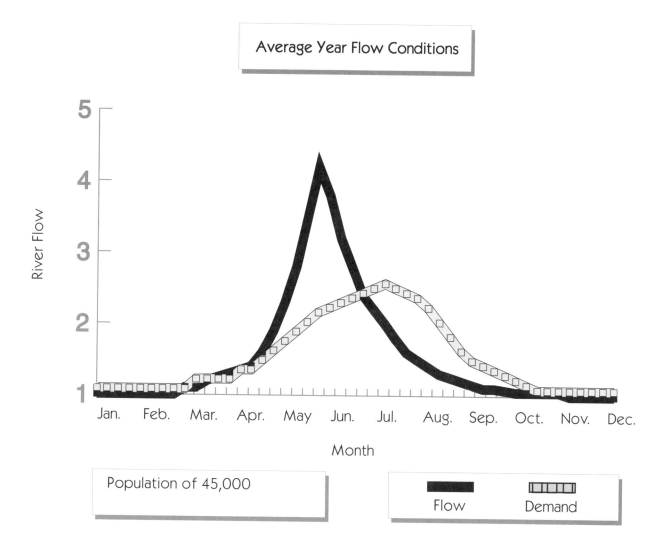

Average Year Flow Conditions

River Flow

5

4

3

2

1

Jan. Feb. Mar. Apr. May Jun. Jul. Aug. Sep. Oct. Nov. Dec.

Month

Population of 45,000

Flow   Demand

Interpretation:

1. The hydrograph shows that this was an average year for flow conditions.
2. Peak runoff occurred in June and subsided by July.
3. Demand exceeded flow beginning in July, until it matched up with flow in October.

Your Hydrologic Deck, continued

Water Usage Report 2020						Population 55,000
Water Use from 2015 Water Usage Report	Domes. Use ____ gpcd		Comm. Use ____ gpcd	Indust. Use ____ gpcd	Public Use ____ gpcd	Total Use ____ gpcd
If Conservation #1					−7%	
If Conservation #2	−2%		−2%	−2%		
If Conservation #3	−3%		−3 %	−3%	−2%	
If Conservation #4	−3%		−3%	−4%		
TOTAL WATER USAGE per day						

1. Average Total Water Demand Per Day:

Total Use Per Day _____ gpcd x Population 55,000 = _____ gal. per day/1,000,000 = _____ MGD

2. SUPPLY FROM GROUND WATER	MGD
Number of Wells 1 well =	0.4 MGD
5 wells =	2.0 MGD

3. Average Daily Demand from Surface Water:

Average Total Water Demand Per Day: _____ MGD
Supply from Ground Water: − _____ MGD
Average Daily Demand from Surface Water: _____ MGD

Your Hydrologic Deck, continued

* Bad Drought Year

Year 2020 Evaluation	Points	Priority	Score*
Customer Needs ·If dam size is equal to or greater than 1 times annual flow, circle	2		
·If dam size is equal to or greater than 1 times annual flow, but surface water demand is less than 7.5 MGD, circle	3		
·If dam size is equal to or greater than 1 times annual flow, and surface water demand is less than 6.5 MGD, circle	4		
·If dam holds 1/2 the annual flow, circle	1		
·If dam holds 1/2 the annual flow, but surface water demand is less than 7.5 MGD, circle	2		
·If dam holds 1/2 the annual flow, and surface water demand is less than 6.5 MGD, circle	3		
·If dam holds 1/4 the annual flow, circle	0		
·If dam holds 1/4 the annual flow, but surface demand is less than 7.5 MGD, circle	1		
·If dam holds 1/4 the annual flow, but surface demand is less than 6.5 MGD, circle	2		
·If dam holds 1/8 the annual flow, circle	0		
·If dam holds 1/8 the annual flow, but surface demand is less than 6.5 MGD, circle	1		
Streamflow (Use same score as for Customer Needs)			
Taxes ·Less than $6, circle	4		
·Less than $16, circle	3		
·Less than $30, circle	2		
·Less than $50, circle	1		
·$50 or greater, circle	0		
·If total water use is above 10 MGD, add $15 in taxes for water treatment plant expansion before you score your points. ·If total water use is above 12 MGD, add another $15 for wastewater treatment plant expansion (note: only around 80 percent of water used reaches the wastewater treatment plant) before you score your points.			
Growth Total points from Customer Needs, Streamflow, and Taxes = ·If 10 or more points, circle	4		
·If 8 or more points, circle	3		
·If 6 or more points, circle	2		
·If 4 or more points, circle	1		
·If less than 4 points, circle	0		
TOTAL SCORE			

*Points x Priority = Score

Your Hydrologic Deck, continued

YEAR 2021: YOUR RECOMMENDATIONS FOR THE NEXT FIVE YEARS			Tax: Cost per person per year (Population: 55,000)	
Increase Supply				Your Choices
Reservoir Size	**Initial Reservoir Capacity** 1/8 of annual river flow (2,000 Acre-Feet)	**Flow Rate** (1.8 MGD avg.)	$0	
	Increase to 1/4 (4,000 Ac.-Ft.)	(3.6 MGD avg.)	$5	
	Increase to 1/2 (8,000 Ac.-Ft.)	(7.1 MGD avg.)	$11	
	Increase to 1 (16,000 Ac.-Ft.)	(14.3 MGD avg.)	$23	
	Increase to 2 (32,000 Ac.-Ft.)	(28.6 MGD avg.)	$41	
Develop Ground Water	Drill 1 well Drill 5 wells	0.4 MGD 2.0 MGD	$1 $5	
Reduce Demand Increase Delivery System Efficiency	#1) Replace/repair leaky water mains and worn water meters (If you have selected leak repairs for 10 years, reduce tax to **$2**)		$5	
Conservation Education	#2) Develop and distribute water conservation information and make public announcements: bill inserts flyers, billboards, etc.		$2	
Conservation Programs	#3) Rebates on efficient appliances, fixtures, and landscape conservation measures		$4	
	#4) Increase water charges to encourage conservation		$5	
No Action Required for Current Conditions			$0	
Total Tax: Add figures in Your Choices column for total cost per person per year				

Your Hydrologic Deck, continued

Hydrograph for the Year 2020

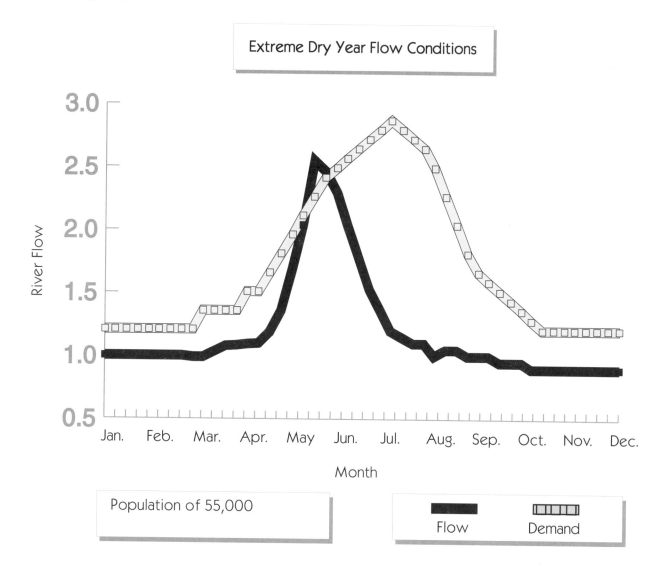

Extreme Dry Year Flow Conditions

Population of 55,000

Flow   Demand

Interpretation:

1. The hydrograph indicates that 2020 was an extremely dry year.
2. The river flow peaked early, in mid-May, and subsided by July.
3. Note how demand exceeded river flow for the entire year, except during the peak flow. When demand exceeded flow, there would have had to be sufficient storage capacity to accommodate customers' needs.

Your Hydrologic Deck, continued

Water Usage Report 2025					Pop. 60,000
Water Use from 2020 Water Usage Report	Domes. Use ____ gpcd	Comm. Use ____ gpcd	Indust. Use ____ gpcd	Public Use ____ gpcd	Total Use ____ gpcd
If Conservation #1				-6%	
If Conservation #2	-1%	-1%	-1%		
If Conservation #3	-2%	-2%	-2%	-1%	
If Conservation #4	-2%	-2%	-2%		
TOTAL WATER USAGE per day					

1. Average Total Water Demand Per Day:

Total Use Per Day _____ gpcd x Population 60,000 = _____ gal. per day/1,000,000 = _____ MGD

2. SUPPLY FROM GROUND WATER	MGD
Number of Wells 1 well =	0.4 MGD
5 wells =	2.0 MGD

3. Average Daily Demand from Surface Water:

Average Total Water Demand Per Day (1): _____ MGD
Supply from Ground Water (2): – _____ MGD
Average Daily Demand from Surface Water: _____ MGD

Your Hydrologic Deck, continued

Year 2025 Evaluation	Points	Priority	Score*
Customer Needs ·If the dam size is equal to or greater than 1 times the annual flow, circle ·If the dam size is equal to or greater than 1 times the annual flow, but surface water demand is less than 7.5 MGD, circle ·If the dam holds 1/2 the annual flow, circle ·If the dam holds 1/2 the annual flow, but surface water demand is less than 8 MGD, circle ·If the dam holds 1/2 the annual flow, but surface water demand is less than 7 MGD, circle ·If dam holds 1/4 the annual flow, circle ·If dam holds 1/4 the annual flow, but surface demand is less than 8 MGD, circle ·If dam holds 1/4 the annual flow, but surface demand is less than 7 MGD, circle ·If dam holds 1/8 the annual flow, circle ·If dam holds 1/8 the annual flow, but surface demand is less than 7 MGD, circle	3 4 2 3 4 1 2 3 1 2		
Streamflow (Use same score as for Customer Needs)			
Taxes ·Less than $6, circle ·Less than $16, circle ·Less than $30, circle ·Less than $50, circle ·$50 or greater, circle ·If total use is above 10 MGD, add $15 for water treatment plant expansion ·If total use is above 12 MGD, add another $15 for wastewater treatment plant expansion	4 3 2 1 0		
Growth Total points from Customer Needs, Streamflow, and Taxes = ·If 10 or more points, circle ·If 8 or more points, circle ·If 6 or more points, circle ·If 4 or more points, circle ·If less than 4 points, circle	 4 3 2 1 0		
TOTAL SCORE			

*Points x Priority = Score

Your Hydrologic Deck, continued

Hydrograph for the Year 2025

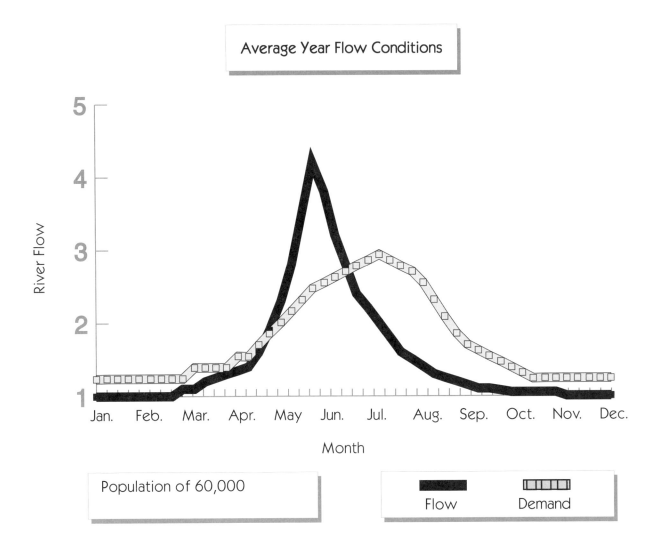

Average Year Flow Conditions

River Flow

Month

Population of 60,000

Flow   Demand

Interpretation:

1. The year 2025 had average flow conditions.
2. The river flow peaked in late May and early June and subsided in August.
3. Note that demand exceeded river flow all year except during the peak flow months of May and June.

Your Hydrologic Deck, continued

Population Growth Chart

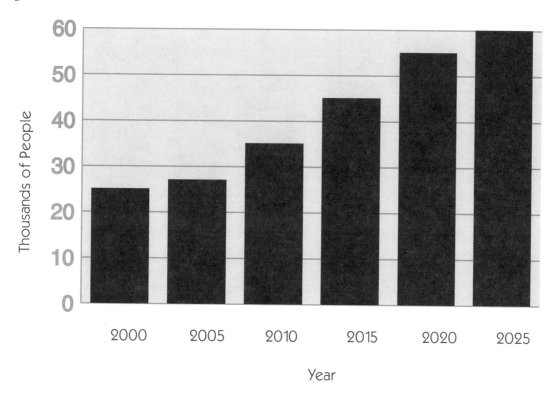

Seven Principles of Xeriscaping

1. Planning and design

2. Soil analysis

3. & 4. Efficient irrigation and careful plant selection

5. Selective use of grass

6. Consistent use of mulch

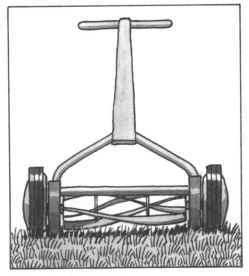

7. Yard maintenance

Xeriscape!™

Summary

Students design a Xeriscape landscape for a "potential client" and learn about native plants and materials.

Grade Level:
Middle School

Subject Areas:
Environmental Science, Ecology

Duration:
Preparation time: 5 minutes

Activity time: 50 minutes

Setting:
Classroom

Skills:
Organize, Analyze, Interpret, Apply, Present

Vocabulary:
Xeriscape, soil pH, drought-tolerant, native plants, mulch, ground cover

Objectives

Students will:
· define the term Xeriscape.
· organize characteristics of water conservative landscapes using the seven principles of Xeriscaping.
· create a water conservative landscape.

Materials

· *Seven Principles of Xeriscaping* Student Copy Page, 1 per student
· *Xeriscape!* Student Copy Pages, 1 set per student or group
· colored pencils and markers
· home and garden magazines
· research material on native plants

Background

The term Xeriscaping means, "landscaping to conserve water and protect the environment." The term is derived from the Greek word, *xeros*, which means "dry." The concept of Xeriscaping actually evolved in the early 1980s during a drought in Denver, Colorado. Water managers and landscape professionals came together to solve a problem: how to provide a common-sense way for people to create beautiful landscapes to enhance their homes and conserve water at the same time.

There are seven simple principles associated with Xeriscaping. In some states (for example, Florida), laws require that the seven principles be applied in landscaping any newly developed property that is state-owned. The seven principles are:

1. **Planning and Design:** The first step toward achieving the goal of creating a beautiful and functional yard while conserving water is to have a plan. You may not be able to totally rework your existing yard, but you can convert small sections at a time. When designing a landscape, assess climate conditions in your yard to help locate where different plants will do well.

2. **Soil Analysis:** To ensure that the plants you wish to include in your yard will thrive, have your soil pH determined first. Plants have different preferences for soil types: acidic, basic, or neutral. Select plants based on this analysis.

3. **Efficient Irrigation:** Group plants based on their water requirements. Drought-tolerant plants should be placed together and separated from grass and plants that require a lot of water.

4. **Careful Plant Selection:** Some individuals do not like Xeriscaping because it appears harsh and uninviting. Many

people have the misconception that Xeriscape materials include only rock and cacti. But you can use lush and beautiful plants to landscape your yard as well. You may select native plants or those that are drought-tolerant. Almost any plant is a Xeriscape plant if it is placed where it can thrive in your landscape. The key is to know the light, water, and temperature needs, and the growth patterns of the plant and then locate it correctly within your yard.

5. **Selective Use of Grass**: Be practical in placing grass in your yard. Grass guzzles irrigation water. When you do irrigate your grass, water thoroughly about once a week. If you only water a little each day, you encourage the roots of the plant to remain shallow as they attempt to tap the water close to the surface. Consider whether or not the grass serves a purpose, such as a play area. If not, eliminate it or replace it with ground covers.

6. **Consistent Use of Mulch**: Mulch is material like pine needles, leaves, or wood shavings. Mulch helps hold moisture in the soil and helps control erosion.

7. **Yard Maintenance**: Although Xeriscaping helps cut down the amount of work to be done in the yard, it does not eliminate it. You must still continue to care for your yard by mowing grass properly, pruning, weeding, etc. Adjust the mower to the correct height

for your type of grass, learn to prune not shear, and remove nuisance weeds.

And just imagine—once you have completed your water conservative landscape, you will have more time, more money, and a beautiful yard!

Procedure

Warm Up

Ask students if they are familiar with the concept of Xeriscaping. Have they ever seen a yard that has been landscaped to conserve water and resources? Share several pictures of Xeriscaped yards. What characteristics do they have in common? List them on the board.

The Activity

1. Review the list of characteristics that students came up with.
2. Distribute the *Seven Principles of Xeriscaping* Student Copy Page to students. Have them organize the characteristics they offered under the seven principles.
3. Tell students to imagine that they all run large landscaping firms. A prospective client has asked a number of firms to submit plans for landscaping his yard. The only stipulation is that the yard must be Xeriscaped. Have students sketch plans for the client's yard. They may work alone, with one other student, or in a small group. The client is someone within their community

who has two children and two dogs.
4. Distribute copies of the *Xeriscape!* Student Copy Pages. Have native plant books with colorful pictures available. Students may wish to study home and garden magazines to find ideas for their design. Remind them to follow the seven principles.
5. Have students submit their designs on the student copy page.
6. Have students present their designs to the class as if they are "pitching a proposal" to the client for their firm.

Wrap Up

Did students group drought-tolerant plants together? Did they take advantage of native vegetation that requires less water? Did they use mulch around trees to retain moisture? Did they suggest gravel, rocks, or mulch for paths leading to the house and around the yard? Did they remember to include some grass as an outdoor play area for the children and pets? Did they select a drought-tolerant ground cover? Did they have a nice balance of ground cover, vines, shrubs, flowers, trees, rocks, logs, wood chips, and so forth? Were students able to tell the prospective client that this design would be low maintenance and that by saving water it would also save him money? Ask students why native plants are often a good choice when designing a land-

© The Watercourse

scape to conserve water. (Native plants have evolved with the climate and rainfall distribution of the area for thousands of years. They are accustomed to being "rain-fed" and do not often require supplemental irrigation.)

Assessment

Have students:
· define Xeriscape (*Warm Up*).
· design a water conservative landscape using native plants and incorporating the seven principles of Xeriscaping (step 4).
· prepare and present a water conservative landscape proposal to the class (step 6).

Extensions

Have students design a water conservative landscape for their own homes or school. If they design a plan for the school, have them research costs and benefits (how much time, water, and money the school would save), and ask the principal to visit the classroom for a presentation by the students. Perhaps the class would like to begin an ongoing project of their grade to progressively convert the school landscape to Xeriscape.

Resources

Division of Public Information. Xeriscape, Landscaping for Water Conservation. Palatka, Fla.:St. Johns River Water Management District (brochure).

Allen, Leslie Frye, Valerie Johnson, Georgann Penson, and Diane Sterling. 1996. *WaterWays: Exploring Northwest Florida's Water Resources*. Havana, Fl.: Northwest Florida Water Management District.

Xeriscape!

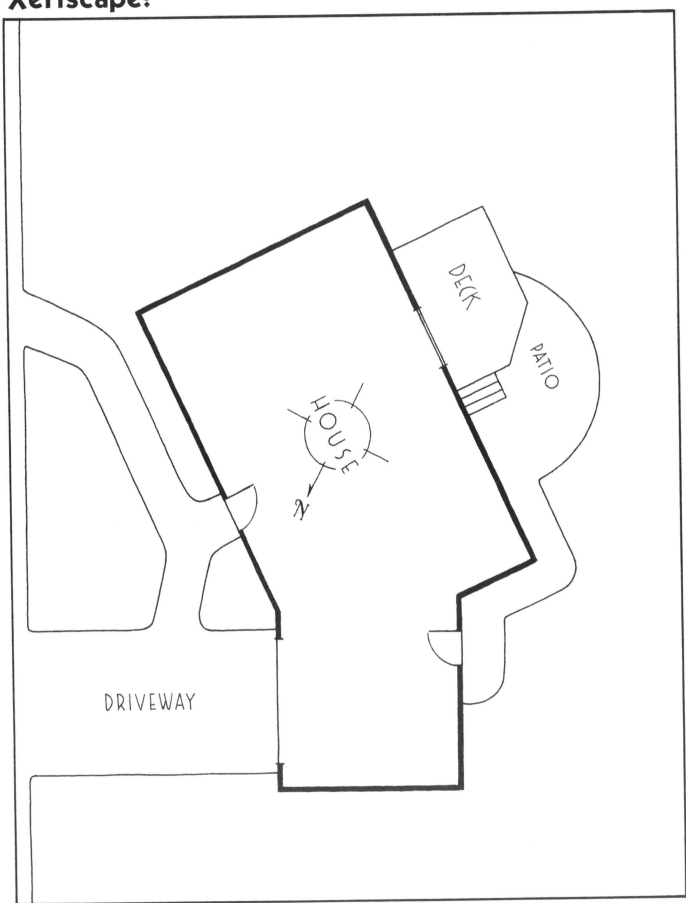

Xeriscape! continued

Landscaping Symbols

Use these symbols, cut photos or drawings out of magazines, or draw your own symbols, to represent different plants in your Xeriscape design.

Evergreen trees

Mulches

Palm trees

Vegetables

Deciduous trees

Grains

Flowers

Ornamental plants

Cacti

Grasses

What Plants to Choose

Almost any plant can fit into a Xeriscape landscape, as long as the right plant is placed in the right spot. Native plant species are good choices for Xeriscaping because they have adapted to local growing conditions. The plants pictured at right are California native plants, and are popular choices for Xeriscaping.

Prickly pear cactus in bloom

Coreopsis

Bunch grass PHOTOGRAPHS BY SALLY UNSER

Our Water Future

Our Water Future Depends on Today's Conservation Choices

Water Conservation Invention Convention

Grade Level:
Middle School

Subject Areas:
Language Arts, Earth Science, Health

Duration:
Preparation time: 10 minutes

Activity time: two 50-minute periods

Setting:
Classroom

Skills:
Gather, Organize, Analyze, Interpret, Apply, Evaluate, Present

Vocabulary:
spinoffs, technology, retrofitting, potable, designed ecosystem, aquaculture, desalinization

Summary
Students examine the technology of water resources conservation and participate in a Water Conservation Invention Convention.

Objectives
Students will:
· describe at least three ways in which inventions are conceived.
· explain the concept of "spinoffs."
· define retrofitting and recognize water-saving devices.
· conduct an experiment, solve a design problem, or do a literary or film review to explore water conservation technology.

Materials
· *Match It Up!* Student Copy Page (1 per group)
· *Retrofitting* Student Copy Page (1 per student)
· *Water Conservation Invention Convention* Student Copy Page (1 per student)
· other materials depend upon the process selected by students

Background
Jonathan Swift, the author of *Gulliver's Travels*, wrote, "Necessity is the mother of invention." Our need for clean and abundant water resources has often inspired, even spurred researchers to seek technological solutions. Many of these solutions have allowed households, industries, and agriculturists to use water resources more efficiently and conservatively.

"Technology is the science and art of making and using things" (*Technology, Eyewitness Science*). Some technological solutions to water resources management problems have included cloud seeding, desalinization, iceberg towing, rainwater harvesting, more efficient irrigation, water-saving plumbing devices, compost toilets, wastewater treatment, and wastewater recycling.

For the most part, we have treated wastewater with chemicals in high-tech environments built of metal and concrete. However, in striving to find a more efficient and less costly method, some scientists are investigating natural systems where water is treated as it passes through the water cycle. In recognizing that this may be possible, scientists are combining technology and nature.

Households and industries in some places use "designed ecosystems" such as constructed wetlands and soil filters to treat wastewater. Constructed wetlands are intended to mimic natural wetlands which soak up rainwater with wetland vegetation removing particles of sediment and metals. Soil also acts as a filter by removing sediment and other pollutants.

What do Phoenix, Arizona, Israel, and Saudi Arabia have in common? A significant percentage of their wastewater is reused. Researchers are looking to turn "waste into resource" by improving wastewater treatment methods.

Where do ideas for inventions come from? Sometimes ideas originate in fantasy or imagination. Albert Einstein wrote, "Imagination is more important than knowledge, for imagination embraces the world." Take the work of early science fiction writer Jules Verne. In the late 1800s, the French writer's novels predicted the invention of submarines, airplanes, television, guided missiles, and even space travel! Today, readers all over the world still enjoy his novels, such as *Twenty Thousand Leagues Under the Sea*, *A Journey to the Center of the Earth*, and *From the Earth to the Moon*.

Sometimes ideas for inventions originate with questions. For example, recognizing that 97 percent of the water on earth is salt water, one might ask, "Can salt water be made drinkable for people living in

coastal communities to supplement their existing freshwater supply?" This question has prompted the development of processes to remove salt from water—desalinization. In arid parts of the world, like Saudi Arabia and Jordan, ocean water is pumped through desalinization plants and made potable. But large-scale desalinization faces economic obstacles. The energy output required to produce pure water makes the process very expensive.

For some purposes, the economics of desalinization makes sense. On board ships, for instance, the weight and bulk of evaporation equipment and the fuel to run it is less than the weight and bulk of fresh water for the voyage. In some regions where water has become more precious than fuel, desalinization is also economical.

Ideas for inventions may also result from the need to solve a problem. How would you solve the problem of providing water for space shuttle crews? Water is both bulky and heavy, so its presence aboard has to be limited. On the other hand, crew members need drinking water to survive. They also need water to provide acceptable levels of humidity, cool the shuttle during exposure to extreme heat, hydrate food and beverages, and so forth.

An extensive team of personnel was charged with the task of developing the Environmental Control and Life Support System (ECLSS) on the shuttle. One solution they found was to install three Fuel Cell Power Plants on board that actually produce water as a byproduct of generating electricity in flight. The power plants are capable of producing water at a rate of 25 gallons every hour.

Some ideas for inventions are out of this world! The National Aeronautics and Space Administration (NASA) has developed technology for space that is making life better for people on Earth. "Spinoffs are technologies which have been transferred to uses different than, and often remote from their original application in the aerospace field" (*Spinoffs, Information Summaries*). Thousands of examples exist of spinoffs, or applications of space technology. A few diverse examples follow:

· Sized for single households or small communities, a water purification system was invented for developing countries that had its origins in the Space Shuttle Orbiter's water purification system. The water moves through a multiple filtration unit that kills pathogenic microbial organisms.

· The work done on purifying water for astronauts has also led to improvements in dialysis, a treatment for patients with

diseased or damaged kidneys.

· From technology originally developed in the late 1960s by NASA engineers, a private company produced an underwater "acoustic pinger." It broadcasts a signal within the auditory range of harbor porpoises, alerting them to the position of gill nets so they can avoid getting caught. The acoustic pinger was originally developed for retrieving NASA payloads from ocean touchdowns.

· To train astronauts in biofeedback so they could condition themselves to relax naturally, one researcher developed interesting computer games. In an interactive baseball video game, players must relax in order to be able to hit the ball. Eventually players can relax at will and can apply this skill to real-life.

· In zero gravity astronauts assume the most restful posture for the human body, a trunk-to-thigh angle of 128 degrees. This research was applied to the development of comfortable, ergonomic chairs that reduce the harmful effects of gravity on individuals who spend a lot of time sitting to do their work (for example, computer work).

· In development is a "pill transmitter" that will allow doctors on earth to monitor astronauts in space. Researchers are working to reduce the size of the pill so that it can be swallowed. This may prove helpful for ulcer patients in determining changes in pressure in the intestine and in stomach acid.

When can researchers or inventors put their ideas to work? Anytime! Some researchers and inventors got their start from Science Fairs sponsored by their schools or other organizations. Several states offer invention conventions. An excellent resource for invention ideas and materials is the US Patent and Trademark Office. Kid Pages at their website offer games, resources, and links to other sites for students, teachers, parents, and coaches. (The "Idea Hatchery" at this site is an interesting way to get students thinking.)

Although water conservation problems may seem overwhelming, the answers to big questions can have small beginnings—in homes, offices, schools, laboratories, science fairs, and invention conventions. The solution begins with the individual who recognizes a problem, asks a question, or perhaps, like author Jules Verne, imagines the fantastic!

Procedure
Warm Up
Discuss Jonathan Swift's idea that "necessity is the mother of invention" with the class. Ask students how they would interpret this quotation and how it could apply to water conservation. Have students define "technology." Are they aware of technological solutions that have been suggested or implemented to manage water resources? (seeding clouds, desalinizing, iceberg towing, retrofitting devices, and so forth).

Have students suggest how inventions are conceived (examples include but are not limited to imagination, questions, or problems). Remind them that science is a way to find the answers to questions. The word "science" comes from a Latin root meaning "to know."

Explain to students that in some cases, technological advances are "spinoffs" from research originally conducted for very different uses. Working in groups, have students complete the *Match It Up!* Student Copy Page. Discuss spinoffs with them and indicate that they may also be interested in visiting the NASA website that describes spinoffs.

Remind students that inventions can be as complex as the "pill transmitter" or as simple as kitchen faucet aerators or low-flow showerheads. Provide each student with the *Retrofitting* Student Copy Page. Define the term retrofit (the installation of new or modified parts or equipment to something that was previously produced). The parts were not originally applied because they were either thought to be unnecessary or were unavailable. Discuss how these simple devices help households and businesses to conserve water by restricting water flow or volume.

Tell students that they have the opportunity to contribute to a classroom Invention Convention. They may base their contribution on their individual interests and skills, and may select from a variety of options.

The Activity

1. Distribute the *Water Conservation Invention Convention* Student Copy Page. Tell students they may work alone or in small groups and will select a project for a classroom Invention Convention. (Some projects have potential for student science fairs.)
2. Students may require library time for research and materials to complete the projects.
3. Help students organize their time by having them outline the procedure for their project. Remind students that they may only proceed with their lab work after their outline and design have been approved.
4. Work with students to identify a reasonable time line for the completion of their projects and determine a date for a classroom Invention Con-

vention. Students may wish to invite other classes, parents, or community members.

Wrap Up

Before the Invention Convention, have students present their projects to the class. Discuss what they found to be the most difficult aspects of solving their problem. What did they enjoy most about the process? Least? Would they be interested in exploring their question or problem further?

Have students list additional water resource questions or problems along with ideas for an experiment or design.

Assessment

Have students:
· interpret the saying, "Necessity is the mother of invention" (*Warm Up*).
· suggest how inventions are conceived (*Warm Up*).
· provide three examples of "spinoffs" (*Warm Up*).
· survey their home and/or school for retrofitted devices (*Warm Up*).
· review literary works or films, conduct an experiment, or solve a design problem to investigate water conservation technology (steps 1—4).

Extension

Students may wish to develop their work so that it can be submitted as a science fair project. They may also wish to conduct research on the World Wide Web and review other

resources to discover NASA spinoffs and other forms of technology.

Resources

Adams, Richard, and Robert Gardner. 1997. *Ideas for Science Projects*. New York: Franklin Watts.

Bochinski, Julianne Blair. 1996. *The Complete Handbook of Science Fair Projects*. New York: John Wiley and Sons, Inc.

Bridgman, Roger. 1995. *Technology, Eyewitness Science*. New York: Dorling Kindersley.

Doran Rodney. 1998. *Science Educator's Guide to Assessment*. Va.: National Science Teachers Association.

NASA. 1990. *NASA Fact Sheet* (December). Write to Marshall Space Flight Center, Huntsville, AL 35812.

NASA Centralized Technical Services Group. 1988. *Spinoffs, Information Summaries, NASA* (February). Write to NASA Scientific and Technical Information Facility, P.O. Box 8757, Baltimore, Washington International Airport, MD 21240.

NASA website: http://technology.ksc.nasa.gov

U.S. Patent and Trademark Office website: http://www.uspto.gov/

SJRWMD. *Retrofit!* Brochure. Write to SJRWMD Division of Public Information; P.O. Box 1429, Palatka, FL 32178–1429.

Water Conservation Invention Convention Match It Up!

Directions

In the column on the left are items that you may actually use at some time in your life or that may benefit other members of your family or community. All these items are the result of research and technology developed by the National Aeronautics and Space Administration (NASA). These items are called "spinoffs" and NASA defines them as "technologies that have been transferred to uses different than, and often remote from their original application in the aerospace field." You can even visit their website and learn how companies throughout the country are working with NASA to develop spinoffs. See if you can match the items with the research that contributed to their development.

Items:

"Pill transmitter"

Acoustic pinger

Biofeedback computer games

Ergonomic office chair

Matches:

A. Floating in zero gravity, an astronaut's body assumes a posture that is the most relaxed state possible for the human body (a trunk-to-thigh angle of 128 degrees). See if you can imitate this position. What invention did this knowledge contribute to?

B. The work of an astronaut is high stress. It was necessary to find ways to train astronauts so that they could learn to relax naturally.

C. This prescription may be just what the NASA doctors ordered to allow them to monitor what happens to astronauts in space. If you develop an ulcer, a doctor may someday ask you to swallow this so that he or she can monitor the pressure within your intestines and changes in stomach acid.

D. Originally developed for locating NASA payloads from ocean touchdowns, this technology helps porpoises avoid sink gill nets by alerting them of the nets' positions.

Water Conservation Invention Convention Retrofitting

What is retrofitting?

To help conserve water, you and your family can quickly install simple devices (that are usually inexpensive) that replace or alter plumbing fixtures within your home. Some devices restrict or reduce the flow of water.

Kitchen faucet aerator

These devices take about five minutes or less to install. They usually result in a water saving of about 20 to 40 percent less of what is currently flowing from the faucet.

Low-flow showerhead with on-off control valve

These devices require ten minutes or less to install. They can save about 4.5 gallons per minute; this represents a 40 to 65 percent water saving.

Low-flush toilets

Plumbers can install them in less than an hour. These types of toilets use 70 to 90 percent less water than conventional toilets.

Toilet dam

Anyone can install a toilet dam in a few minutes. About 20 percent less water is required for the proper functioning of the toilet.

Other water saving tips:
· Check for water leaks throughout your home. During a time when no one is using water within your home, read your meter before and after a period of two hours. If the water meter does not read the same, you probably have a water leak.
· Check for toilet leaks.
· Don't let the water run while brushing your teeth, washing your hands, etc.
· Run dishwashers and washing machines when they are fully loaded and at the proper water levels.
· Instead of using a garbage disposal, consider a compost pile.
· Insulate your water pipes, so you get hot water faster.

Source: St. Johns River Water Management District, Division of Public Information, Palatka, Fla.

Water Conservation Invention Convention

Directions

1. Review the options.
2. Decide if you would like to work alone or in a small group.
3. Select a project.
4. Outline how you will complete the project by the date of the Water Conservation Invention Convention. Have your outline approved.
5. After you have completed your work, produce a report and decide how you will present and display your efforts.

Options:

I. Write or Film

1. Review the work of several science fiction writers or watch science fiction films. Examine how they solve water resource issues:
   a. for a future society on Earth.
   b. for space travel.
   c. for life on other planets.
   d. for life under the sea in marine cities.

2. What scientific concepts has the author introduced?

3. Are the concepts presented accurately?

4. Do you believe that any of these inventions of the imagination might really help provide or conserve water in the twenty-first century?

5. Select your favorite invention and draw and label it (if appropriate).

6. Create a display of your findings or produce a science fiction video to demonstrate how water resource issues may be resolved in the future.

II. Experiment

1. Select a topic and, using the scientific method, design an investigation.

2. Possible topics to investigate related to water conservation:
   a. water purification.
   b. water filtration.
   c. efficient (water-conserving) lawn-watering patterns for your community.
   d. salt removal using desalinization or reverse osmosis.

III. Design

1. Solve a design problem or improve an existing design.

2. Possible design challenges:
   a. design a water-efficient house.
   b. design a water-efficient fountain.
   c. design a car wash that conserves water.
   d. create a safe, effective, water-efficient pet watering device.
   e. engineer a device to cause household members to take shorter showers.
   f. plan a water catchment system for your home or school.
   g. design a Xeriscape.

Come Celebrate With Us!

Water Conservation Activities for the Whole Community

"I learned that we wouldn't have anything without water."
—a parent

"The water festival was very well organized and my students said it was their best field experience of the year. The selection of the classes and exhibits was exceptional."
—a teacher

Water Conservation Celebration!

WHAT Is a Water Conservation Celebration?

It's education. It's networking. It's fun!

A Water Conservation Celebration is a free, one- to three-day event to entertain and educate your community about the importance of water conservation. Although most celebrations have been organized as a one-day event for middle school students and their teachers, a Water Conservation Celebration can be tailored to meet the needs of any audience or age group.

A celebration can range anywhere from a special one-hour class in school to a half-day event in a park, to a weekend-long water fair at a convention center. It can target school children, an entire community, or a special-interest group.

Celebrations organized for school children can include classroom activities, exhibit areas, contests, games, and teacher networking opportunities. Children and adults learn together. A Water Conservation Celebration for adults can range from water conservation conventions to forums on wise water use to public debates on water rights.

To be successful, a water celebration should expose participants to the wide variety of water uses and present all sides of an issue. Opening the festival to various points of view allows participants to learn firsthand about many water resource topics. They learn to compare environmental and economic perspectives and to gather the necessary information to make informed decisions about water use and protection.

A Water Conservation Celebration is a high-profile educational activity that will increase the awareness and appreciation of water re-

sources and issues in your area. Adults and students will take home current information that will be used in the classroom and referred to for months after the event. Local water resource organizations will begin working together closely, often for the first time. Service groups will start looking for ways to get involved with water issues. Organizers will suddenly receive requests for more information on organizing water celebrations in other parts of the state or region. Clearly, water celebrations are highly contagious, not to mention educational and fun!

WHO Can Organize a Water Conservation Celebration?

You can!

Any group with a desire to generate an interest in water resources can sponsor a Water Conservation Celebration. All it takes is a commitment to educating the public about the importance of water resources, the ability to work with large numbers of people and a willingness to put in the amount of time and energy required.

A Water Conservation Celebration, whether targeted at a community or at local schools, requires a lot of work. From identifying a suitable time and place to hold your event, to scheduling speakers and presenters, to keeping everyone informed, you are looking at a commitment of six months to a year in preparation time. The real logistical challenge comes immediately before and during the event.

The results of the Water Conservation Celebration, however, will more than compensate for your investment in time and energy, and if you organize well, the media coverage will be extensive.

WHERE Should a Water Conservation Celebration Be Held?

Anywhere you want (though some places are better than others)!

In general, you need a facility with a large meeting area—like an auditorium, gymnasium, or community center—where you can assemble a large number of exhibits and activities. The facility should be well secured and have rest rooms and ample parking. You also need additional classrooms or smaller meeting areas with desks or tables and chairs and access to audiovisual equipment like VCRs, microphones, slide and overhead projectors, and blackboards. The ideal location also includes an outside area where you can set up a weather station or hold a fishing derby. And don't forget one of the most important ingredients for any water celebration—running water!

Unless arrangements have been made for an alternate indoor site, we don't recommend holding a Water Conservation Celebration in the local park or in an open-air facility. One celebration in Nebraska was held successfully at an outdoor recreation area, with an indoor site ready if necessary.

When picking a site, be sure to match potential crowd size with facility capacity and parking. Many water celebrations have been held on a first come, first served basis, with the building capacity met early. Good advance planning can prevent disappointing a large number of young people and adults.

WHEN Is the Best Time for a Water Conservation Celebration?

Anytime (except summer if planning for school children)!

Water celebrations have been held throughout the year. The ideal time for a school-based event is generally in the spring. Keep in mind that off-site travel budgets can be low, and plan ahead to ensure that schools will be able to participate.

Despite more reliable weather, summer is not the best time to hold a Water Conservation Celebration. Unless year-round schools operate in your region, attendance could be low. However, summer can be a good time for a community-oriented celebration.

If you intend to use a university or college facility, plan the event to occur during a break in their schedule. Otherwise, logistics like classroom availability and parking could be very challenging.

HOW Much Will a Water Conservation Celebration Cost?

Maybe a lot less than you think!

In general, expect to spend anywhere from $1,000 to $10,000 to stage a daylong Water Conservation Celebration. This includes the costs of printing brochures, paying for postage and supplies, renting space (if necessary), and providing food and drink for your volunteers. If this is more than you can afford on your own, do not despair. Many sources of support exist within your community, from corporate volunteers to sponsors. In-kind assistance and the cumulative value of small grants can keep a community celebration up and running. In-kind services are contributions of time and goods.

Ready? Let's Go!

Getting Organized

You will find that organizing a Water Conservation Celebration involves a special combination of ingredients including finding partners, deciding on a theme, raising funds, soliciting presenters and exhibitors, and finding dedicated volunteers—the key to your success. As you read this chapter, note the "Words of Wisdom" and other special information highlighted in the boxes. These words of advice come from seasoned water celebration organizers.

Your Team

No one person can organize an entire Water Conservation Celebration. You will need the help of schedulers, planners, and dedicated volunteers. You will also need financial and in-kind support from groups throughout your community. So where do you start? You may already know a handful of individuals who would be willing to help you organize a Water Conservation Celebration. If so, great. Get them all together and move on to the next step. If not, then what?

Identify community members who are interested in water resources and in providing quality educational experiences. Make a list and get on the telephone! If you have gone this far, you are probably willing to assume a leadership role. But you will need to identify at least three or four other individuals with whom you can share the large number of tasks equitably. They should be willing to commit the time it will take.

Give your team a name. Be productive, but have fun!

Sample Nine-Month Schedule

Month 1
- organize your team
- set theme
- identify celebration location, confirmed in writing
- prepare time line of events
- plan press release schedule (Appendix C)

Month 2
- form committees

Month 3
- send initial inquiry letter to sponsors, exhibitors, presenters (Appendix B)
- contact food/beverage vendors for donations of goods

Month 4
- confirm presenters/exhibitors with confirmation letter and form (Appendix B)
- send Celebration Announcement to administrators and teachers (Appendix A)

Month 5
- prepare, print, and distribute brochures

Month 6
- send registration packets to schools (Appendix D)
- recruit volunteers

Month 7
- schedule all schools (Appendix D)
- create logistical package (maps, schedules, etc.)

Month 8
- send final information packet to schools, presenters, etc. (Appendices A, B, D, E)
- make final phone calls as needed to exhibitors and presenters
- contact the press again

Month 9
- Water Conservation Celebration!

Month 10
- send thank-you letters and surveys to everyone involved (Appendix F)
- start planning for next year!

Learn from Experience: Form Partnerships

In northeast Colorado, several organizations came together to form the Northeast Colorado Interagency Water Quality Committee. This committee, which consists of Colorado State University Cooperative Extension Agents, the Northeast Colorado Health Department, Soil Conservation Service personnel, and managers of eight Ground Water Management Districts, sponsors an annual Youth Waterfest.

Your Theme

As a team, your planning committee needs to decide on the overall goal of your Water Conservation Celebration. In addition to being educational and fun, your celebration should cover basic water quality, water supply, and water conservation topics. A classroom or school might select a theme like wetlands, watersheds, the water cycle, or water conservation.

What are the important water resource issues in your community? If your region has been plagued by consistent low rainfall or drought, for example, focus on water conservation: bring together displays and exhibits that demonstrate how everyone can work together to conserve water. If your area is heavily reliant on agriculture, concentrate more on this water use. If ground water quality is a pressing concern, focus on that topic. Or, if battle lines are being drawn over how water should be used in your area, highlight the many points of view. Regardless of your goal, it is important to present all sides of the story.

Your Plan of Action

Now that you have selected your team and your theme, it is time to sit down and do some serious planning. In this section, refer to the *Sample Nine-Month Schedule.*

The more organized you are early on, the better off you will be in the long run. Some water celebration organizers have allotted a full year to organize the event; others have worked on nine-month, six-month, or even three-month schedules (although the general consensus is that even six months is not much time to plan—particularly if it is your first event).

Since your location may dictate when you can hold the event and, therefore, how much time you have to plan, your first assignment is to identify a celebration location.

Many organizers have found that local community colleges are the ideal location, since they often have outreach and support services available to the community at no cost. They are interested in having prospective students visit their campus, and they usually have excellent facilities, but scheduling can be difficult and cost can be high. Public schools and county fairgrounds are other possibilities.

The size of the space will dictate the numbers of students and adults you can invite. Or, you may find that you have plenty of room but want to keep the crowds—and the logistical challenges—to a minimum. Now is the time to think this through.

This is also a good time to organize committees and assign responsibilities. Tasks include fund-raising, handling logistics, organizing presentations, setting up the exhibit hall and the teachers' resource room, and so forth. Although one person should chair the event, you should plan to enlist many volunteers.

Your Partners

You will need financial supporters, exhibitors, presenters, and volunteers to round out your event. The individuals and organizations you enlist to participate in the Water Conservation Celebration will make your event a great success.

Financial Supporters

Once you have a place and time in mind, the next step is to arrange financial and in-kind support.

Finding support for the event may be as simple as having the organizations represented by your team members contribute the necessary funds. Or, you may want to contact foundations, local trust funds, businesses, or individuals in your community with an interest in promoting education, conservation, or the wise use of water resources.

Local market owners, soft-drink distributors, and restaurateurs may be willing to provide food or drink for your speakers and volunteers. Local print shops or newspapers may help with layout and printing costs.

Once you have decided on an overall theme, it is easier to find and approach individuals and organizations with an interest in that theme for financial and in-kind support.

Sample Budgets

Budget #1
(Approximately 210 children and 20 adults attended this event.)

Postage	$75
Printing	$200
Teacher Resource Packet	$200
Student Resource Packet	$200
Meals	$300
TOTAL	$975

Note: This celebration also received approximately $4,000 of in-kind services.

Budget #2
(Approximately 1,100 children and 100 adults attended this event.)

Meals	$380
Teachers' Packets	$600
Supplies	$140
Graphics	$326
Brochures & Buttons	$387
TOTAL	$1,833

Note: This celebration also received rooms and postage as in-kind support.

Budget #3
(Approximately 1,800 children and 300 adults attended this event.)

Postage	$500
Printing	$800
Balloons & Decorations	$200
Food	$500
Miscellaneous	$500
TOTAL	$2,500

Financial Supporters
Here are just a few of the organizations and groups that have sponsored Water Conservation Celebrations:
- City Governments
- State Game and Parks Commissions
- Departments of Natural Resources
- State Departments of Agriculture
- Universities
- Extension Service Offices
- Soil/Water Conservation Districts
- Environmental Protection Agency
- Local Trust Funds
- Local Banks
- Agricultural Supply Companies
- Recreation Groups
- Ground Water Protection Districts

Volunteers

Volunteers you recruit to work with you the day of the big event are important players on your team. Ask members of special-interest groups (4-H, Future Farmers of America, League of Women Voters) or service-related groups to help out. You will need volunteers to greet buses, stay with a particular class during the day, make food runs for presenters, help with cleanup, and generally assist throughout the day. They should arrive early to tour the building and become familiar with presentation locations. A few extra-dedicated people will be needed for cleanup chores.

Exhibitors and Presenters

For maximum success, plan on having a combination of exhibits, classroom presentations, and half-day outdoor activities. Ideally, a student on a half-day visit at the celebration should be able to attend three to five classroom presentations and have an hour in the exhibit hall.

An exhibit is an ongoing demonstration of water-related activities such as gold-panning, water-quality testing, or solar-driven pumping. Exhibits may be located in the exhibit hall or in the outdoor activity area.

The best place to start lining up exhibitors is with a list of individuals and organizations interested in water resources and your theme. Contact your state Project WET (Water Education for Teachers) coordinator for ideas and suggestions. These people have a wealth of water-resource activities on hand and will likely want to help. Chances are you will know most of the players already. If not, or if you are looking for additional ideas, your local telephone directory and the director for the state capital are good references for contacts. Also, contact state, federal and local government agencies and groups responsible for natural resources, agriculture, and tourism.

When selecting presenters, review their credentials and, most importantly, consider individuals with a passion for the subject and a willingness to communicate directly with children and adults. All presenters must know how to make learning fun.

After you have identified your ideal exhibitors and presenters, contact them by letter (see Appendix B). Tell them about your plans and ask them to join in the celebration. Your first contact with exhibitors is an opportunity to solicit additional financial and in-kind support for your event. Do not be shy. If they are interested in the program, they may also be willing to provide some type of support.

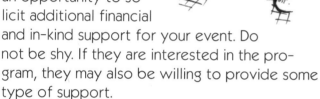

Follow up a week or two later by telephone to gauge their interest. Once you have everyone signed up, ask your exhibitors and presenters to prepare an overview of what they plan to do. If you do not agree with their approach, take time to work with them. Knowing the capabilities and style of each presenter is critical!

Ask if exhibitors and presenters will need special audiovisual equipment or any assistance during their presentations. One organizing team discovered the day of the event that some presenters needed video players and slide projectors. These are difficult requests to fill at the last minute.

If school children are your primary audience, ask exhibitors and presenters to keep activities at their level. That does not mean presentations and exhibits cannot be technical; the more hands-on, however, the more attentive and involved the audience will be.

Examples of Exhibits

Exhibit areas are chaotic and noisy. Be sure they are organized in an open area (gymnasium, civic center, etc.) that can handle both the crowd and the decibels! The following ideas work for either exhibits or presentations:

Water Cycle: Put together models of how the water cycle works and how water eventually makes its way to the ocean.

Underground Patrol: Using a ground water flow model, demonstrate how water under Earth's surface moves and how it is pumped for human and livestock use.

Water Power: Demonstrate a small hydroelectric plant.

Pivot Patrol: Show how computers are helping farmers irrigate efficiently.

Gold Rush: Design a gold-panning operation.

Liquid Treasure: With the help of turn-of-the-century water artifacts, early photographs, and the participation play *Mrs. Alderson*, demonstrate how water was transported and used by our ancestors.

Sunshine to Water Tanks: Set up a photovoltaic-powered water pump and demonstrate how the sun can be used to fill livestock tanks.

Bubbleology: Let students take turns making life-size bubbles. This is one of the most popular exhibits of all!

> Words of Wisdom
> "Bubbleology is very fun but can be messy and slick. Use great care to contain the mess and keep the area safe."

Fishy Business: Invite a hatchery representative to demonstrate how fish are raised for stocking favorite fishing holes.

Can I Drink It?: Set up a demonstration drinking-water plant.

Cleaning It Up: Set up a demonstration waste-water treatment plant.

Name That Fish: Provide a fish tank of native species and have students try to identify them.

Keeping It Clean: Ask local industries (miners, loggers, ranchers) to demonstrate how they protect the region's ground and surface water.

Out of Sight, But Not Out of Mind: Make your own ground water model and demonstrate ground water pollution.

4-H and Water: Let 4-H and other organizations provide information on their water-related programs.

Creepy Critters: Set up a microscope so students can see what's lurking in water.

Pollution Solution: Provide hands-on demonstrations on how students can prevent water pollution.

Science Projects: Have a viewing area for award-winning water science projects.

Wetland Wonders: Create wetland models and explain how wetlands work and why they are important. Conduct a contest for students to build their own.

Examples of Presentations

Presentations may be twenty to twenty-five minutes in length and are repeated throughout the day in classrooms. The more varied your presentations, the more successful they'll be. They should address a range of water resource topics such as the water cycle, water chemistry, and water law. Consider including math, science, music, art, history, and dance. A multidisciplinary approach helps ensure that the program will be fun for everyone.

Hydrologist for a Day: Invite a local hydrologist to talk about—and demonstrate—how water is measured and administered.

People's Water Court: Let students work on resolving water disputes—in twenty minutes or less!

Water Rappers: Make rap water-music or organize a water sing-a-long!

Water Pioneers: Who helped bring water to your region? Who irrigated the first tract of land? Who dammed the river for hydroelectric power? Bring the history of water in your re-

gion to life!

Where Does Water Come From? Where does water go? Present an overview of the water cycle.

Hometown Water: Where does YOUR water come from? Invite someone from the city or water treatment plant to explain.

It's Good Chemistry: Demonstrate the physical and chemical properties of water through hands-on activities.

Safe Waters: Invite the Red Cross to discuss water safety.

WET Waters: Try any one of the Project WET activities.

Acid Rain: Analyze water samples to see if local lakes are at risk.

Smart Water: How do you know if you have smart water? Give it a test! Invite someone from the Health Department to show students how.

Dancing Water: Talk about the cultural significance of rain dances and traditional instruments. Let students express themselves through creative dance and movement.

Look Out Below: Ask the USDA Soil Conservation Service or similar organization to teach students about the dangers of erosion.

Puppet Shows: Use puppet figures to teach young students about endangered species, water history, water pollution, water conservation or any other water-related issue you want to present.

Watercolors: Bring the fine art of watercolors into your life!

Learn From Experience
Consider including a contest or two as part of your celebration. Examples of past contests include: poster (to advertise the event), art (the best twelve drawings were used for a fund-raising calendar the next year), water poetry, wetland building, and school yard habitat design. Winners can be announced the day of the celebration and their work displayed. Information on the contests should go out in the school registration packets.

© The Watercourse

Examples of Outdoor Activities

Weather permitting, outdoor events can provide a welcome break form indoor activities. Here are just a few ideas:

Weather Station: Set up a weather station and demonstrate how it works.

Fishing Derby: Using barbless hooks, run an ongoing catch-and-release fishing derby.

Tree Planting/Adopt a Tree: Allow each class to plant a tree and mark it with a plaque to commemorate the event. If there isn't a natural area for planting, allow each class to adopt an existing tree and mark it with a plaque. Provide information about each kind of tree and the role trees play in the environment.

Native Plants: Conduct a walking tour of the area, pointing out native plants and trees, and relating some of the history and lore about them.

Dowsing: Dowse for water! Demonstrate the many ways water has been located through time.

Games

Offering a fun and educational alternative to the other presentations, games are a regular feature of celebrations, with "watered-down" versions of Pictionary® (Puddle Pictures) and other board games. Water Wizards consistently receives high marks from both organizers and students. Using a trivia format, Water Wizards teams from different schools answer water-related questions, competing against each other for ribbons or awards. In the Bucket Brigade, participants haul water in a relay competition and discover the challenge of transporting water from a historical perspective. (See *Games and Contests* in Appendix E.) Enlist the help of a local radio or television personality or government leader to host a game.

Scheduling and Communications

Once your exhibitors and presenters are lined up, it is time to start getting the word out to schools and media.

Working with Educators and Communities

A brochure is an easy way to get everyone excited about attending the celebration. The design should be fun, with eye-catching graphics and easy-to-follow information. Mail brochures to all schools and libraries in the area, school system newsletters, the media, local government groups, state water organizations, and interest groups. Include them in registration packets too.

Teachers need information on registration, choice of events, and scheduling. Limit the number of classroom events each group may attend (four to six usually works best), and limit the group size to twenty-five or less if possible. Activities selected by each group should be diverse. Allow time between events for leg stretching and moving from room to room.

You will need to prepare individual schedules to send to teachers, presenters, exhibitors, and volunteers, and a series of master lists and matrices for the coordinators. Send teachers a schedule with descriptions of selected activities. Encourage them to share this information with students so that everyone is prepared (see Appendix D for sample schedules).

The most important reference tool for celebration coordinators is the *Master Scheduling Matrix* shown in Appendix D. Create this matrix by using the information received from teachers. This matrix should include columns for location, topic, and time slots.

If you are planning a community celebration, you might want to have a registration table where participants sign up for presentations. This will ensure that the size of the audience does not exceed room capacity or the presenter's expectations.

Working with the Media

With a little planning and organization, a Water Conservation Celebration can be THE media event in your community. But you need to get the word out early and keep the media informed as the project progresses. The celebration is a newsworthy event that can provide you with additional opportunities for educating people in your community. Small-town papers are often news hungry and are willing to use good information sent to them.

You should contact as many newspapers, radio stations, and television newsrooms in your area as possible, determine their interest, and identify who might be assigned to the story. As information and plans develop, you can call on that person. Check Appendix C for ideas on press releases.

One way to grab the attention of major media is to invite prominent government figures or radio and television personalities to be hosts for Water Wizards, Puddle Pictures, or Bucket Brigade.

Consider setting up a pressroom during the celebration where you can distribute additional information to the media and acknowledge your sponsors. The more recognition sponsors receive, the more apt they will be to support you again.

Teachers' Resource Room

In a teachers' resource room, provide exhibitor handouts, curriculum information from other states, speaker and video lists, and other pertinent materials. This room offers the opportunity for educators to meet one another and find out how their colleagues are teaching about water resources. A coffee pot and muffins or donuts are sure to encourage visitors.

Lunch

If you plan to have events stretch over the lunch hour, arrange for everyone to bring his/her own lunch. An option for community celebrations is to provide food concessions, since these events often have morning and afternoon sessions. Options for handling the lunch hour include asking students to have lunch off-site or providing a lunchroom at the celebration. Be sure to arrange this with the building manager in advance.

Wrapping It All Up

After the event, send teachers, exhibitors, presenters, volunteers, and sponsors thank-you letters and short surveys. For a community event, you may want to consider placing a thank-you note in a local newspaper. Through a survey, find out what went well, what didn't go well, and what participants would like to see more of in the future. The survey should be designed to solicit suggestions from students (see Appendix F). Also, send a short press release to media contacts to generate interest in a follow-up story.

The perfect time to start organizing the celebration for next year is when the team gets together to review the surveys.

Words of Wisdom
One celebration organizer highlighted the importance of sending information to school administrators AND to teachers. "If they're sent exclusively to administrators, too often these kinds of brochures get lost in the shuffle."

Words of Wisdom
One organizer said, "Establishing relationships with small-town papers, by putting a hometown focus on each press release, is our group's next challenge."

Words of Wisdom
"Lunch can be the most challenging part of organizing a celebration, not because of the logistics—but because of the litter! Plan for a 'litterless lunch' by encouraging students and teachers to bring everything in their lunches— from milk to potato chips—in recyclable containers. Have someone responsible for maintaining recycling bins. Make this 'greening of lunch' challenge part of the educational experience and the fun!"

Helpful Hints

· Allow plenty of lead time for planning.
· Confirm the availability of the school or facility early for the day you are planning to hold the celebration.
· Try to organize the entire event to be litterless. Your cleanup crew and host facility will thank you for it and you will be setting a good example for participants.
· In case a busload of students arrives early, have an overflow space ready. Also, have a contingency plan in case groups arrive late.
· Put someone in charge of bus parking.
· Provide all teachers and organizers with maps indicating where activities are located.
· The noise level will be high in the exhibit hall. Let exhibitors know that noise may provide a challenge.
· Arrange backups for presenters or exhibitors who call in sick.
· Make directional signs and title plates for exhibits and classrooms. Attach balloons to them to get everyone's attention.
· Use balloons, banners, and other decorations to make the celebration festive.
· Have a telephone number for teachers to call if weather might threaten the event.
· Rent walkie-talkies (or borrow them from a sponsor) to facilitate communications between celebration organizers the day of the event.
· Request that volunteers arrive early for a group tour of the facility.
· Have volunteers deliver sodas and lunch to presenters.
· Have someone make sure that presenters keep to the schedule.
· Postfestival cleanup must be thorough and complete. This is a thankless task, so reward your volunteers with an extra treat and a big thank-you.

Appendices

The following forms, schedules, and announcements can give you a head start in preparing your own celebration. Feel free to adapt these materials to fit your needs. Special or generic directions and messages for you have been placed in brackets.

A. Communications with Participants

Initially, you will be corresponding with many different people to solicit their support and involvement in your Water Conservation Celebration. To get you started, we have included sample materials. Use what is helpful and ignore the rest.

Flyer: Celebration Announcement

Either by hand or on the computer, you can quickly and inexpensively produce a one-page flyer announcing your Water Conservation Celebration. Distribute flyers to your target audience at least six months prior to the celebration. Early notification allows schools time to plan and budget for the event.

To the right is an example of a simple flyer.

Sample Flyer

Announcing A Water Conservation Celebration

Mark your calendar
[date]
for a day of water education and fun at

[location]

You and your students may
· pan for gold
· become a water wizard
· find out how smart your water is (test it!)
· discover a hidden treasure—ground water!

You'll receive additional information in a registration packet in about two months, or call for information now.

[name]

[phone]

© The Watercourse

Registration Packet

Include the following letter and registration form in the registration packet. If you have prepared a brochure, enclose it in this packet as well. Mail the packet about four months prior to the planned celebration.

Sample Registration Form

[TITLE OF CELEBRATION]
[DAY OF WEEK, MONTH, DAY, YEAR]
[FACILITY, LOCATION, CITY, STATE]

Please return no later than [date; set this date two months before the celebration].

Yes, my _____ grade class would like to attend the Water Conservation Celebration. Preferred time slot: _____ a.m. [8:30 a.m.–12 noon] _____ p.m. [12 noon–3:30 p.m.] Number of students in class: _____ [Do you have a maximum number? If so, indicate here.]

Please print:

School	Address
Teacher's Name	Phone Number

Teacher's Signature

If possible, my class would like to attend the following five activities (please indicate your preference by marking 1 through 5, with 1 being your first choice; see enclosed brochure for more details). Every attempt will be made to assign you your four highest-ranked activities.

_____ Water Chemistry
_____ History of Water
_____ Fishing for Words
_____ Water Rappers
_____ Watercolors
_____ Pictionary
_____ [...etc.]

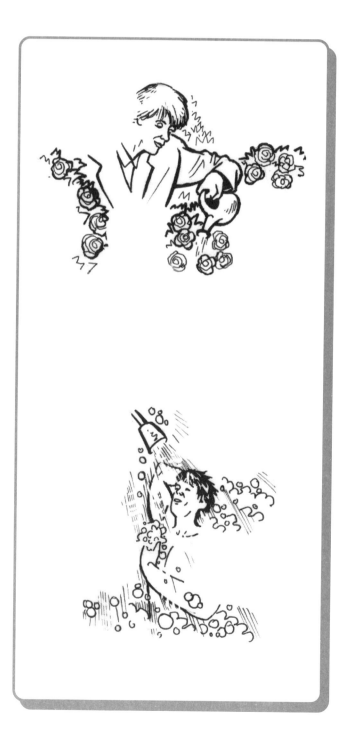

Sample Inquiry Letter

Dear [educator's name]:

Water resources are of vital importance to our region's future—and, thus, to the future of our children. Young people need to understand how this critical natural resource affects healthy watersheds and water-dependent activities like agriculture, recreation, local industry, and wildlife habitat. They also need to learn how they can contribute to its wise use and protection.

For that reason, [names of sponsoring organization(s)] are planning the first Water Conservation Celebration in [place] on [date].

Modeled after several successful Water Conservation Celebrations attended by thousands of children nationwide, our celebration will feature concurrent hands-on presentations highlighting topics like water conservation, water chemistry, water habitats, and other topics of interest to our region. Students will have the opportunity to participate in games and contests and even make bubbles as large as they are! An exhibit hall will house numerous educational exhibits designed for fourth- through sixth-grade students; we are also setting up a teachers' resource room. It will be a fun and educational day for everyone!

There is no registration fee but reservations are required so that we can schedule groups through the various activity areas. Schools are required to provide adult supervision for each group of students. [Note that you may want to limit the number of students in a group to twenty-five.] If food will be consumed at the celebration site, participants must bring their own litterless lunches.

We've enclosed a registration form and a tentative list of activities [or brochure if you have one]. Please fill out the form and indicate your preference for morning or afternoon sessions. Indicate five activities that you and your students would like to attend. ALL ACTIVITIES WILL BE ASSIGNED ON A FIRST-COME, FIRST-SERVED BASIS. Return your registration form at your earliest convenience, but no later than [date]. [Give yourself plenty of lead time.]

We look forward to hearing from you soon! In the meantime, if we can answer any questions, please feel free to call us at:
[type in contact name and phone number/address here]

Hope to see you on [date]!

Sincerely,

Final Information Packet

This will be your last opportunity to communicate with teachers before the celebration—unless you also choose to contact them by telephone prior to the event. The following confirmation letter should be sent out with maps, schedules, rules, and other important notes.

Sample Confirmation Letter

Dear [teacher's name]:

Thank you for your interest in attending the Water Conservation Celebration. We have been thrilled by the response from teachers throughout [location], and we expect a capacity crowd of [number] students on [date].

To keep things running as smoothly as possible, we have enclosed for your review:
1. An updated schedule of activities for the day (on green paper).
2. A list of activities assigned to your class (on yellow).
3. A map of the [facility] indicating where the various activities will be conducted. Note that bus parking is [give location] but that there is a safe loading/unloading area at the [entrance] of the building. Someone will be there to greet your class when it arrives and to ensure that buses move in and out of the area quickly. The teachers' resource room is [give location]. We've compiled some excellent resources for your review with a complete packet of take-home materials. This is a great place to meet other teachers with an interest in water resources.
4. If you have been assigned to a game, you will also find enclosed a copy of rules and sample questions.

Lunch may be eaten on- or off-site. To keep cleanup to a minimum and to promote a conservation ethic, we are requesting that students and teachers who eat at the celebration site bring litterless lunches. Everyone is encouraged to bring lunch items in reusable containers. Assuming good weather, picnic tables are available for lunch breaks [give location/directions]. Rooms will be set aside for lunch in the event of inclement weather.

Please let us know if you have any questions about the enclosed materials or if we can be of any assistance to you or your class prior to the celebration. If not, we'll see you on [date]!

Sincerely,

Teacher Communications Checklist

___ 1. Send flyer: Celebration Announcement (Month 4)

___ 2. Mail Registration Packet (Month 6)
   - inquiry letter
   - brochure or list of activities
   - registration form

___ 3. Send Final Information Packet (Month 8)
   - confirmation letter
   - list of activities scheduled for the class (see Appendix D)
   - game rules/sample questions (see Appendix E)
   - contest rules/instructions (see Appendix E)
   - maps

___ 4. Send thank-you letter and surveys to everyone involved within one month after celebration (see Appendix F; remember to include forms for students)

B. Communications with Exhibitors and Presenters

The best way to enlist support from and ensure smooth sailing for your exhibitors and presenters is to keep the lines of communication open. Your first letter should explain who you are and what you are planning. Adapt the sample letter and send it out at least six months before the event. Follow up with a telephone call to determine interest and identify specific topics for presentations and exhibits. Once exhibitors and presenters have agreed to come, send a thank-you letter confirming their participation. A sample confirmation letter is also provided. Two or three weeks prior to the event, contact them again with last-minute information on logistics. Ask each presenter and exhibitor to arrange for a backup and to give you the name and telephone number of that individual. Be prepared to call the stand-in if the exhibitor or presenter cancels.

© The Watercourse

Sample Initial Inquiry Letter

Dear [exhibitor/presenter]:

Water resources are of vital importance to our region's future—and the future of our children. Young people need to be aware that water is critical to many water users including farmers, recreationists, and wildlife. With this understanding, they can contribute to its wise use and protection.

For these reasons, [names of sponsoring organizations] are planning the first Water Conservation Celebration in [place] on [date]. We would appreciate your support and involvement in [presenting/ exhibiting] information on [water ecology, water dancing, or whatever].

Modeled after several successful Water Conservation Celebrations attended by thousands of children nationwide, this event will include hands-on sessions featuring topics like water conservation, the history of water use in our area, water chemistry, aquatic wildlife and ecology, and other regional water-related topics. We hope to present all aspects of these important water resource issues. You would provide a vital contribution to the event's overall success.

The celebration will include an area where students can visit educational exhibits. We are also organizing a teachers' resource room.

Although we have no set guidelines on presentation methods, please remember that the audience will be fourth- through sixth-grade children. The more hands-on the presentations and exhibits are, the more the students will enjoy them. More adult-oriented material can be distributed in our teachers' resource room.

Please feel free to call us if you have any questions; otherwise, a member of our team will contact you to follow up. We welcome your ideas, interest, and participation and look forward to a successful Water Conservation Celebration!

Sincerely,

Sample Confirmation Letter

Dear [exhibitor or presenter],

Thank you for agreeing to participate in this year's Water Conservation Celebration. We are looking forward to an educational and fun-filled day!

There are a few things you should know when preparing your [exhibit or presentation]:

1. The Water Conservation Celebration will be held on [date] in the [location] from [time] to [time]. We are asking all presenters and exhibitors to be set up and ready to go no later than [time] a.m. We have access to the [location] the night before; please let us know if you would like to set up at that time.

2. The exhibit hall will be open from [time] to [time]. Presentations will be twenty minutes long, with a ten minute break in-between, and will run throughout the day in assigned classrooms.

3. We will provide lunch and soft drinks for exhibitors and presenters. We cannot, however, reimburse participants for travel or expenses. We truly appreciate your willingness to donate your time and energy to this worthwhile event.

4. The Water Conservation Celebration targets fourth- through sixth-graders. They are most attentive when they have an opportunity to be involved actively with the subject. In general, they do not enjoy lectures, slide shows, or videos, unless they are given an opportunity to become part of the action. Try to make your exhibit or presentation as hands-on as possible. If you have any questions about how to adapt your presentation as a Water Conservation Celebration activity, please give us a call.

5. Please complete the enclosed confirmation form and return it no later than [date]. Note that we have asked for the name and telephone number of a backup in case you are unable to attend the celebration. This is very important and will help ensure that we have a successful day. Please let us know if you have any special needs (access to power or water, audiovisual equipment, microphones, and so on).

Once our schedule is complete and we have our teacher confirmations in hand, we will contact you again with last-minute details. Thanks again for agreeing to participate. We look forward to seeing you on [date].

Sincerely,

© The Watercourse

Sample Exhibitor/Presenter Confirmation Form

[TITLE OF CELEBRATION]
[DAY OF WEEK, MONTH, DAY, YEAR]
[FACILITY, LOCATION, CITY, STATE]
Please return no later than [date].

Yes, I plan to participate in this year's Water Conservation Celebration on [date] at [location]. I will be presenting or exhibiting the following information:

My presentation/exhibit (please circle one) will include the following hands-on activities:

If at the last minute I cannot attend, my backup is:

_____

Name   Phone

I need access to the following for my exhibit/presentation:
_____   running water
_____   audiovisual equipment
           (slide projector/overhead projector/VCR/TV—please circle)
_____   electricity
_____   table(s) (indicate size and number)
_____   other (please indicate) _____

I plan to set up on _____ at _____ [date and time]

_____

Your Name (please print)   Organization

_____

Address, including zip code   Phone Number

_____

Signature   Date

Exhibitor/Presenter Communications Checklist

_____ 1. Send Initial Inquiry Letter (Month 3)

_____ 2. Follow up with a telephone call

_____ 3. Send Confirmation Letter and Form

_____ 4. Identify backup

_____ 5. Mail out Exhibitor/Presenter Final Information Package (Month 8)
  · letter listing where to park and unload and special instructions about the facility
  · exhibitor/presenter's individual schedule (Appendix D)
  · brochure
  · maps
  · list of local motels and restaurants

_____ 6. Recheck by telephone that exhibitors' and presenters' needs are clear (Month 8)
  · a.v. equipment
  · electricity
  · tables/chairs
  · running water
  · other?

_____ 7. Send out thank-you letters and surveys to everyone involved (see Appendix F)

C. Communications with the Media

For your Water Conservation Celebration to be a community-wide educational success, you should contact the media often and provide them with as much detailed information as possible. As specific events occur during the planning of your Water Conservation Celebration, let the media know about them through a series of news releases. Press releases should provide the following information: 1) What is happening? 2) According to whom? 3) When/where is it taking place? 4) Why is it important? 5) How can the community get involved—or who can they call for more information? Be sure to acknowledge all financial and in-kind supporters. A follow-up call to media contacts will ensure a better response!

Sample Press Release

Nearly 400 elementary school children from [give names of counties] counties will converge at [location] on [date] to participate in the [number] annual Water Conservation Celebration.

[Name of person], president of the local chapter of [name of organization], and other event organizers report that students attending the daylong event near [city, state] will experience firsthand the importance of water for all water users. Young people and educators will participate in a variety of activities designed to promote awareness, knowledge, and stewardship of water resources.

Children will build their own aquifer to take home, compete in a nonpoint source pollution scavenger hunt, examine aquatic organisms, learn about nitrates in ground water, enter a mural contest, and join in other hands-on activities.

Community support for the Water Conservation Celebration continues to grow. Funds have been provided by [name funding organizations/groups]. The event is sponsored by [name sponsoring organizations/groups].

For more information, contact [name], [organization], at [phone number].

© The Watercourse

D. Scheduling (Master Lists and Matrices)

Teachers, volunteers, presenters, and exhibitors each need a schedule so they know where they should be during the day. In addition, celebration organizers need master lists and schedules of all teachers, volunteers, presenters, and so forth. The following lists have been compiled based on materials from other successful celebrations.

These lists are abbreviated and provide only samples of content. They should be prepared so that individual sections can be used by volunteers and posted in different areas of the facility. For example, a volunteer working the information booth needs that portion of the Master List.

INFORMATION BOOTH VOLUNTEERS	
ROOM [name/number] BUILDING [name/location]	
Time	Volunteers
8:30 a.m.– 10:30 a.m.	Jane Smith and John Doe
10:30 a.m.– 12:30 p.m.	Debbie Dumas and Hannah Smith

BUBBLEOLOGY VOLUNTEERS	
ROOM [name/number] BUILDING [name/location]	
Time	Volunteers
9:30 a.m.–11:30 a.m.	Adrian Carrasco
11:30 a.m.–1:30 p.m.	Sam Brown

TEACHERS' RESOURCE ROOM VOLUNTEERS	
ROOM [name/number] BUILDING [name/location]	
Time	Volunteers
9:30 a.m.–12:30 p.m.	Suzie Q.
12:30 p.m.–3:30 p.m.	Kate Gill

SCHEDULE FOR THE EXHIBIT HALL	
Time	Teachers
9:00 a.m.	Free time
9:30 a.m.	Mr. Glenn (5th grade) Mr. Jones (4th grade) Ms. Smith (4th grade) Mrs. Wilson (5th grade)
10:00 a.m.	Mr. Anderson (4th grade) Mrs. Scott (6th grade) Mr. Nelson (5th grade) Ms. Carnegie (4th grade)

Master Scheduling Matrix (for use by Celebration Coordinators)

Expand to several poster boards for large-scale format. Numbers in parentheses are grade levels; other numbers indicate class size.

ROOM	TOPIC	9:00 a.m.	9:30 a.m.	10:00 a.m.	10:30 a.m.	11:00 a.m.
General Services 224	Open					
[Name of Hall] 511	Water Cycle [Name]		[Teacher] (4) 37	[Teacher] (5) 38	[Teacher] (4) 32	[Teacher] (4) 25
[Name of Hall] 513	Teachers' Resource Room					
[Name of Hall] 516	Water History "Mrs. Alderson"			[Teacher] (4) 28	[Teacher] (5) 31	[Teacher] (4) 19
[Name of Hall] 517	Water Power [Name]		[Teacher] (4) 25	[Teacher] (4) 37	[Teacher] (5) 27	[Teacher] (5) 25
[Name of Hall] 525	Fishy Business [Name]		[Teacher] (5) 27	[Teacher] (4) 32	[Teacher] (4) 27	[Teacher] (4) 27
[Name of Hall] 557	Pollution Solution [Name]		[Teacher] (5) 25	[Teacher] (4) 19	[Teacher] (5) 25	[Teacher] (5) 17
[Name of Hall] 558	Wetland Wonders [Name]			[Teacher] (4) 17	[Teacher] (5) 32	[Teacher] (5) 38
[Outdoor Location]	Weather Station [Name]			[Teacher] (4) 25	[Teacher] (4) 37	[Teacher] (5) 27
[Name of Hall] 568	Hydrologist for a Day [Name]			[Teacher] (5) 27	[Teacher] (4) 17	[Teacher] (5) 31
[Name of Hall] 510	Water Wizards [Name]		[Teacher] (4) 27 [Teacher] (5) 31	[Teacher] (4) 27 [Teacher] (5) 31	[Teacher] (4) 28 [Teacher] (4) 19 [Teacher] (5) 28	[Teacher] (5) 32 [Teacher] (4) 17 [Teacher] (4) 33
Physical Education Building	Exhibit Hall		[Teacher] (4) 17 [Teacher] (4) 19 [Teacher] (5) 32	[Teacher] (5) 25 [Teacher] (5) 32 [Teacher] (5) 28 [Teacher] (5) 19	[Teacher] (4) 25 [Teacher] (5) 38 [Teacher] (4) 34 [Teacher] (5) 19 [Teacher] (4) 33	[Teacher] (4) 37 [Teacher] (4) 28 [Teacher] (5) 26 [Teacher] (4) 32 [Teacher] (4) 34
Etc.	Etc.	Etc.	Etc.	Etc.	Etc.	Etc.

11:30 a.m.	12:00 p.m.	12:30 p.m.	1:00 p.m.	1:30 p.m.	2:00 p.m.	2:30 p.m.	3:00 p.m.
[Teacher] (5) 16		[Teacher] (4) 29	[Teacher] (5) 27	[Teacher] (4) 26	[Teacher] (5) 28		
[Teacher] (4) 33		[Teacher] (4) 18	[Teacher] (5) 17	[Teacher] (4) 15	[Teacher] (4) 17	[Teacher] (4) 26	[Teacher] (5) 29
[Teacher] (4) 20	[Teacher] (4) 33	[Teacher] (4) 19	[Teacher] (4) 27	[Teacher] (5) 28	[Teacher] (5) 26	[Teacher] (4) 15	[Teacher] (4) 26
[Teacher] (4) 23	[Teacher] (4) 20	[Teacher] (4) 30	[Teacher] (5) 24	[Teacher] (5) 26	[Teacher] (5) 25	[Teacher] (5) 30	
[Teacher] (5) 38	[Teacher] (5) 17	[Teacher] (4) 27	[Teacher] (4) 18	[Teacher] (4) 19	[Teacher] (4) 18	[Teacher] (4) 21	
[Teacher] (4) 28	[Teacher] (4) 34	[Teacher] (5) 24	[Teacher] (4) 30	[Teacher] (4) 18	[Teacher] (4) 19	[Teacher] (5) 29	[Teacher] (4) 19
[Teacher] (4) 34		[Teacher] (4) 18	[Teacher] (4) 23	[Teacher] (5) 25	[Teacher] (5) 27	[Teacher] (4) 19	[Teacher] (4) 21
[Teacher] (5) 32	[Teacher] (5) 24	[Teacher] (4) 23	[Teacher] (5) 25	[Teacher] (4) 17	[Teacher] (4) 20	[Teacher] (4) 12	[Teacher] (5) 30
[Teacher] (4) 32 [Teacher] (4) 29	[Teacher] (4) 18 [Teacher] (4) 27	[Teacher] (5) 17 [Teacher] (5) 16	[Teacher] (4) 17 [Teacher] (4) 20	[Teacher] (5) 20 [Teacher] (5) 27	[Teacher] (5) 19 [Teacher] (5) 21	[Teacher] (5) 26 [Teacher] (5) 28	[Teacher] (4) 15 [Teacher] (4) 12
[Teacher] (4) 18 [Teacher] (5) 24 [Teacher] (4) 27 [Teacher] (4) 30 [Teacher] (5) 17	[Teacher] (5) 16 [Teacher] (4) 23 [Teacher] (4) 30 [Teacher] (4) 29	[Teacher] (4) 20 [Teacher] (5) 20 [Teacher] (5) 25 [Teacher] (4) 17 [Teacher] (5) 27	[Teacher] (5) 20 [Teacher] (4) 18 [Teacher] (4) 19 [Teacher] (5) 26 [Teacher] (5) 28	[Teacher] (4) 12 [Teacher] (4) 19 [Teacher] (5) 29 [Teacher] (4) 21 [Teacher] (5) 30	[Teacher] (4) 12 [Teacher] (4) 29 [Teacher] (4) 30 [Teacher] (5) 15 [Teacher] (4) 26	Overflow	Overflow
Etc.	Etc.	Etc.	Etc.	Etc.	Etc.	Etc.	Etc.

Each presenter should also be given a schedule of his/her involvement during the celebration.

Each teacher should be given a schedule of activities for his/her class.

PRESENTER'S SCHEDULE

Dr. Emmett Brown, Water Rappers, Room [name/number]

Time	Teacher/Class
9:00 a.m.	Free time
9:30 a.m.	Mrs. Ernst and Mrs. Emmert (4th & 5th grades)
9:50 a.m.	Break
10:00 a.m.	Mr. Glenn (5th grade)
10:20 a.m.	Break

STUDENT/TEACHER SCHEDULE

Mrs. Ernst, [name of school] Elementary, and Mrs. Emmert, Home School
TOTAL NUMBER OF STUDENTS: 25

Time	Activity	Location
8:30 a.m.	Arrive	[give location, ie., east parking lot]
9:00 a.m.	Water Pumping	[room name/ number]
9:20 a.m.	Break	
9:30 a.m.	Water Rappers	[room name/ number]
9:50 a.m.	Break	
10:00 a.m.	Water Wizards	[room name/ number]
10:20 a.m.	Break	
10:30 a.m.	Exhibit Hall	[room name/ number]
10:50 a.m.	Exhibit Hall	
11:00 a.m.	Exhibit Hall	
11:30 a.m.	Depart	

SCHOOL AND TEACHER, GRADE, NUMBER OF STUDENTS

School & Teacher	Grade	Number of Students
[name of school] Elementary		
Mrs. Ernst	4th	15
Mr. Glenn	5th	35
[name of area] Home Schoolers		
Mrs. Emmert	4th–5th	10

(Keep listing until you have each group accounted for)
TOTAL NUMBER OF STUDENTS: _____
[fill in total number of students]

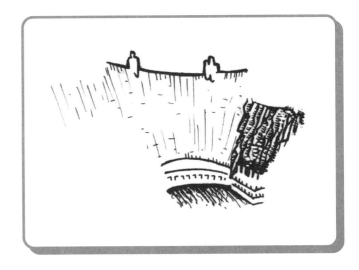

© The Watercourse

E. Games And Contests

All game schedules and rules should be distributed to organizers, participating teachers, and masters of ceremony (hosts) prior to their arrival. Here are sample schedules, host procedures, and ideas for games.

ACTIVITY NAME (e.g., Puddle Pictures, Bucket Brigade, or Water Wizards)	
HOST [name of host, e.g. Mayor Jones] LOCATION [room number/name]	
Time	Activity, Teacher/Class
9:00 a.m.	Free time
9:30 a.m.	Mr. Anderson (4th grade) vs. Mrs. Johnson (4th grade)
9:50 a.m.	Break
10:00 a.m.	Mr. Glenn (5th grade) vs. Mr. Wilton (5th grade)
10:20 a.m.	Break
Etc.	Etc.

Host Procedures

ACTIVITY NAME (e.g., Puddle Pictures, Bucket Brigade, or Water Wizards)

1. Each team has four players on the stage.
2. Introduce yourself and welcome both schools.
3. Explain the rules.
4. Have team captains roll dice to determine starting team.
5. Start game.
6. Have fun!
7. End on time.
8. Congratulate both teams and present prizes/awards.

Water Wizards

Teams

Water Wizard teams consist of four players from each school or group. Some celebrations rotate members through the teams so everyone gets a chance to play; others use the same four players selected by the school in advance for the entire game.

Timekeepers/Scorekeepers

Choose one person from each school. Team members and scorekeepers should be selected by the schools in advance.

Equipment

Water Wizards questions, a die, scorecards (or paper), timer, pencils, small table for scorekeepers, podium for host, chairs for participants.

Game Time

Fifteen minutes.

How to Play

1. Teams take their places and the host reviews the rules. Correct answers are worth 3 points and bonus questions 5 points. If the team answers the question correctly, it receives 3 points and a chance to answer a bonus question. If the team gives the wrong answer, the opposing team has a chance to respond for 3 points. Bonus questions are asked only if the first team of each round answers correctly. Questions are rotated through individuals on the team, but the individual can discuss the answer with his/her teammates. Each team has 1 minute to answer. If no team answers correctly, the host reveals the correct answer.
2. Captains roll the dice; the team with the highest roll goes first (Team #1).
3. The host asks Team #1 the first question. If the question is answered correctly, the team gets 3 points and a chance to answer a bonus question; if not, the host asks the same question of Team #2 for 3 points, but they get no bonus question.
4. The host asks Team #2 the next question first, and play continues.
5. Awards, ribbons, or certificates can be pre-

sented at the end of the game. If more than one school is represented in a group, both schools should receive a certificate or ribbon.

Sample Questions
Game questions and answers should be forwarded to the teachers prior to the celebration so students can practice. Some schools write the questions and answers on opposite sides of note cards so they can use them like flash cards. Plan on having at least 100 water-related questions prepared for the game. Here are a few ideas:

In the water cycle, after precipitation, name two things that can happen to water next.	Evaporate; flow into a stream or lake; enter an aquifer; stay in place as a solid/liquid
What is the correct spelling of the word aquifer?	Aquifer
What is the difference in degrees Fahrenheit between water freezing and boiling?	180 degrees
What mineral is used to recharge water softeners?	Salt
Where is the most famous geyser in the world located?	Yellowstone National Park
What is heavier, a kilogram of water or a kilogram of snow?	They weigh the same
What ocean mammal is known for communicating with "songs"?	Humpback whale
What is the saltiest sea in the world?	Dead Sea
What fruit has water as part of its name?	Watermelon
What medium involves the use of pigment mixed with water?	Watercolor
List two ways you can conserve water in the kitchen?	Efficient dishwasher; using a sinkful of rinse water instead of running water; low-flow aerators on taps; fix leaks; compost food vs. garbage disposal
Give an example of standing surface water.	Lake, pond, swamp, bog, or marsh
Name three of the five oceans of the world.	Atlantic, Pacific, Indian, Arctic, Antarctic
Name two ways the body uses water.	To regulate temperature; remove waste; transport oxygen and food; aid in digestion
Who has the responsibility to protect ground water?	All of us

© The Watercourse

Sample Questions

How long is the Panama Canal?	44 miles
Who was the mythical god of the sea?	Neptune or Poseidon
Explain why even though Earth is three-fourths covered with water, water is often called a limited resource.	Most of Earth is covered with salt water, which cannot be consumed by humans
What is the second leading cause of accidental death in the U.S.?	Drowning
How many gallons of water does it take to produce a hamburger, fries, and a soft drink?	1,500 gallons
What is the chemical symbol for water?	H_2O
What does a fish breathe with?	Gills
Of all Earth's water, what percentage is in the ocean or seas?	97 percent
About how much water should a person consume each day to maintain health?	8 glasses
What happens to the velocity or speed of water in a river when it is channelized?	The speed increases
What were the first water pipes in the U.S. made of?	Logs

Bucket Brigade: A Race!

Teams
Divide each class into two equal teams, each representing a brigade of fire fighters from the 1890s.

Timekeepers/Scorekeepers
Choose one person from each school. Team members and scorekeepers should be selected by the school in advance.

Equipment
Four 30- to 50-gallon trash cans, one 75-foot garden hose and spigot, two stopwatches or watches with second hands, ten 1-gallon buckets (five for each team).

How to Play
1. Have the host explain the components of a municipal fire-fighting system (a source of water, a method for storing enough water to fight a fire, the means to transport water to a fire, an early warning system, and people and equip-ment to fight the fire). Explain that over time, technical advances have drastically improved our ability to fight fires. Review the progression from the bucket brigade to today's sophisti-cated equipment.

2. The goal of each team is to transport the water filling its 30-gallon trash can to an empty trash can placed 75 feet away to try to "extin-guish" the fire by forming a bucket brigade from the "water source" to the "fire."

3. When each team has filled their trash can, the scorekeepers and group members should record answers to the following questions:
· How long did it take the winning team to transport all the water to its trash can?
· How many buckets did each group haul?
· If 1 gallon of water weighs 8.34 pounds, how many pounds of water did each group haul?
· How many gallons of water did each group haul per minute? Per hour?

4. Extensions

Ask two students to represent a 1990s fire-fighting team and ask them to use an outdoor spigot and water hose to move water to the hypothetical fire. One student will turn on the water, and the other will run with the hose to put out the fire.

· How long did it take the 1990s fire fighters to fill the trash can?

· How many gallons of water could the 1990s group deliver per minute? Per hour?

· How much more water did the 1990s fire fighters transport than the 1890s fire fighters per minute? Per hour?

Invite your city fire chief to discuss the relationship between the city fire department and the city water supply.

Contact The Watercourse for additional background information on this activity.

Puddle Pictures

Teams

Puddle Picture Teams consist of four players from each school or group. Some celebrations rotate members through the teams so everyone gets a chance; others use the same four players, selected in advance by the school, for the entire game. NOTE: Puddle Picture words should **not** be distributed in advance.

Timekeepers/Scorekeepers

One person from each school. Team members and scorekeepers should be selected by the schools in advance.

Game Time

Fifteen minutes.

Equipment

Large easel, markers, paper, stopwatch/timer, game cards, score pads, chairs, small table for timekeepers/scorekeepers, and a die.

How to Play

1. Team captains roll die to determine who goes first.

2. A person from Team #1 selects a card from a pile and has one minute to draw a picture that communicates the word to his/her team members. No fair using words, letters, or symbols! If the team correctly identifies the word, it wins 1 point and gets to draw another word.

3. If Team #1 does not identify the word, Team #2 has an opportunity to guess the word. If it does, it wins the point.

4. If Team #1 and Team #2 both miss the word, the school audience from the team that drew the word (in this case Team #1) has an opportunity to shout out the word. If the audience guesses the word, play stays with that team. If it doesn't, play goes to the opposing team. NOTE: Be sure the school audience understands that it may not participate until both teams have been stumped.

Sample Words

The words to be used in competition should not be sent to participating schools, but written on cards for use the day of the game. You may want to send schools a few sample words to get them started, however.

water	duck
puddle	swimming
cloudburst	sea
gallons	surf
rapids	bath
waterbed	lake
liquid	drink
irrigation	skating
snow	wetland
drip	well
icicle	ice cube
water tower	submarine
squirt gun	rainbow
drop	etc.

© The Watercourse

F. Surveys

It is always a good idea to find out how you did by distributing surveys to celebration participants (including students, exhibitors, presenters, and teachers). Here are two sample surveys you may want to build on:

Sample Teachers' Survey

Which presentations did you attend during the day?

How would you rate the presentations you attended [from 1 (poor) to 5 (great)]? (Please rate them individually.)

Which presentation did your class like the best?
Why?

Was the resource room adequate for your needs?

How can we improve the Water Conservation Celebration?

Are there other water resource topics we should add?

If we have a Water Conservation Celebration next year, will you and your class attend?

Other comments:

Sample Students' Survey

What presentation did you like the best at the Water Conservation Celebration?

What exhibit did you like the best?

How would you rate the celebration [from 1 (poor) to 5 (great)]!

List one or more important facts you learned about water conservation at the celebration:

What other topics would you like to learn about?

Case Studies

"...We are all adrift on an intergalactic ocean with limited supplies...among the most essential resources necessary to our survival is our need for fresh water that we drink, use to manufacture materials, flush wastes away, play on, irrigate our vegetables, and are tethered to in a far more fundamental way than we normally realize."

Case Studies and Prediction Problems
Introduction and Procedural Guidelines

Overview

The case study scenarios that follow are taken from real-life situations faced by individuals, industries, cities and towns, ranchers, and even sailors lost at sea. They lend a tangible dimension to the discussion of water conservation. Students and teachers can theorize about issues and conflicts, research statistics, and discuss philosophy, but in real life, economic reality, the force of habit, cultural biases, and self interest intrude to muddy the picture.

These case studies put students in the position of a rancher trying to make a living in the Texas panhandle, of a water authority official responsible for supplying several million users, or of a space shuttle engineering team that determines the role water will play on the voyage. How do you balance conservation philosophy with the economic bottom line? What do you do if you're dying of thirst? How can you save water and maintain the lifestyle you're accustomed to?

The case studies illustrate individual ingenuity, advances in technology, the impact of growing environmental awareness, and the power of commitment to an ideal. Through them, it becomes clear that we are all part of the problem, as well as part of the solution.

By working through the same complexities that face the subjects of these case studies, students experience the difficulties presented by real-life choices on water issues. They experience the process of brainstorming, discussion, research, and documentation to reach conclusions, and are then asked to defend their positions. Along the way, students will need to collect and evaluate evidence to support their decisions, cooperate with their peers to seek solutions, and match theory and philosophy with such realities as economics, environmental responsibility, design limitations, and politics.

The success stories presented here are not meant to imply that nothing more needs to be done. In almost every case, more can be done, or the process can be made more efficient or broadcast more aggressively and holistically. The following examples offer a sampling of efforts that have met with some success, and provide students and teachers with the inspiration to do more.

Embedded in each of the case studies is a prediction problem. The real-life story is interrupted at a certain point, and students are asked to assess the problem as if they were in the shoes of the NASA space shuttle team, the industry official, or the ranch owner. Before students go on to the conclusion of the story, they should work through the process of brainstorming and strategizing ("The Prediction Process") in order to engage themselves in the same dilemma that faced the parties in real life. Teachers should stress that the strategy adopted ("What Really Happened") isn't necessarily the only, or even the best, solution to the problem. There is no such thing, in most cases, as a single correct response. Their own solutions may be as sound and potentially successful as any.

Handling Small Groups

Small-group decision making is the method of choice for these case study problems because that is the process by which decisions are most often made in life (even in the case of a rancher, the family and ranch crew usually collaborate on a plan of action). Small group work can be problematic, however. Motivated students can give other participants a free ride, discussion can be dominated by strong or loud students, and assessment of individual contributions is often difficult.

Teachers will find it important to assign well-defined roles to group participants (spokesperson, recorder, brainstorm leader, etc.) and to rotate these in subsequent case studies. The group's final product or summary should reflect contributions from all members and be the result of an interdependent process. Teachers should circulate and moderate the group interaction, encouraging participation from quiet or shy students, making suggestions to groups that are bogged down, and so on.

Try variations on the group theme to showcase different students' abilities and to help assess individual student contributions. For instance, some case studies lend themselves to role-playing scenarios (using real-life roles such as city commissioner, industry official, environmental lobbyist, etc.), which can bring out issues and perspectives in a lively way. Or, each student in a group could adopt a solution to the case study scenario and defend it in a debate format. Following the debate, the entire class could be asked to rank the choices. Another approach would be to go through the small-group process, but then assign each individual a written summary statement and defense as homework.

The Prediction Process

Follow these steps to respond to the scenarios set up partway through each case study. Students (either as a class or in groups of four to six) should be given adequate time to go through all the steps and make their presentations. They may use the "Case Study Worksheet" to record their work. Some scenarios will require more work at certain stages (Summary and Research, for instance) and less at others. Feel free to adapt the structure to fit individual circumstances.

1. **Summary and Research**. Start by asking the group to summarize the situation, given the information provided. They may find it useful to write a quick list of the salient points. This is also the time to identify other pieces of information that they will need in order to make an informed decision. You may want to allow time for groups to research such things as climate, topography, culture, and so on.

2. **Brainstorm**. Have the students brainstorm possible approaches and solutions to the conservation dilemma. In this phase, no in-depth discussion is allowed, and students should refrain from criticizing any suggestions. Even zany or improbable options are important. Solutions often evolve from the suggestions that seem the least likely at first. One person should record the ideas on the blackboard or a flip chart. Allow the process to continue until all ideas are exhausted.

3. **Narrow Choices.** Discuss strategies with an eye toward narrowing the field to the best two or three options. These may combine elements from the brainstorm list. Encourage students to discuss the rationale behind their positions and to remain open-minded about conflicting points of view. By the end of this discussion, they should have clearly defined one or more possible courses of action.

4. **Evaluation.** Have the students weigh the pros and cons of each strategy. At this stage, students may combine aspects of several options into one or two more comprehensive choices.

5. **Selection.** Have the students choose one option as their recommendation.

6. **Summary and Defense.** Have the students formulate a clear summary of their strategy, identify its strengths and weaknesses, and prepare to defend it. If time allows, ask the group/s to select a spokesperson who can

make a persuasive statement in defense of their recommendation.

After completing the prediction process, have the students read on and discover what really happened. It will be interesting and instructive to compare students' suggestions and strategies with the real-life choices. Your class may develop ideas that weren't even considered, and that might add new dimensions to the whole picture.

The Prediction Process

Follow these steps to respond to the questions raised in "The Prediction Predicament." You will be given adequate time to go through all the steps and make your presentations. Use the "Case Study Worksheet" to record your work. Some scenarios will require more work at certain stages (Summary and Research, for instance) and less at others. Feel free to adapt the structure to fit individual circumstances.

1.   **Summary and Research.** Start by summarizing the situation as a group, given the information provided. You may find it useful to write a quick list of the salient points. This is also the time to identify other pieces of information that you need to make an informed decision. You may want to research such things as climate, topography, culture, and so on.

2.   **Brainstorm.** Discuss and brainstorm possible approaches and solutions to the conservation dilemma. In this phase no in-depth discussion is allowed. Please refrain from criticizing any suggestions. Zany or improbable options are important. Solutions often evolve from the suggestions that seem the least likely at first. One person should record ideas on the blackboard or a flip chart. Continue until all ideas are exhausted.

3.   **Narrow Choices.** Discuss strategies with an eye toward narrowing the field to the best two or three options. These may combine elements from the brainstorm list. Discuss the rationale behind your positions, and remain open-minded about conflicting points of view. By the end of this discussion several clearly defined courses of action will be left.

4.   **Evaluation.** Weigh the pros and cons of each strategy. At this stage, it may be possible to combine aspects of several options into one or two more comprehensive choices.

5.   **Selection.** Choose one option as your recommendation.

6.   **Summary and Defense.** Formulate a clear summary of your strategy, identifying its strengths and weaknesses, and be prepared to defend it. If time allows, select a spokesperson who can make a persuasive statement in defense of your recommendation.

Case Study Worksheet

Use this form to record the evolution of your group decision-making process and to help you refine and clarify your arguments along the way. Some case studies will require several worksheets, one for each question posed. Or the class may be split up, with each group asked to tackle one facet of the overall problem, and may then meet to compare notes at the end of the session.

1. Write a two- to three-sentence summary of the problem, the particular challenge being faced, or the circumstances outlined so far.

2. List any important information you may be able to supply from general knowledge or add through research.

3. After the brainstorming and narrowing procedures, record the handful of possible solutions or responses your group has settled on as the most promising.

4. Once you've processed the options, perhaps combining several responses into a single, more comprehensive one, record the option you've selected.

5. Outline the main points of a defense of your strategy in several sentences or in a list. Briefly explain your reasoning and describe why this solution is superior to those not selected.

Adrift

In 1981, Steven Callahan set off on an ambitious sailing circuit in his 21-foot (6.5-m) cruising sailboat, Napoleon Solo. He planned to sail from his home in New England down to Bermuda, across the Atlantic to England, south along the coast of Spain, and then back west to the Caribbean, circumnavigating the North Atlantic in a boat not much longer than a tandem canoe. For a good part of the trip, he hoped to sail single-handed.

By late January, 1982, he had completed all but the final long leg of this journey. He set off for the Caribbean islands from Tenerife in the Canary Islands (Spain) late in the sailing season. On the night of February 4, the seas were rough and Callahan had settled into an uneasy sleep below deck, wearing little clothing, a wristwatch, and a string necklace with a whale's tooth dangling from it.

Around midnight, he was jolted awake by the sound of a tremendous collision. Ocean water poured in through a gaping hole in the hull. In the pitch black night, Steven was able to climb to the deck, retrieve his survival duffle and a few odds and ends, including some scraps of food and a bit of water, and escape onto an inflatable life raft. Napoleon Solo stayed barely afloat for some time, and Callahan tethered his raft to her, hoping to reboard in daylight and salvage more supplies, but the rough seas severed his ties and set him adrift before dawn.

Callahan's raft was 450 miles (720 km) from the nearest shipping lanes and 1,800 nautical miles from the closest Caribbean island. Besides the small amount of food and water, he had a few critical pieces of equipment. These included a harpoon spear gun, several untested solar stills designed to produce fresh water condensed from seawater, a space blanket, a sleeping bag, a Tupperware container full of notebooks and pencils, several signal flares, some cord, and some general repair and survival gear.

Even under normal circumstances, water conservation is a daily concern for sailors. Water weighs roughly 8 pounds (3.5 kg) per gallon and takes up precious space on board ship. Twenty gallons uses up a significant portion of a sailboat's storage area.

For Callahan, water conservation had changed abruptly from a matter of sailing habit to a matter of survival. Along with his other gear, he had managed to rescue a single gallon of water, an amount that most of us lose down the drain every time we brush our teeth.

In addition, Callahan was exposed to ocean storms, brutal sun, frigid water, inevitable hunger, and other basic obstacles to his survival. He had no idea how long he'd be adrift before he was rescued—or before he met his end.

Stop now and work through the Prediction Predicament

Prediction Predicament

Put yourself in Steven Callahan's shoes (though, actually, his feet were bare) and imagine the challenges you'd face. Ask yourself what some of the questions were foremost in Callahan's mind, and try to come up with your own answers.

Consider these questions:

1.   How long can you survive on a gallon of water? What's the minimum ration you can allow yourself and how long would that make your water supply last?

2.   What other ways can you come up with to collect fresh water, given the materials at hand?

3.   What food could you hope to get, and how would you get it?

4.   What other challenges will almost certainly face you?

5.   Given that you are a sailor with a working knowledge of sea currents and prevailing winds, how would you figure your position? Look at a map marked with ocean currents and wind patterns and try to estimate where your next landfall might be. Any guesses as to how long it will take you to get there?

Refer to the prediction process to answer some or all of these questions. Use the worksheet to record your progress.

What Really Happened...

As it turned out, Callahan spent a staggering 76 days adrift before fishermen rescued him near the tiny Caribbean island of Marie Galante. As you'd expect, his biggest enemies were hunger, thirst, and exposure.

Several times, waves swamped his raft. He fended off repeated shark attacks. Once, Callahan accidentally sliced open one of the inflated tubes as he struggled to subdue a fish he'd speared, and he spent more than a week testing various patches (by which time he was nearly dead from exhaustion) before he got one that held reasonably well. About ten days into the drift Callahan speared his first Dorado (a large fish), and was able to spear fish after that with enough regularity to stave off actual starvation. Even so, he lost 44 pounds (20 kg) in two and a half months.

His battle with the elements and his struggle to maintain his life-support system were constant. He devoted much of his time to pumping up leaky compartments, hunting for fish, and trying to calculate his drift and position. By timing how long it took a floating bobber attached to a string of known length to travel to the end of the line, he approximated his rate of speed. He constructed a crude triangular sextant out of lashed together pencils in order to make sightings on stars.

At first Callahan rationed himself to one-half pint of water per day, a single eight-ounce glass. He couldn't get his solar stills to work at all in the beginning, but by tinkering with them, then fussing over them constantly, he was able to coax a consistent meager output that allowed him to increase his ration to a pint, and sometimes a pint and a half, every day.

During infrequent rainstorms he collected water in the Tupperware container and spread out the space blanket to trap rainwater, thereby adding to his stock. However, in mid-March, the first solar still quit working, and on day 73, his final still was damaged beyond repair.

Nine times during the drift, Callahan spotted ships, several at close range, but none saw his flares or responded to his signals. On the morning of his 76th day, Callahan awoke to the sight of land for the first time since leaving port almost three months earlier. He drifted toward a rough headland, and was making preparations for a difficult landing in surf when he heard an engine.

A small fishing boat with a crew of three men roared up to him. The fishermen were amazed to find a raft with an emaciated figure aboard. They brought him to the local town, where he was treated and later reunited with his family.

The impact responsible for sinking Napoleon Solo on that fateful February night remains a mystery. Callahan's best guess is that it was an accidental collision with a whale, an occurrence that is surprisingly common for small boats at sea.

Callahan's story is told vividly in his book, *Adrift*, published by Houghton Mifflin Company, 1986.

TRP in NYC

By the late 1980s, New York City was entering a water use crisis that had been developing gradually for the two previous decades. Since the 1960s, the city's demand for water supplies had significantly outstripped the dependable yield from its reservoir system. To make matters worse, the wastewater flowing to treatment facilities either approached or exceeded the permitted levels. During the 1980s, three drought warnings or emergencies severely tested New York's water supply and treatment infrastructure.

Historically, New Yorkers have been a particularly thirsty population, consuming as much as 100 gallons per person per day. That number is especially high when you consider that irrigation is a negligible water use in that area.

It became very clear that something had to give. New sources of water had to be developed, new treatment facilities built, and/or the water use habits of the entire city had to radically change. Keep in mind, too, that in the late 1970s, New York City faced the very real threat of municipal bankruptcy. The last thing the taxpayers needed was a whopping water development bill.

A great many options were discussed, including expensive development projects, elaborate leak detection programs, meter-based billing (rather than the traditional flat-rate billing), installation of hydrant locks to curtail the unlawful opening of hydrants on hot days, and more.

One other suggestion was to replace the old, water-hungry toilets and showerheads with more efficient models. Studies showed that roughly 75 percent of household water use was concentrated in bathrooms, and that approximately 350 million gallons per day (MGD) flowed down the toilets of New York City residents. Planners estimated that there were as many as 4.5 million toilets within the city's jurisdiction.

Stop now and work through the Prediction Predicament

Conserve Water! Educators' Guide © The Watercourse

Prediction Predicament

Let's look at the New York City toilets alone—just one facet of the overall plan—and think about what the impact of change and the subsequent problems would be.

Consider these questions:

1. What do you think is a reasonable estimate of the percentage of toilets you can expect to retrofit or replace?

2. How many gallons could you save every day, given the answer to the question above, and assuming that you replace toilets that use 5 gallons per flush with ones that use 1.6 gallons with every flush?

3. How might you motivate the population to embrace the project?

4. What logistical problems do you anticipate along the way?

Refer to the prediction process to answer some or all of these questions. Use the worksheet to record your progress.

What Really Happened...

The mayor of New York City decided, among other measures, to institute a Toilet Rebate Program (TRP) that would actually pay homeowners and apartment building owners to replace their toilets. This water conservation program would be administered through the Department of Environmental Protection. Essentially, the mayor decided it would be cost-effective for the city to issue rebates to property owners who contracted with licensed master plumbers to purchase and install hundreds of thousands of new toilets. Homeowners could claim rebates of up to $240 if they contracted to install low-flow showerheads at the same time. New York was, in effect, buying new water supplies through the conservation savings inherent in the TRP.

In 1994 the program began, first with property owners in the Bronx, then in Manhattan, and by the end of the year, city-wide. Within a year and a half, just under 500,000 toilets had been replaced, with applications in place for some 300,000 more. At that point, water savings had reached about 20 million gallons per day (MGD) and rebates had amounted to a cost of about $90 million.

The program has several side benefits. For one thing, property owners save money on their future water bills by reducing their consumption. Also, local economies (especially the plumbing trade) get a welcome boost in business.

The long-range goal of the TRP is to replace up to 1.5 million toilets and achieve daily water savings of some 90 MGD. Brochures, videos, school programs, and other forms of publicity have been developed to keep promoting the effort.

Cost comparisons between the TRP program and the development of new supply and treatment facilities underscore the advantages of conservation. Although rebates amount to what seems like a lot of money over the years, they add up to less than one-third the estimated cost of expanded supply/treatment facilities. Figures show that the TRP costs about $4 million for every one MGD saved, while expanding supplies and/or building more treatment facilities would cost $12—14 million per one MGD.

The combination of a number of conservation programs (leak detection, metered billing, hydrant locks, TRP, educational programs, etc.) has had a substantial impact on New York's water consumption. Since 1991, the city's water consumption has dropped by about 250 MGD, even through some of the hottest summers on record. Through 1999, all the city wastewater treatment facilities were consistently operating below their permitted levels.

The city continues to pursue some long-range options to increase water supplies and expand treatment facilities, but the earlier pressure caused by the water crisis has dramatically eased. Because of conservation measures like the TRP, New York is no longer struggling with a crisis management situation, but has literally bought itself the time to pursue the best combination of long-range, cost-effective strategies.

One Scoop or Two?

The Friendly's Foodservice Division manufacturing facility in Wilbraham, Massachusetts, supplies over 650 Friendly's Restaurants and a vast number of supermarkets around the country. What do they make? Ice cream! Each year roughly 300 employees at the 350,000 square-foot (31,500 square-meter) facility (one-third of this is storage space) produce 5-10 million gallons of ice cream, frozen yogurt, sherbet, and dessert toppings.

In order to fill those freezers with our favorite flavors, the facility uses 34 million gallons of water each year, which mounts up to an annual water bill of $221,000 in combined water and sewer costs. Add to this the cost of treating wastewater at the plant prior to discharge, and the costs of oil, gas, and electricity used to heat water for certain applications, and the bill more than doubles. As you can see, water conservation would have a significant impact on the operating cost of the Friendly's plant.

Here's how the plant works. Trucks deliver the raw materials required for ice-cream production (milk, condensed milk, cream, liquid sugar, etc.) to 10,000-gallon storage tanks. Following homogenization and pasteurization, the ingredients enter central blending tanks where a base mix of ice cream or yogurt is made. The base mix is then piped to freezing stations where a variety of goodies like chocolate chunks, nuts, and cookie dough are added to create flavors. Each final mixture is packaged in four-gallon cans, half-gallon cartons, and specialty items (sundae cups, pies, cakes, and rolls). The four-gallon cans are hardened for six to eight hours in a -40-degree Fahrenheit freezing tunnel, while the half-gallon cartons are hardened for 90 minutes in a plate freezer. The final product then proceeds to cold storage where it awaits shipping to restaurants and stores.

In addition to ice cream and yogurt, the Friendly's facility whips up a variety of dessert toppings. Items such as whipped topping, fruit sauce, and fudge are created in the Syrup Department. Portions of these tantalizing toppings are sent to the flavoring area where they are added to base mixes of ice cream or yogurt. The rest of the toppings not used for flavoring are prepared for shipping to stores and restaurants.

As you might have guessed, all this ice cream, frozen yogurt, and fudge production can get a little messy! So cleaning and sterilization are both high priorities. Both automated and manual washing play parts in the daily ritual of Friendly's employees. The plant operates four clean-in-place (CIP) automated washing systems. These systems clean in a series of stages, just like a dishwasher. An initial freshwater pre-rinse that removes the large chunks of ice cream left on the equipment is followed by a recovered-water pre-rinse. The wash, post-rinse, and sanitizing stages complete the cycle.

Stop now and work through the Prediction Predicament

Prediction Predicament

Now you've been introduced to the inner workings of this particular ice-cream plant.

Consider these questions:

1. If you were one of the engineering advisors charged with making recommendations for water conservation, what would some of your first recommendations be?

2. What areas of the ice-cream-making process do you suspect use the most water? How might you make cuts to water use in those applications?

Refer to the prediction process to answer some or all of these questions. Use the worksheet to record your progress.

What Really Happened...

As you already know, the Wilbraham plant uses 34 million gallons of water each year to make its delicious desserts, keep the products cold, maintain the cleanliness of the facility, and support the employees in a comfortable environment. The allocation of water is broken down in the chart at the right. As one might suspect, evaporative condensers, which use water for refrigeration, freezing, and air conditioning, consume the most water. Manual and automatic washdown procedures also use a significant amount of water. Together, these two uses account for 48 percent of the 34-million-gallon total. Interestingly, the water used in the product itself is relatively insignificant (just 500 gallons per day). Rather than working with small uses that would not result in significant savings, Friendly's decided to target the largest users in developing its water efficiency measures.

To address these two water consumption areas, the Friendly's plant adopted several efficiency measures, reduced their overall annual usage by 6 million gallons, and cut their water bill by $15,000 in water, sewer, and heating costs. When wastewater treatment conservation is included, the savings jump to $28,000 every year.

Water Use at Friendly's

Uses	Consumption (gal/day)	Consumption (gal/yr)	% of Total
Top Uses			
Evaporative Condensers	32,640	8,160,000	24%
CIP Systems	20,400	5,100,000	15%
Domestic (toilets, etc.)	17,680	4,420,000	13%
Manual Washdown	12,240	3,060,000	9%
Other Uses			
Fudge Heat Exchanger	9,520	2,380,000	7%
Lawn Watering	5,440	1,360,000	4%
Truck Washing	4,080	1,020,000	3%
Evaporative-Condenser Bleed	4,080	1,020,000	3%
Can Washer	2,720	680,000	2%
Homogenizer Piston Cooling	2,720	680,000	2%
Main-Filter Backwash	2,720	680,000	2%
Water Added to Product	500	125,000	0%
Miscellaneous	21,760	5,440,000	16%
TOTAL		34,125,000	100%

What Really Happened...continued

First, Friendly's decided to look at its flavor sequencing pattern in order to maintain maximum productivity and minimal need for thorough washing. For example, if a chocolate-based flavor was run, the equipment would have to be thoroughly cleaned before running a vanilla-based flavor. Otherwise, you run the risk of discoloring and tainting the vanilla product. Under the new ordering scheme, flavors like chocolate marshmallow are run after flavors like mint chocolate chip and chocolate chip cookie dough whenever possible. Only minimal cleaning is necessary between these flavors.

Second, Friendly's took measures to improve the efficiency of its automated washers, or CIP systems. Under the old system, several long stretches of pipe were washed twice. Reprogramming the CIP to eliminate duplicate washings saved 7,000 gallons of water every day. This amounted to a financial saving of $11,000 every year in water and chemicals. Additionally, the CIP systems were programmed for worst-case scenarios, or for the dirtiest conditions possible. By measuring water conductivity to assess purity, the water conservation team found that items were often adequately washed and rinsed before the end of the cycles. The team recommended shortening the cycles.

Also, in wash stages and some rinse stages that used recirculated (recovered) water, the water was often discharged before its cleaning potential was exhausted. By installing a series of pH-monitoring sensors in the CIP system, Friendly's was able to measure more precisely when water was used up in terms of its cleaning potential. This saved another 3,500 gallons of water every day—an annual savings of $5,460 in water and chemical costs.

Finally, Friendly's decided to fit more actual production time into each day by adding a third shift to make the Half-Gallon Department a 24-hour operation. The basis and stipulations on how long Friendly's production could run before a cleaning was based on USDA regulations. Formerly, the department would shut down and clean up every day after the two shifts. A full-time production schedule avoided the daily interruptions in production and, if no changes in flavor are scheduled, the department can feasibly run for days without breaks for the water-guzzling washdowns and still adhere to USDA regulations. As a result, the CIP runs were reduced from six to three per week, saving 2,250 gallons of water every week (120,000/year). Financial savings are estimated at $5,700 per year. An added benefit of the shift addition is that it cuts the need for storage, since the plant can produce more product on shorter notice.

Once these three changes were instituted throughout the plant, Friendly's was able to reduce water use to 28 million gallons a year, down 6 million gallons.

As in any business venture, the cost of conservation measures has to be figured into overall financial efficiency. It cost money to reprogram the CIP controls, to add pH sensors to the system, and to re-pipe some ice-cream transport lines. It also cost money to add a third shift and to resequence the order of ice-cream flavor production.

Friendly's had to study the "payback" of these measures, or assess the estimated costs against the potential savings. For example, consider the CIP system adjustments. The total estimated savings in water and chemical costs after reprogramming the CIP and adding pH probes came to $16,460. Reprogramming costs were estimated at $3,000 for the three CIP systems. Installing the pH sensors and tying them into the central controls would cost $8,000 for all three CIP. The total system adjustments come to

© The Watercourse

What Really Happened...continued

$11,000. The payback for these water conservation measures is figured by dividing the cost by the annual savings—$11,000/$16,460 or 0.67 years (eight months). In other words, the savings would exceed the costs after eight months.

Keep in mind that taking these measures involves a one-time expense, while the savings continue to be realized year after year. Once the savings pay for the initial cost, the investment is making a profit. The resulting manufacturing gains from these changes were major.

Next time you bite into an ice-cream cone, you might think about the teamwork, resourcefulness, and creativity involved in saving water in an industrial setting!

Thanks to Marsha Gorden and Scott Craig at the Massachusetts Water Resources Authority, and to Christine Castonguay at Friendly's, for providing the first draft of this case study.

Water Trouble on the High Plains

Since the mid-1940s, around the end of World War II, farmers and other water users on the Texas High Plains have been mining the underground water stored in the vast Ogallala Aquifer. Hydrologists say an aquifer is being mined when water is withdrawn faster than it can be recharged. The Ogallala, in fact, underlies much of the High Plains ecosystem in several western states and has been heavily tapped for irrigation water.

Back then, the dominant irrigation method was furrow (or flood) distribution, where water is directed through ditches—or underground pipeline—and surface gated pipe, and released to flow throughout a field by gravity. Maintaining an even distribution of water through surface irrigation is nearly impossible, and average efficiency ratings achieved with flood irrigation top out at only 50-60 percent.

These inefficient parameters could be tolerated as long as the ground water supply remained adequate. Although ground water depletion began with the onset of widespread pumping, the Ogallala Aquifer withstood the incredible demand on its supplies for decades. By the mid-1970s it had become clear, however, particularly in the southern Texas plains, that the supply was disappearing.

Estimates confirmed, in fact, that some 40 percent of the region's ground water supply had been mined without being replenished. Most wells were producing less than half what they had yielded in the past. The resulting inadequate irrigation translated into poor crop yields.

Some farmers reacted to the problem by investing in more efficient center-pivot sprinkler irrigation systems. These sprinklers rotate across fields and spray water under high pressure in an even pattern over crops. However, pivot irrigation has its problems, too. To start with, the initial expense and continuing energy costs are high.

Even more problematic, the climate in the High Plains region is one characterized by high winds, low humidity, and intense summer heat. Much of the water sprayed into the air was lost to evaporation or blown away by winds. When winds blow at 20 miles per hour (32 km)—and these wind speeds are quite common—evaporation losses climbed to more than 30 percent!

Stop now and work through the Prediction Predicament

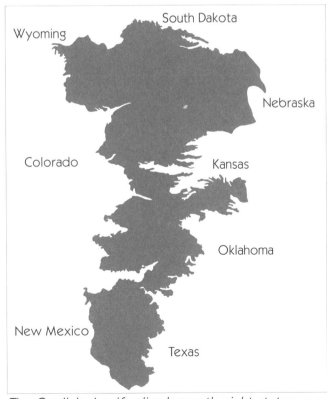

The Ogallala Aquifer lies beneath eight states.

Prediction Predicament

If your job was to give these Texas farmers helpful advice, what would your suggestions be?

1. Should they move away and change careers, or can you think of some things they might try first?

2. Think about all aspects of the picture, from crop selection to water technology, when you come up with your recommendations.

Refer to the prediction process to answer some or all of these questions. Use the worksheet to record your progress.

What Really Happened...

Researchers at the Texas A & M University Agricultural Experiment Station understood well that they were dealing with a water crisis. It had already forced some people to change their farming practices, forced others to another location, and it threatened many more with the same fate.

In the face of that reality, they developed technology known as Low Energy Precision Application (LEPA). It uses the overhead pipeline, just as the traditional high-pressure center-pivot sprinklers do, but instead of shooting water out under great pressure, LEPA uses drop tubes with special applicator devices that deposit water on or near ground level in alternating furrows. LEPA requires minimum water pressure (usually only 4-6 psi at the end of the pipeline) while overhead sprayers require 30 psi or more. Water is discharged so close to the soil surface that it has a minimal chance of evaporating or being blown away in the wind. The alternate furrow placement greatly reduces soil surface evaporation of water.

The LEPA concept is tied to a holistic management picture that encourages farmers to manage their soil and vegetation to maximize the soil's ability to store water, thereby reducing runoff and erosion. Pivot speeds are set to ensure that the water volume doesn't exceed the soil storage capacity and lead to waterlogging or runoff. Careful consideration was given to nozzle spacing, crop row orientation (to avoid erosion and runoff), and the rigidity of the drop hoses (to reduce the effects of wind).

Results have been impressive. Application efficiency with LEPA rose to 96-99 percent (remember, surface irrigation only managed 50-60 percent). Crops responded to the uniform application of water with significantly higher yields. A three-year study of cotton yields in Lamesa, Texas, for example, documented an average increased yield of 12.9 percent over traditional spray irrigated crops. Increased yields of 20-30 percent have been reported. Increased profits on crops can be applied to pay off a LEPA sprinkler system in as little as one year's time.

When LEPA is coupled with careful "basin" tillage, which traps runoff (either rain or irrigation water), retention of water in the soil and an improved crop yield will result.

In dry climates, like that in much of the High Plains region, benefits to farmers from LEPA technology (and other practices) are significant. Farmers feel the relief with markedly lower energy expenses and more efficient water application.

Perhaps even more important, there is a chance to reduce demand on the Ogallala Aquifer, and to make strides toward the long-term goal of letting the ground water supply recharge itself.

LEPA system

What Really Happened, continued

Examples of LEPA Systems in Use

Precise application of water characterizes LEPA technology.

Furrow irrigation reduces soil surface evaporation.

Drop tubes with special applicators deposit water on or near ground level.

PHOTOGRAPHS COURTESY OF TEXAS A & M UNIVERSITY AGRICULTURAL EXPERIMENT STATION

Operation Water Sense

Consider yourself a board member for the newly created Massachusetts Water Resource Authority (MWRA). The year is 1985. The Massachusetts legislature has handed you the responsibility for maintaining and preserving the water supply for the city of Boston and its metropolitan area. The area encompasses 45 towns and cities with a stable population of more than 2 million people.

It is a critical moment. The water system has been chronically underfunded, largely ignored, and taken for granted for decades. Citizens, experts, and officials have been raising serious concerns over the region's water supply and water quality for more than fifteen years. Among other things, the MWRA faces the burden of constructing a new wastewater treatment facility at a cost of some $4 billion.

Your main concern, however, is with water supply. For many years, the Boston metropolitan area has depended on several large reservoirs—the Quabbin and Wachusett in the central part of the state, connected to the city by aqueducts. The problem is this: though the reservoirs can safely supply 300 million gallons per day (MGD) on a long-term basis, demand has consistently outstripped that level since the mid-1960s. In 1980, for example, demand exceeded 340 million gallons per day. In effect, for twenty years the region has lived on borrowed time (and water) and has gotten away with it. It can't last, however. Sooner or later a prolonged period of drought or increased demand will saddle the region with an unavoidable crisis.

You and your fellow board members must choose between two options: one would increase your water supplies, the other would decrease the demand.

Increasing Supply:

In the 1960s, the Army Corps of Engineers developed plans to divert a large portion of the Connecticut River in western Massachusetts into the reservoirs, which would augment supplies by several hundred million gallons per day. The project would involve dams and a system of aqueducts, canals, or pipes, and long-term maintenance. Construction costs were estimated to run to $118 million (1985 dollars).

Environmental groups protested vehemently that such massive diversions will radically alter habitat, threaten wildlife species with extinction, shrink wetlands, and create a host of unexpected problems. Downstream users, notably the state of Connecticut, have also expressed strong opposition.

Still, the Boston area's thirst is an undeniable long-term need that won't go away. The Connecticut River is the only reasonably accessible source for such a large quantity of water. If increased supply is the strategy, the Connecticut is the logical source. Once the diversion project is completed, the water supply crisis will be over, at least for the foreseeable future.

Decreasing Demand:

The only way to decrease demand would be to institute conservation measures to the tune of 50—100 million gallons every day, and to make that level of savings permanent. It would be like asking a city to go on a permanent crash water diet.

The major components of a water conservation scheme of this magnitude would include:

1.   Leak detection and repair. The antiquated delivery system for greater Boston's water is notoriously decayed and full of holes. Estimates

Overview, continued

of losses range as high as 50 percent for some sections.

2. Industry audits aimed at the many factories, hospitals, universities, and other large institutions in the area.

3. Residential programs that will educate homeowners and provide them with water-saving devices.

4. A system of pricing that will reflect the true value of water and address the costs of the conservation effort. A homeowner who now pays $70 per year for water might end up paying $700 per year by 1995. Substantial rate increases are already certain in view of the costs of the new wastewater treatment project.

You and your fellow board members must now evaluate the pros and cons of both options. Although costs for the conservation program would initially be much less than the river diversion option (estimates you've come up with run about $30 million), the logistical challenge of coordinating the various aspects of the campaign are daunting, and there is no guarantee that conservation alone will solve the problem. There is a real risk that, after years of effort and millions of dollars spent, you could end up back where you are now, still needing to increase supplies.

Stop now and work through the Prediction Predicament

Prediction Predicament

As a class or in small groups, discuss the MWRA's quandary in an effort to define what you think would be the best strategy for dealing with their water supply.

Address the following issues:

1. What else do you need to know to make an informed decision?

2. What are some short-term costs and benefits for each option?

3. What are some long-term costs and benefits for each option?

4. Can you come up with other strategies to address the water supply dilemma facing Boston?

5. Extend the scenario out 10 or 20 years and predict the concerns and issues the city will face then.

6. What things might you do now to mitigate these long-range concerns?

Refer to the prediction process to answer some or all of these questions. Use the worksheet to record your progress.

At the end of the session, select a spokesperson for the class or each small group can present the strategy as if you are the MWRA board addressing the city of Boston.

What Really Happened...

When the MWRA assumed responsibility for greater Boston's water supply, they inherited a system that had been ignored and neglected for decades.

Their first job was to make an assessment of the situation, of their available resources, and of their realistic options. After much discussion, they decided to pursue a rigorous conservation program. The river diversion, they concluded, would cost too much initially and would be fraught with environmental controversy and battles over water appropriation.

By 1987, they were ready to begin the conservation push. They had established a full-time staff of a dozen employees to work on it. Their strategy was four-pronged:

1.   A leak detection program using sophisticated listening instruments, followed by repair of all the leaks.

2.   Industry education, audits, and improvements in overall efficiency.

3.   Residential retrofitting, more sophisticated home metering, and general education.

4.   A pricing regime that included dramatic increases to cover the costs of rehabilitating the water and wastewater treatment system and to pay for the conservation campaign.

Impressive results were achieved almost immediately. Leak control alone, by 1989, had reduced water usage by some 35 million gallons per day.

Workshops and free audits of industries and large institutions encouraged the use of more efficient equipment, recirculation of water, and increased user awareness of the need for conservation. The Gillette Company's plant in Boston cut its water use by more than half simply by installing a recirculation system. Many other large water users achieved similar results.

Within several years, industrial and institutional users were contributing another 10 million gallons per day in savings. In another important demographic trend, office buildings were replacing industries known for their heavy demands on water supplies. Over the past decade, this trend has provided another 5—10 million gallons a day in savings.

The MWRA invested a great deal in public education. They had presentations at schools and workshops in communities; they developed activities for teachers and sent brochures with residential water bills. They have now established a home page on the Internet.

The MWRA also began a program called Operation Water Sense, which, in addition to serving an educational function, began to retrofit residences with toilet dams, aerated faucets, and efficient showerheads. Using contracted labor, Operation Water Sense contacted and upgraded some 400,000 residences. This project saved an additional 5—8 million gallons per day. Largely as a result of the education drive, the Massachusetts State Plumbing Board set a new industry standard nationwide for toilets that use 1.6 gallons per flush (traditional toilets use 5 gallons).

COURTESY OF MWRA

What Really Happened...continued

The entire MWRA project cost has been covered by increased rates charged to water users. Water and sewer bills have increased tenfold in the last decade, bringing water costs up to the approximate level of home energy expenses, inevitably, incurring the wrath of water users.

Higher rates, however, have proven to be the single most effective incentive for adopting water conservation practices. The fact is that when bank accounts are noticeably affected, people pay attention.

By 1989, the MWRA district had dropped water demand to 285 million gallons per day. In 1996, the figure was roughly 255 million. MWRA officials predict that water use will plateau at about 250 million gallons per day, substantially below the magic 300-million-gallon figure. Unless the region's population grows substantially (which planners say is unlikely), supplies will be adequate to meet demand. As a side benefit, reduced water consumption has relieved the pressure on the wastewater treatment facility, saving millions of dollars.

For the time being, the MWRA has reduced its water conservation staff to three. The board has formulated a 20-year, $2 billion master plan that concentrates on repairing and constructing major aqueducts, expanding water treatment facilities, replacing old and decrepit water mains, and installing a modern metering system that will make the water-monitoring process much more accurate and useful.

Native Landscapes

In 1977, Denver, Colorado faced severe drought conditions that threatened to cause citywide water shortages. The Denver Water Board—a committee of five appointed by the Mayor of Denver to oversee water distribution—was charged with developing an appropriate response to the potential water emergency. The Board decided to issue a mandate to control water consumption while drought conditions continued. All water users in the area served by Denver Water—urban, commercial, recreational, rural, and industrial— were subject to the mandate.

Before implementing the mandate, the Denver Water Board studied citywide water use and predicted that lawn-watering would again place a great demand on water supplies during the summer months when annual water use reached its peak. Based on its study, the Board developed simple guidelines to address the impending water shortage. The resulting mandate stipulated that Denver Water users—some 840,000 customers—could only water lawns every third day for three hours. A steep fine was set as a penalty for violating the mandate. In addition, water users were asked to be mindfully sparing in all their other water uses.

The mandate successfully carried Denver through the drought period. However, Denver's water reserves had fallen below normal during the drought, and water users supplied by Denver Water had resumed their normal pattern of water consumption as soon as the mandate was lifted. The Water Board realized that further action would be necessary to maintain adequate water supplies for the immediate future.

The city of Denver sits a mile above sea level on the high plains east of the Continental Divide. The Rocky Mountains rise above Denver in the west and the Great Plains roll away to the east. Snow blankets the high peaks of the Rockies most months of the year, and several major waterways have their headwaters in Colorado, including the Rio Grande, Colorado, and Arkansas rivers. Though seemingly rich in water resources, Denver's climate is considered semi-arid. The average precipitation is just over 14 inches a year (about one-third of the average precipitation that most cities east of the Mississippi receive in a year) and the humidity is very low.

Again the Water Board was faced with the ongoing water shortage dilemma. This time, they focused on ways to increase the water supply, and two options emerged. The first was to build a larger holding dam on the river, to be paid for by raising water use rates. The new dam would enlarge water storage capacity and effectively increase water reserves. Though this option would satisfy the need to increase the water supply quickly, it was met with opposition. Several citizens' groups protested the dam, citing its potential financial and environmental impacts. Also, many water users remained unconvinced that the threat of water shortage was real and imminent. In the face of such opposition, the Water Board decided to consider another option to increase the water supply.

Option two was to build a larger water treatment plant. This option also would increase the water supply immediately, but as Denver's population grew, the treatment plant would require continual expansion. The cost of such construction would be borne by taxpayers. As a short-term solution, this appeared to be a fairly cost-effective alternative, but as a long-term solution, it did not.

The Board concluded that increasing the water

supply was not the solution. They refocused their attention on conserving the supply of existing water.

The Denver Water Board faced several big tasks, including convincing the public that it was necessary to use water more efficiently. In this, the Board faced the same problems many city water planners face—how to encourage citizens to manage their own water use.

Stop now and work through the Prediction Predicament

Prediction Predicament

You collectively form the Denver Water Board. You know first-hand the threat that Denver faces. Your responsibility as a board is to ensure that Denver Water users have adequate water for years to come. What are some of the dilemmas you might face, and which of these do you consider to be the most critical?

In addition, consider the following questions:

1. What mandates would you develop to address the immediate water shortage? Would these mandates also remedy a long-term shortage? Why or why not? Consider examples of other water conservation mandates set in times of water crisis. (Note: Water crises may be brought on by floods as well as drought conditions.)

2. To address the possibility of a long-term water shortage, you and the members of your board must develop water conservation measures. How would you encourage Denver Water users to adopt these measures? How would you implement a voluntary conservation program?

3. What other short-term/long-term options would you recommend for Denver Water users?

Refer to the prediction process to answer some or all of these questions. Use the worksheet to record your progress.

What Really Happened...

The Denver Water Board decided not to impose further mandates to control water consumption. Instead, the Board implemented an education and incentive program to teach and encourage Denver Water users to manage their own water use. The Board intended to use the program to help water users understand why conservation was important and how each water user could influence future water availability. This option had the potential to successfully address a long-term water shortage, and would give the people of Denver the tools to help themselves conserve their own water.

Denver Water—the staff working under the directive of the Water Board—launched an education campaign that began by pinpointing Denver's water consumption dilemmas. Lawn-watering was again identified as a water use that placed the greatest demand on water supplies during the peak use months of spring and summer.

Under this premise, Denver Water developed a campaign based on conservation landscaping. They coined a term—Xeriscape™—from the Greek word *xeros* meaning dry. Xeriscape is based on the principle of planting regionally native plants or vegetation that is well-adapted to the local climate. To demonstrate conservation landscaping's potential, Denver Water built a Xeriscape garden. Dedicated in 1981, the garden served Denver Water as a place for public education and community involvement. Local landscape architects and contractors helped to build and maintain the garden, while Denver Water provided community tours and social events within the 200 x 35 foot Xeriscaped area.

The Water Board held Xeriscape contests. Homeowners, artists, painters, landscapers, and others entered. Winners received cash prizes and were featured, along with their award-winning Xeriscaped lawns, in the newspaper and on radio programs.

From the beginning, the Xeriscape program was designed to be applicable in diverse areas. It was not simply a list of plants for Colorado, but a set of "seven principles for intelligent horticulture" that could easily be applied in all climates, all topographies. The seven principles are:

1. Plan and Design . . . for conservation and beauty from the start
2. Create Practical Turf Areas . . . to make manageable sizes and shapes of lawn areas
3. Select Low Water Requiring Plants . . . and group plants with similar water demands
4. Use Soil Amendments . . . like compost or manure
5. Use Mulches . . . like woodchips to reduce evaporation and keep the soil cool
6. Irrigate Efficiently . . . by using properly designed irrigation systems
7. Maintain the Landscape Properly . . . by mowing, weeding, pruning, and fertilizing

The Xeriscape program was a success from the start. In the decade after it was introduced, population in the Denver area increased steadily but water use remained relatively stable. Education and incentive programs proved effective as a means of promoting conservation awareness and voluntary self-regulation of water consumption. According to phone surveys of Denver Water customers, 26 percent reported using Xeriscaping in their landscaped lawns.

The principles of conservation landscaping have spread far beyond their original Denver Water boundaries, and have been adopted and adapted on a global scale. In 1983, shortly after the dedication of the first Xeriscape garden, the state of California established its own Xeriscape program with conferences, education programs, and gardens. Soon after, Texas, Florida, Massachusetts, Georgia, and Utah established conservation landscaping programs.

What Really Happened...continued

Internationally, in 1997, the province of Saskatchewan, Canada released *Creating the Prairie Xeriscape* to promote water conservation landscaping, and in 1998, Spain began plans for a Xeriscape demonstration garden.

To date, the Denver Water Board has successfully maintained water availability for all Denver Water users, and has bought itself the time to continue researching and planning for future water needs.

Examples of Xeriscape gardens.

PHOTOGRAPHS COURTESY OF DENVER WATER

Planning With Vision

Back in 1961, the Irvine Ranch Water District (IRWD) was a sleepy agricultural enclave in southern California's Orange County, serving some 300 residents. Even then, though, people knew that change was coming; substantial growth was inevitable. By 1972, the populace had grown to 14,500 and predictions estimated a population as high as 300,000 by the year 2000!

Southern California is a region so dry and so populous that it can't supply its own needs for water. Roughly half the area's water is imported, mostly from the Colorado River. Despite that fact, water conservation was not a real topic of conversation a generation ago, even in semiarid California. Luckily, planners at the IRWD were ahead of their time.

Communities were traditionally set up with separate water and sewage districts. Water was used once, sent to the treatment facility, then piped directly into the ocean. Had the IRWD chosen to set up a water system similar to those in other communities, they would have paid between $38 and $58 million for discharge pipes alone, even in the '60s.

Nowadays the IRWD encompasses about 77,950 acres (31,558 ha) and includes the city of Irvine and the University of California at Irvine. The IRWD has been touted as a showcase of forward-thinking water conservation practices (ironically, it is one of the lushest spots in the area), due to the planning decisions made by a handful of experts more than 30 years ago.

Stop now and work through the Prediction Predicament

Prediction Predicament

Put yourself in the position of the planners who oversaw the IRWD when the area was just beginning to see its population grow. In many ways you can start fresh. There is no existing system that has to be reworked or replaced. The residents are few and scattered. You are free to look ahead and plan for a crowded future with high demands for water (and high levels of wastewater).

Consider the following questions:

1. What are your thoughts on how to supply water and get rid of wastes?

2. What steps would you recommend to facilitate the planning process?

Refer to the prediction process to answer some or all of these questions. Use the worksheet to record your progress.

What Really Happened...

The single most important aspect of the IRWD's plan was to depart from the tradition of separating the water and sewer districts. By combining the two, they were able to consider the entire supply/use/treatment/discharge cycle as a single entity. The real key to their success, however, was the fact that Irvine was a master planned community in which reclaimed water was designed in from the beginning. Rather than seeing wastewater as something to be disposed of, IRWD saw wastewater as a resource in a drought-prone area.

The IRWD realized that reclaimed water that received tertiary treatment was pure enough to qualify for irrigation use. Instead of footing a whopping bill for sending treated wastewater into the Pacific, they saw that with additional treatment, they could pipe it to farmers, parks, and other large irrigators who would be happy to pay less for their supply (90 percent of the cost of fresh irrigation water).

To facilitate their plan, the IRWD became the first water agency in California to obtain a "producer-primary user permit" from the Department of Health, which allowed them to reuse and resell treated wastewater. Now the district could sell reclaimed water directly to users, rather than having each user pursue a separate permit from government officials.

Reclaimed water is distributed to users from the IRWD's Michelson Water Reclamation Plant. After treatment at the plant, the reclaimed water is ready to be used for irrigation and other purposes in the community, or it can be sent to storage in one of several reservoirs constructed for this purpose. In the summer time when demands are highest, reclaimed water is distributed directly from the plant to the farmers, parks, and other large irrigators. In the cooler months, some of the final effluent is sent to storage. The IRWD has two open (lake-type) reservoirs and six enclosed (tank-type) reservoirs for reclaimed water. These storage

facilities are in addition to 15 enclosed drinking water reservoirs that are completely separate.

Reclaimed water used for irrigation actually acts as a fertilizer, so it saves farmers money in fertilizer and mineral applications. The water's relatively high levels of nitrogen and phosphorus, for example, have translated into a fertilizer value of roughly $120 per acre per year. And, purchasing reclaimed water from the IRWD rather than importing it from the Colorado River saves farmers another $140 per acre-foot per year. As a result, reclaimed water is in high demand.

The IRWD also uses reclaimed water to water golf courses, city parks, school grounds, and some residential areas at a similar savings. The growing public clamor for reclaimed water is a testimony to the IRWD's success. Since 1991, office buildings, commercial sites, and high-rises have been hooked up to reclaimed water for use in toilets and urinals, and have reduced their fresh water use by as much as 70 percent.

The decision to combine water and sewer districts influenced the many smaller choices that came with growth. New subdivisions were constructed with dual piping systems, one for fresh water and another for reclaimed water. Industries building in the area faced restrictions on the hard-to-remove contaminants they could send through the sewage pipes.

Today, the dual distribution system is extensive. There are over 300 miles of pipelines that carry reclaimed water to the various users in the district, and 900 miles of drinking water pipelines.

Since instituting the water recycling program, the IRWD has cut back on the amount of water it imports each year by more than 10,000 acre-feet. To boost these efforts, the Metropolitan Water District pays a $154 rebate for every acre-foot of reclaimed water it buys from the

What Really Happened...continued

IRWD. Those sales earn the IRWD roughly $1.5 million a year.

Most of the rest of southern California (and the rest of the United States, for that matter) is subject to the threat of water quotas and shortages during times of drought or water stress. The IRWD is sitting on a 15-million-gallon-per-day buffer of reclaimed water that no one can turn off! Future plans call for supplying as much as 33 million gallons of reclaimed water a day.

Pumps like these transport reclaimed water from the plant into 300 miles of reclaimed water pipelines.

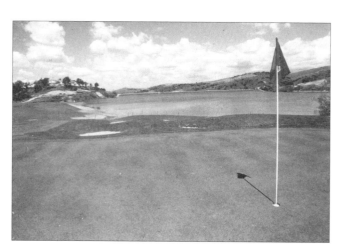

Reclaimed water is now used to irrigate golf courses (above) and to flush toilets in office buildings (below) in Irvine.

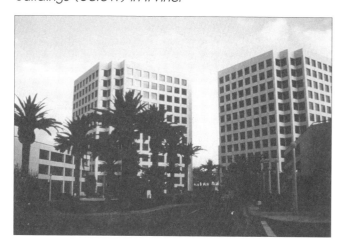

PHOTOGRAPHS COURTESY OF IRVINE RANCH WATER DISTRICT

Used Up Country

When the Weatherly family bought 250 acres (101 ha) of the Texas panhandle in 1968, the neighbors probably thought they were a little bit crazy. It was sand hill country, land that had been farmed intensively in cotton and milo for decades. It had been hit hard during the Dust Bowl and Depression years of the 1930s.

"It was farmed-out land," admits Joe Weatherly. "Pretty much abandoned, used-up country."

Once the land was theirs, the family had some choices to make. The overriding concern was what direction to take their new property in.

The Weatherly family could have gone in one of several directions.

1. They could continue using fertilizers and pesticides along with irrigation water at current levels, and hope crop prices would be high enough to cover their expenses (equipment, cost of planting, harvesting, and shipping to market).

2. They could leave the land as it was and stock it with the number of cattle it would support.

3. They could treat it as a simple investment property and hope that the land value appreciated.

4. They could risk an additional investment of money and energy in restoring the "used-up country," in hopes that it might come back to some semblance of its historic health and perhaps become viable farm/ranch country again on a sustainable basis.

Stop now and work through the Prediction Predicament

Texas Panhandle in the Dust Bowl years.

COURTESY OF PANHANDLE-PLAINS HISTORICAL MUSEUM

Prediction Predicament

As you work through the case study, address the following:

1. If you were in the Weatherly's situation, what would you want to do?

2. Sketch out the pros and cons of each of the possible courses of action, considering the investment concerns, farming future, and environmental impacts.

3. Discuss both the short-term and long-term merits and pitfalls of each option. Remember to weigh ethical and personal concerns alongside the economic bottom line.

4. The best of all worlds would unite ethics and financial success, but is that always possible?

Refer to the prediction process to answer some or all of these questions. Use the worksheet to record your progress.

What Really Happened...

Joe Weatherly had a vision for his new property. He knew that beneath the overgrazed, overworked, eroded surface of the land lay the potential for ranchland rich with vegetation and wildlife. Plenty of surface and ground water existed to support a ranching endeavor—a land that could be both beautiful and profitable. Joe envisioned a landscape that had existed there for millennia before settlement and farming impacted the region in the early part of the twentieth century. The question was, could Joe and his family bring it back?

First off, the Weatherlys decided that grazing cattle would be the best use of the property. Crops were simply too hard on the land and required too great an investment of pesticides, fertilizers, and water.

Water is always the major concern in that semi-arid region. Right from the start, the Weatherlys committed themselves to capturing what surface runoff they could, reusing water where possible, and streamlining the efficiency of their operation so they didn't have to deplete the ground water supply any more than necessary.

The centerpiece of the Weatherly family's water conservation program is a system of manmade collection ponds situated strategically across the property to capture runoff and wastewater; those are connected by a series of pipes. By the time water reaches a final reservoir, solid wastes have settled out, and the water is pure enough to irrigate the crops grown to augment the grazing forage for cattle. The ranch employs two center-pivot irrigation systems. Some water that can't be channeled by gravity alone is pumped back to the central reservoir.

Supplying the stock tanks in the feedlot once demanded the full-time work of two ground water pumps. More recently, the Weatherlys have installed two large storage tanks at the highest elevation of the feedlot. These release a constant trickle of fresh water. A float automatically shuts off the pumps when the tanks are full. The use of storage tanks has cut the need to pump ground water by 50 percent, and has saved roughly $8,000 per year in energy costs. Water savings under the new system amount to 111,000,000 gallons every year.

The family cleans accumulated animal wastes from pens and reservoirs and spreads them on the fields as natural fertilizer to increase productivity. The same land that produced 40 pounds (18 kg) of beef per acre (half-hectare) in 1968 now produces 1,500 to 2,000 pounds (675 to 900 kg) per acre (half-hectare), a productivity leap of more than 40 times in less than 30 years.

"Compared to just about any crop you can name, that's a pretty good return," says Weatherly.

Over the decades, that used-up, worn-out landscape has been transformed into a 6,000-acre (2,429-ha) oasis of lush grassland, wildlife sanctuary, and productive ground. The Weatherlys have elected to set aside roughly 1,000 acres as wild land. There, wild turkeys, white-tailed deer, porcupines, bobcats, and many other species thrive on the same land that was barren, overworked, and stripped of its life-giving water only a generation ago.

"Somebody driving through the other day said that our place was the only spot of green

What Really Happened...continued

between Amarillo and Oklahoma City," Weatherly says. "Looking east out my office window, I can see probably 300 cattle grazing on 120 acres. What I'm most proud of," he concludes, "is that we've taken what people often see as waste products—wastewater and animal waste—and turned them into a profitable operation."

Collection pond.

Productive grassland.

Runoff and wastewater are collected in manmade collection ponds on the Weatherly's property.

Center-pivot irrigation system.

PHOTOGRAPHS COURTESY OF THE WEATHERLY FAMILY

The Problem With Silt

In 1994 and 1995, city planners in Louisville, Kentucky, were playing the juggling game that all urban officials are saddled with—trying to match inadequate funds and personnel to burgeoning municipal demands. The issue of the day involved Riverside Park, a strip of land along the Ohio River that they hoped to upgrade to an attractive and highly visible community resource.

Their funds were, of course, limited, and the maintenance staff consisted of only a few full-time employees. They had enough money to hire a landscaping/irrigation firm to establish the site, but could provide only minimal money and staff for the park's long-term upkeep.

In terms of water, the park's problem, as often as not, is one of oversupply. The Ohio River floods regularly, and exceptional flooding has occurred at least once a decade in the last half of the twentieth century. When the river floods, it leaves behind a layer of silt as much as 4 inches (10 cm) thick. If the silt hardens, it turns to a concrete-like coating that smothers vegetation and leaves the landscape under an ugly veneer.

At the same time, water has become a political issue, even in climates that receive adequate precipitation. Louisville doesn't yet have to conserve water, but conservation has become an important theme, and the park could showcase Louisville's commitment to conservation efforts.

In summary, the city planners needed a plan for Riverside Park that would include appropriate landscaping, irrigation, and a strategy for coping with periodic flooding. On top of that, the plan had to provide for minimal long-term upkeep on a bare-bones budget.

Stop now and work through the Prediction Predicament

Prediction Predicament

Assume that you are one of the landscaping/ irrigation firms that has been contacted by the Louisville city planners.

You need to:

1.   Come up with a proposal that will address their circumstances and offer them an efficient and economical plan appropriate for the long term.

Refer to the prediction process to come up with the general components of a landscaping and irrigation system that you think will meet Louisville's unique needs. Use the worksheet to record your progress.

What Really Happened...

A California firm called Brookwater was one of the companies bidding on the Louisville contract. They accurately established the overriding concerns as:

1. coping with floodwater and silt deposits,
2. installing a landscape and irrigation system that would require minimal maintenance and expense and that could be touted as an example of water conservation at work.

To address the flooding issue, Brookwater developed their landscape irrigation scheme to avoid the ravages of high water as much as possible. Brookwater discussed with the landscape architect (Hargreaves & Associates) the type of irrigation equipment that could be used in the flood prone areas and the likelihood of its survival in flooding. Based on the type of irrigation equipment that would withstand flooding, the landscape architect chose hardy, native sedges and forbs that could survive a certain amount of flooding and would not require extensive watering under normal conditions. However, Brookwater still had to provide for the effects of extraordinary flooding. Part of the plan involved locating pumps and other sensitive equipment safely above the "nuisance flooding line." The other facet of Brookwater's proposal caused some concern and required some selling on their part.

Brookwater proposed a sophisticated Central Control System (CCS) that would employ a computer and some sophisticated software to run the irrigation system. The CCS would boost the initial cost of the project by roughly $70,000. When city planners expressed concern about the price tag, Brookwater stressed how much less maintenance a CCS-run system would require than a traditional irrigation scheme and how amazingly flexible a CCS could be. And, Louisville would have the distinction of being one of the few locations east of the Mississippi to use a CCS.

Brookwater pointed out that a CCS would use at least 20 percent less water than a traditional irrigation system (and possibly as much as 50 percent), that most of the monitoring tasks would be handled by the computer, and that the extra expense of the CCS would be paid back in energy savings and reduced maintenance within five years.

When silt built up, the irrigation system would operate at high pressure (140 psi) and would use powerful, 15-horsepower pumps. "Quick coupling" fittings for 3-inch (7.5-cm) diameter hose attachments would be spaced along the pipes so fire hoses could be used to wash silt away before it hardened. Pressure-reducing valves and regulators would slacken water pressure at sprinkler heads and other points where necessary.

Most important, the CCS would allow the park managers to program in such factors as soil type, slope, evapotranspiration figures, rate of flow, vegetation types, and even wind speed. Irrigation could then be controlled almost surgically. The CCS could water different zones to fit specific parameters, immediately pinpoint leaks and faulty fittings, and, in the event of water shortages, cut water back to the minimum required by vegetation, based on climatic data. On windy days, when a great percentage of sprinkler water is lost to evaporation, the CCS would automatically stop watering.

Finally, the CCS would be expandable. It could potentially handle other city properties within a 20-mile (32 km) radius, adjust to monitor park expansion in the future, and even be programmed to manage such jobs as lighting and security.

What Really Happened...continued

In the end, Louisville chose the Brookwater bid over a traditional sprinkler system. Despite the higher initial investment, the planners saw the long-term benefits inherent in the CCS, as well as the tremendous contribution to water conservation the Brookwater proposal could guarantee.

Shuttle Water

The NASA space shuttle faces challenges and conditions that are, you might say, out of this world. The shuttle endures temperature extremes and atmospheric pressures beyond anything found on Earth. It has to blast itself free of the atmospheric envelope, cope with the unique conditions of outer space, and then punch its way back through the atmosphere to a safe landing.

Since a huge quantity of fuel is required to boost the craft free of Earth's gravitational pull (as much as two-thirds of the payload is taken up by fuel), every other object on board has to be as light and compact as possible.

Stop now and work through the Prediction Predicament

Space shuttle lifting off.

COURTESY OF NASA PUBLIC AFFAIRS

Conserve Water! Educators' Guide © The Watercourse

Prediction Predicament

Put yourself in the role of an engineer working on the space shuttle's overall life-support system, and consider the role water will play in the craft's day-to-day operation. Some of the issues will be obvious, while others are more obscure and will require some creative thinking to come up with.

Consider the following:

1. Water is both bulky and heavy, so its presence on board has to be kept to a minimum.

2. At the same time, water is essential to life support on board and may well have some other pivotal roles to play, too.

Refer to the prediction process to come up with a list of water's main functions on the space shuttle, as well as to brainstorm some possibilities for other uses for water in space. Use the worksheet to record your progress.

What Really Happened...

An extensive team of personnel were charged with the task of developing the Environmental Control and Life Support System (ECLSS) on the shuttle. Their domain included the function and management of air, water, heat, and waste. As it turns out, water is a major player in many facets of ECLSS operations.

The team's challenges included maintaining ambient humidity between 30 and 75 percent, controlling the proper (nontoxic) mix of carbon monoxide and carbon dioxide, and keeping the cabin temperature in a comfortable range despite extremes of searing heat and numbing cold outside. Waste disposal, cabin ventilation, potable water supplies, and many other issues came under the purview of the ECLSS.

It quickly became apparent that despite fuel and water's essential parts in the space shuttle's operation, the shuttle couldn't carry all the necessary fuel and water supplies required on a long voyage. The team's solution was to install three separate Fuel Cell Power Plants to generate power and actually manufacture water in flight. Water produced by the fuel cells is then used for drinking and cooking, filling cooling loops, supplying the Flash Evaporator, and other needs. This water is stored in three tanks pressurized with nitrogen from the crew cabin. The tanks hold roughly 20 gallons or 165 pounds (74 kg) each. The power plants are capable of producing water at a rate of 25 gallons (92.5 kg) every hour.

Water circulating through a lengthy system of pipes throughout the shuttle both cools the confines and functions as an air/water heat exchanger. Other water is sent to the Flash Evaporator, where its main purpose is to cool the space shuttle during exposure to extreme heat (mostly as the craft leaves and reenters the atmosphere).

Temperature sensors along the water lines detect any freeze-up problems; if one occurs, water is shunted along an alternate line to another tank. A purity sensor measures the pH balance of drinking supplies before the water is sent through a microfilter and receives a precautionary dose of iodine. Wastewater is collected and stored in a pressurized tank below the cabin flight deck.

A unique aspect of the water produced by fuel cell power plants is that it is overly rich in hydrogen. Because of this, the water has to pass through a set of silver palladium tubes (hydrogen separators) that draw hydrogen ions out of the water and vent them to the outside.

Once an astronaut leaves the 2,325 cubic feet (67 cubic meters) of airlocked space on the shuttle, he or she must wear a space suit that, in microcosm, performs the same life support functions. Again, water plays a pivotal role. In the space suit, for instance, water is used for cooling, just as it is on board ship. Ten pounds (4.5 kg) of water are stored in three bladders. The water circulates through a system of sewn-in tubes 300 feet (90 meters) long! The wearer can control the suit's temperature by turning a knob that adjusts the rate of flow. The space suit is also fitted with a $1/2$-quart ($1/3$ l) drink bag with a strawlike drinking tube. The Liquid Cooling and Ventilation Garment (LCVG) is a 6.5 pound (3 kg), one-piece suit made of Spandex that has the 300 feet of tubing distributed throughout it. Even under the strain of rigorous exercise, the LCVG is capable of maintaining a comfortable body temperature.

When crew members don their space suits, they can survive for up to eight hours outside the shuttle. For longer periods of time, they are connected to the mother ship by a thick umbilical line that houses communication and electrical wires and water and oxygen supply and drain lines. Just as a baby could not survive without its umbilical cord, so too would an astronaut without the connecting lifeline to the shuttle.

What Really Happened...continued

Next time you see the space shuttle on the evening news, consider the vital part water plays in the success of NASA's program of exploration and research in outer space!

Space shuttle.

Appendices

Glossary

Page numbers following the definitions indicate where each word appears in the text.

ADAPTATIONS: The modification, over time, of the structure, function, or behavior of an organism, which enables it to be better suited to its environment. 27, 75-76, 78-79

ADHESION: The attraction of water molecules to other materials as a result of hydrogen bonding. 31, 33

AQUIFER: An underground bed of saturated soil or rock that yields significant quantities of water. 71, 230, 260, 262

ARTIFACT: A handmade object characteristic of an earlier time or cultural stage. 101, 104-106, 108, 217

AUDIT: To examine or inspect, to evaluate the efficiency, appropriateness, or safety. 27, 122, 147, 153-155, 212, 265, 267

COHESION: The attraction of water molecules to each other as a result of hydrogen bonding. 31, 33

CONDENSATION: The process by which a vapor becomes a liquid; the opposite of evaporation. 27, 31, 34

CONSUMPTIVE USE: The use of a resource that reduces the supply (e.g., removing water from a source such as a river or lake without returning an equal amount). Examples are the intake of water by plants, humans, and other animals and the incorporation of water into the products of industrial or food processing. 128

DENSITY: The compactness or crowdedness of matter (e.g., water molecules) in a given area. 31-33

DESALINIZATION: The process of salt removal from sea or brackish water. 36, 41, 53

DESIGNED ECOSYSTEMS: Human-made environments consisting of constructed wetlands, soil filters, and various combinations... to mimic natural environments to treat wastewater from both households and industries. 201

DILEMMA: A situation in which a choice must be made from among different alternatives; a difficult or complex set of circumstances. 85

DIRECT WATER USE: Use of water that is apparent (e.g., washing, bathing, cooking). 85

DISCHARGE: An outflow of water from a stream, pipe, ground water system, or watershed. 66, 125, 140, 162, 255, 258, 262, 274, 276

DIVERSIONARY WATER USE: Use that takes water out of a stream, lake, aquifer, or other body of water. 161

DROUGHT: An extended period with little or no precipitation; often affects crop production and availability of water supplies. A-15, 121-122, 125, 133, 135, 139, 143, 187, 195-196, 214, 252, 264, 269, 271, 276-277

DROUGHT TOLERANT: Capable of surviving for extended periods with little or no rainfall. 195-196

ELECTROMAGNETIC FORCES: The fields created by positive and negative charges of atoms, which influence the formation of molecules and the attraction or repulsion (push and pull) of molecules to and from each other. 43

EPIPHYTE: A plant growing attached to another plant, but not parasitic; an air-plant. 75, 80-83

EVAPORATION: The conversion of a liquid (e.g., water) into a vapor (a gaseous state) usually through the application of heat energy; the opposite of condensation. 27, 34-35, 38, 80, 107, 125, 136, 260, 262-263, 272, 284

EVAPOTRANSPIRATION (ET): A combination of evaporation and transpiration of water into the atmosphere from living plants and soil. 37, 134, 284

FURROW IRRIGATION: Water is put into furrows through the use of pumps, pipes, or siphons and gravity moves the water through the field. 132

GROUND COVER: A plant with a low growing, spreading habit, grown specifically to cover the ground. 196

GROUND WATER SYSTEM: All the components of subsurface materials that relate to water, including aquifers (confined and unconfined), zones of saturation, and water tables. 65

HYDROGEN BONDING: A type of chemical bond caused by electromagnetic forces, occurring when the positive pole of one molecule (e.g., water) is attracted to and forms a bond with the negative pole of another molecule (e.g., another water molecule). 32

HYDROGEOLOGIST: A scientist who studies the occurrence, distribution and movement of water below the surface of the earth, with a greater emphasis on geology. 66

HYDROGRAPH: A graphic plot of changes in the flow of water or in the elevation of water level plotted against time. 160, 173, 177, 181, 185, 189

HYDROLOGY: The study of Earth's waters, including water's properties, circulation, principles, and distribution. A-18-19, 30, 161

ICE CARD: A card placed in the window of a home to notify the local ice company that a delivery was needed. 101, 108, 115-122

INDIRECT WATER USE: Uses of water that are not immediately apparent to the consumer. For example, a person indirectly uses water when driving a car because water was used in the production process of steel and other parts of the vehicle. 85

INSTREAM FLOW: The minimum amount of water required in a stream to maintain the existing aquatic resources and associated wildlife and riparian habitat. 161

INSTREAM WATER USE: Uses of water within a stream's channel (e.g., by fish and other aquatic life, or for recreation, navigation, and hydroelectric power production). 161

IRRIGATION: The controlled application of water to cropland, hay fields, and/or pasture to supplement that supplied by nature. 27, 52-54, 59, 85, 119, 122, 124, 130-146, 173, 194-197, 238, 252, 260, 262-263, 272, 276, 278, 280-284

MICROIRRIGATION: Frequent application of small quantities of water as drops, tiny streams, or miniature spray through emitters or applicators placed along a water delivery line. 133, 138, 142-143

MICROSYSTEM IRRIGATION: Method of precisely applying irrigation water to the immediate root zone of the target plant at very low rates.

MULCH: An organic or inorganic soil covering, used to maintain soil temperature and moisture and to discourage the growth of weeds. 194, 196, 272

NATIVE PLANT: A plant occurring naturally in an area and not introduced by humans. 195-197, 219, 272

NONCONSUMPTIVE: Instream use of water that does not reduce the supply; or, removing water and returning it to the source without reducing the supply (e.g., navigation and fisheries). 128

OSMOSIS: The diffusion of water through a membrane. 31, 36, 40-41, 208

PER CAPITA USE RATE: The amount of water used by each person each day, expressed in gallons. 161-162

PERENNIAL: A plant whose life cycle lasts for three or more seasons. 133, 139

PERMEABILITY: The capability of transmitting water (e.g., porous rock, sediment or soil). 91

Glossary, continued

PHREATOPHYTES: Plants that send their roots into or below the capillary zone to use ground water. 77

PLASTICITY: The capability of being molded, receiving shape or being made to assume a desired form. 91

POROSITY: Full of pores; the state of permeability by water, air, etc. 91

POTABLE WATER: Suitable, safe, or prepared for drinking. 147, 149, 288

PRE-ASSESSMENT: A teaching strategy that is used to determine students' level of understanding or competencies related to a concept prior to instruction. Pre-assessments are often compared to assessments performed after instruction to determine if progress has been made. 23

RADIAL ROOT SYSTEM: A shallow root system where roots extend in a radial (or rayed) manner. 77

RECHARGE: Refers to water entering an underground aquifer through faults, fractures, or direct absorption. 44, 66, 236, 260, 262

RESERVOIR: A pond, lake, tank, or basin (natural or human made) where water is collected and used for storage. 38, 81, 89, 124-126, 166, 168,

170, 172-173, 176, 180-181, 184, 188, 252, 264, 276, 280

RETROFITTING: To modify or update equipment. 207, 267

RIPARIAN AREAS: Land areas directly influenced by a body of water; usually have visible vegetation or other physical characteristics showing this water influence. Stream banks, lake borders, and marshes are typical riparian areas. 123

SALINIZATION: The condition in which the salt content of soil accumulates over time to above the normal level; occurs in some parts of the world where water containing high salt concentration evaporates from fields irrigated with standing water. 53, 131, 134-135

SNOWPACK: A field of naturally packed snow that ordinarily melts in early summer months. 125-126

SOIL PH: pH stands for potential hydrogen and is a measure of acidity and alkalinity of the soil. 195

SPINOFFS: Technologies which have been transferred to uses different than, and often remote from their original application in the aerospace field. 202

SPRINKLE IRRIGATION: Method of irrigation in which the water is sprayed, or sprinkled,

through the air to the ground surface. 132-133, 138-139, 141-142

STOMPER: A hand-held, hand-operated piece of equipment that worked as an agitator to wash and rinse clothes. 108

STREAMFLOW: The discharge of water from a river. 125, 166-167, 170, 173, 175, 179, 183, 187, 191

SUBIRRIGATION: The application of irrigation water below the ground surface by raising the water table to within or near the root zone. 27, 132-133, 138-139

SURFACE IRRIGATION: A broad class of irrigation methods in which water is distributed over the soil surface by gravity flow. 132-133, 136, 138-139, 141

TAILWATER: Applied irrigation water that runs off the lower end of a field. Tailwater is measured as the average depth of runoff water, expressed in inches or feet. 132, 145

TECHNOLOGY: The science and art of making and using things. 107, 132, 206, 243, 261-263

TEST WELL: A well hole drilled for experimental or exploratory purposes. 66

TOPOGRAPHY: A description, model, or drawing of mountains, valleys, hills, rivers, roads,

Glossary, continued

bridges, and other things found on the surface of a place. 131-132, 135, 137, 244, 246

TRANSPIRATION: The process by which water absorbed by plants (usually through the roots) is evaporated into the atmosphere from the plant surface (principally from the leaves). 34-35, 50, 52, 80, 134, 284

VALUES: Principles, standards, or qualities considered worthwhile or desirable by the person who holds them. 115

WASHBOARD: A rectangular board or frame, typically with a corrugated metallic surface, on which clothes are rubbed in the process of washing. 107, 110

WASTEWATER TREATMENT: Any of the mechanical or chemical processes used to modify the quality of wastewater in order to make it more compatible or acceptable to humans and the environment.
• Primary treatment: settling and chlorinating.
• Secondary treatment: biologic processing using microbes.
• Tertiary treatment: involves oxidation and the spraying of effluent on croplands. 152, 187, 217, 254, 257, 264-265

WATER ALLOCATION: A hydrologic system in which there are multiple uses or demands for water, the process of measuring a specific amount of water devoted to a given purpose. 123-126

WATER BAG: A bag for holding water, especially one designed to keep water cool for drinking by evaporation through a slightly porous surface. 92, 101, 107, 109

WATER DIVERSION: The transfer of water from a stream, lake, aquifer, or other source of water by canal, pipe, well or other conduit to another watercourse or to application on the land. 124, 147-148

WATER DOWSING: The use of divining rods (of wood or metal) for locating water. 101-102

WATER RIGHTS: A legal right to use a specified amount of water for beneficial purposes. 27, 91, 96, 123-129, 132, 134, 212, 214

WATER TABLE: The level below the earth's surface at which the ground becomes saturated with water. 66, 68, 71, 133-134, 139

WATERLOGGING: Occurs when excess water accumulates in the root zone preventing plants from obtaining adequate oxygen. 131, 134, 262

WATERSHED: The land area from which surface runoff drains into a stream channel, lake, reservoir, or other body of water; also called a drainage basin. A-19, 66, 79, 161-163, 165-166, 214-216, 224

WATER-STRESS: Plants are not able to get enough water from the soil to replace the water lost from transpiration. 131

XERISCAPE: A form of landscaping that utilizes a variety of indigenous and drought-tolerant plants, shrubs, and ground cover. 27, 31, 37, 115, 195, 208

XEROPHYTE: A plant adapted to live under conditions of drought. 75, 77

Glossary Sources

http://www.mstf.org/~meaqua/
index.html
Maine Aquaculture Innovation Center
*Water Conservation Invention
Convention*

www.sti.nasa.gov
NASA Scientific and Technical
Information, Spinoffs, 1980 and 1984
*Water Conservation Invention
Convention*

http://www.tec.org/tec/
terms2.html#d
Texas Environmental Center Encyclo-
pedia of Water Terms
*Water Audit; Water Conservation
Invention Convention; Get the
Ground Water Picture; Your Hydro-
logic Deck*

http://www.gardenweb.com/
glossary/
GardenWeb Glossary of Botanical
Terms
*Xeriscape; Alligators, Epiphytes,
and Water Managers; Irrigation
Innovation*

http://frost.ca.uky.edu/agripedia/
index.htm
Agripedia (University of KY) College
of Agriculture Glossary
Irrigation Innovation

http://www.usbr.gov/cdams/
glossary.html#T
Irrigation Innovation

http://water.usgs.gov/pubs/
chapter11/chapter11M.html
USGS National Handbook of Recom-
mended Methods for Water Data
Acquisition
*Irrigation Innovation; Get the Ground
Water Picture*

http://www.edwardsaquifer.net/
glossary.html
Edwards Aquifer Homepage –
Glossary of Water Resource Terms
*Water Audit; Water Conservation
Invention Convention; Alligators,
Epiphytes, and Water Managers; Get
the Ground Water Picture; A Hydro-
logic Primer; Your Hydrologic Deck*

http://www.prairiefrontier.com/
pages/families/rootsystems.html
Prairie Frontier Wildlowers and
Prairie Grass Seed
*Alligators, Epiphytes, and Water
Managers*

http://www.state.nv.us/cnr/ndwp/
dict-1/waterwds.htm
Nevada Division of Water Planning
Water Words Dictionary Index
*Irrigation Innovation; Pass the Jug;
Get the Ground Water Picture*

http://www.allwords.com/
All Words Dictionary
*Water Conservation Invention
Convention*

http://lcweb.loc.gov/lexico/
Library of Congress Thesauri Home
Page
*Mrs. Alderson Early Lessons in
Water Conservation*

http://www.utexas.edu/depts/
grg/virtdept/workshops/1997/
test/roebuck/physgeog/common/
glossary/gloss.htm
Roebuck, Paul, University of Colorado, Colorado Springs, Self Paced
Introductory Courses in Physical
Geography-glossary
Your Hydrologic Deck

http://www.epa.gov/oiamount/
tips/scws.htm#wastewater
EPA-Constructed Wetlands for
Wastewater Treatment and Wildlife
Habitat, EPA/832/R-93/005 (PB95-
209136)
*Water Conservation Invention
Convention*

http://www.waterrecycling.com/
engineeredenviron.htm
Alternative Wastewater Treatment
Overview, Water Recycling
*Water Conservation Invention
Convention*

1999. *The Project WET Curriculum
and Activity Guide.* Bozeman, MT:
The Watercourse.
All activities except-*Mrs. Alderson
Early Lessons in Water Conservation;
Water Audit;* and *Water Conserva-
tion Invention Convention*

*Random House Unabridged Dictio-
nary.* Second Edition.
*Mrs. Alderson Early Lessons in
Water Conservation; Water Audit;
Water Vessels; Alligators, Epi-
phytes, and Water Managers; Water
Conservation Invention Convention*

1995. *Technology, Eyewitness
Science.* New York:Dorling
Kindersley. *Water Conservation
Invention Convention*

*The Watershed Manager Teacher's
Guide.* The Watercourse.
*Water Conservation Invention
Convention; Your Hydrologic Deck;
Water Audit*

Supplementary Resources

Publications
Activity Guides and Books

STUDENT BOOKLETS

Celebrate Wetlands!
Published in cooperation with Wild Outdoor World (W.O.W.), this 16-page full-color booklet is for upper elementary and middle school aged students. Through hands-on investigations, games, intriguing articles, a poster, and other activities, readers learn about the types and functions of wetlands; the plants, animals, soil, and water found in wetlands; and about the language and culture of the people who inhabited these special places.

The Water Story
Published in cooperation with Wild Outdoor World (W.O.W.), Phillips Petroleum Company, National Association of Conservation Districts (NACD), National Wetlands Conservation Alliance and Project WET, this 16-page supplement is designed for upper elementary and middle school aged students. In telling the story of water, this publication provides young readers with a variety of creative, hands-on activities, projects, games, a poster and valuable information about water. This supplement was honored for Distinguished Achievement in Educational Publishing, EdPress Award Winner.

Conserve Water
This colorful 16-page booklet designed for upper elementary and middle school aged students was published in cooperation with the Wild Outdoor World (W.O.W.) and the Department of the Interior, Bureau of Reclamation. Through engaging graphics and text, students are challenged to participate in investigations such as assembling a sun-powered still or experimenting with catchment. Activities invite students to "soak up" intriguing water facts; play a board game to learn how water moves through their homes and how they can conserve it; conduct a simple home water audit; and discover how a person's latitude can affect their attitude about water conservation. This supplement was honored for Distinguished Achievement in Educational Publishing, EdPress Award Winner.

Fish & Fishing
Produced through a partnership with the Wild Outdoor World (W.O.W), and in conjunction with U.S. Department of Commerce, NOAA—National Marine Fisheries Service, Office of Habitat Conservation; Nebraska Game and Parks Commission; Arizona Game and Fish Department; U.S. Fish and Wildlife Service; and the Future Fisherman Foundation, Youth Education Office of American Sportfishing Association—this full-color, 16-page booklet is intended for upper elementary and middle school aged students. Included in the booklet is the story of fish and fishing through hands-on activities such as "Something Fishy," "Fishing for Facts," and "No Bones About It"; and stories such as "Fish Stories," "Hook, Line and Sinker," "Count the Ways," and "Fine Kettle of Fish."

Explore Oceans
Together with Wild Outdoor World (W.O.W), and the National Marine Fisheries Service (NOAA), The Watercourse has published this 16-page, full-color booklet for upper elementary and middle school aged students. This booklet contains hands-on activities such as "Where in the Universe?" "The Ocean Market," and "Weather Maker, the Big Picture." A board-game entitled "Coastal Connection" demonstrates how water travels in a watershed and how it is affected by all water users. This supplement is a finalist for a Distinguished Achievement in Educational Publishing Award from EdPress.

Supplementary Resources, continued

Water Works

Published in cooperation with Wild Outdoor World (W.O.W), and The U.S. Department of the Interior, Bureau of Reclamation, this 16-page, full-color booklet highlights Hoover Dam. Upper elementary and middle school aged students will discover how dams such as Hoover ensure that we have water to drink, to use for recreation, to provide power to our homes, to provide water for agriculture and business, and to provide habitat for fish and wildlife.

Big Rivers

Students explore big rivers and their watersheds in North America, meet famous river explorers, calculate a river's rate of flow, discover how the river environment is unique, investigate the many ways that rivers are important, and recognize the role of water managers in this fun, hands-on activity booklet. Fully illustrated pages contain directions for making a model of a watershed and a simple paddleboat. This 16-page booklet for students in grades 4 to 6 is published in conjunction with Wild Outdoor World (W.O.W.) magazine and the U.S. Department of the Interior, Bureau of Reclamation.

Discover Ground Water and Springs

(Available Fall, 2000)
Published in cooperation with the Perrier Group of America, this 16 page, full-color booklet will help readers explore and discover information about ground water and spring water. Students will: identify underground rock formations in "Get the Ground Water Picture;" learn how water suppliers locate, retrieve and deliver water to people for use; locate underground water by playing the Ground Water Game; and learn about the importance of springs to past and present cultures.

Discover the Colorado

(Available in 2001)
The Colorado is one of the great rivers of North America. This 16 page, full color student booklet, developed in cooperation with the Lower Colorado Region of the Bureau of Reclamation, will explore the Colorado River from its headwaters high in the Rocky Mountains to its confluence in the Gulf of California. The booklet will include information and hands-on activities on the Colorado River and its vast drainage basin; hydrology; history and culture; water users; ecological communities; and priority management topics and issues.

Native Waters Student Activity Booklet

This 32-page student booklet will contain student-centered information and activities to introduce students to water resource issues from American Indian perspectives. The Watercourse has extensive experience in publishing student activity booklets. The *Native Waters Student Activity Booklet* will contain information similar to the Native Waters Teachers Guide, but will be written for young people in grades 4 to 6. The activities will be hands-on and fun!

GETTING TO KNOW SERIES
Exploring the Waters of Our National Parks: Everglades, an Educator's Guide

Developed by The Watercourse with The National Park Foundation and the Interpretive Staff of Everglades National Park, the fun and informative activities in this guide offer ways for educators and students in grades 4 to 6 to learn more about the role of water in one of the largest wetland ecosystems in the world. Participants may journey through the hydrologic cycle, create an alligator hole in their classroom, or design a newly authorized Wetlands National Park and explore the concept of the "national park idea."

Getting to Know the Waters of Yellowstone National Park

The Greater Yellowstone Ecosystem (an area of nearly 18 million acres, with 2.2. million-acre Yellowstone National Park at its core) is dramatically shaped and characterized by water. Places like

Supplementary Resources, continued

Old Faithful, the travertine terraces at Mammoth, or the Grand Canyon of the Yellowstone are, in some basic way, water phenomena. Illustrated with fun graphics, informative maps and diagrams, the activities introduce learners to the wonder of Yellowstone's waters. Build a mini geyser or track the water journey of a glacial erratic boulder—the waters of Yellowstone have many stories to tell.

WATER HISTORY
The Liquid Treasure Water History Trunk: Learning From the Past
This 64-page booklet contains stories, activities, and information for procuring artifacts needed to assemble a water history trunk. Other less expensive and time-consuming options are suggested for developing a water environmental history program, such as creating a water history scrapbook or building a water history home.

Lewis and Clark Bicentennial Planning Kit
(Available Spring, 2002)
Be prepared to commemorate the bicentennial of the Lewis and Clark Expedition with The Watercourse's user-friendly Lewis and Clark Bicentennial Planning Kit. It describes all of the best primary resources available to educators and community event planners as

well as includes the teaching materials you need to get started.
   The Lewis and Clark Bicentennial Planning Kit will contain:
·*Discover a Watershed: The Columbia Reference and Activity Guide for Educators*
·*Discover a Watershed: The Missouri Reference and Activity Guide for Educators*
·*Discover a Watershed Columbia Student Activity Booklet*
·*Discover a Watershed Missouri Student Activity Booklet*
·*The Lewis and Clark Bicentennial Resource Guide*
·*The Lewis and Clark Student Activity Booklet*
·Video clips
·Teaching materials

REFERENCE
Water Gift of Nature
Become familiar with the many faces of water: clouds, rain, hail, snow, icebergs, geysers, rainbows, and waterfalls. See the animals and plants that depend on water: from wetland beavers to the desert chuckwalla, from a coral reef to a saguaro cactus. Co-published with K.C. Publications, Inc., *Water a Gift of Nature* is grounded in the social and natural sciences. It provides interpretive text and full-color photographs.

A Landowner's Guide to Western Water Rights
Produced with Roberts Rinehart Publishers, this guide provides the layperson with a

user-friendly introduction to western water rights systems. It includes a reference section on western water rights, commonly asked questions (and answers) about water rights with cautions for prospective landowners, information on federal and tribal reserved water rights, and profiles of western states' water rights systems. A 1997 EdPress Gold Award Winner.

CHILDREN'S WATER BOOKS
The Rainstick, a Fable
Produced with Falcon Press Publishing Co., *The Rainstick, a Fable* is drawn from the riddles, myths, and traditions of West African people as well as from descriptions of tropical rainforests by early adventurers and present-day scientists. The book contains a fable about a young boy's journey from the savanna to the rain forest to solve the riddle, "A slender staff touches earth and sky at the same time." Factual information about this early sound instrument is included, as well as easy-to-follow directions to build a rainstick.

Spring Waters, Gathering Places
Throughout time springs have been places of ecological, social, and cultural importance. Many Native Americans revered the life-giving waters, communities grew up around them and adopted their names,

Supplementary Resources, continued

and people of diverse cultures have visited them for health and healing. Sponsored by Perrier Group of America, this beautifully illustrated book is designed for children ages 8-12, their parents, teachers, and librarians. Gathering Places tells the story and science of springs through original vignettes, myths, legends, interactive games and activities.

MODULES—resources containing a reference section and 15 to 50 activities focused on a single topic.

WOW!: The Wonders Of Wetlands

This module, co-developed by The Watercourse and Environmental Concern Inc., is based on the highly successful *WOW!: The Wonders Of Wetlands* activity guide for K-12 educators originally created by EC. The new *WOW!* Guide includes a reference section, new activities (in addition to the originals), and a new format.

DISCOVER A WATERSHED SERIES

Discover a Watershed: The Everglades

Developed for formal and nonformal educators of middle and high school students, this comprehensive guide is divided into three parts: a reference section that includes the natural and human history of the watershed; contemporary issues and potential

solutions; and learning activities. Build a model of the Kissimmee-Okeechobee-Everglades watershed or plot a hurricane and predict if it will make landfall. Explore a unique and endangered watershed where unprecedented solutions are being tested to "find the balance." Produced through a partnership with the South Florida Water Management District, this resource provides examples of restoration concepts.

Discover a Watershed: The Rio Grande/Rio Bravo

This international effort involved a team of educators and water managers from Mexico and the United States. Published in Spanish and English editions, the *Discover a Watershed: The Rio Grande/Rio Bravo Reference and Activity Guide* provides a comprehensive and contemporary exploration of the challenges and opportunities of this great international watershed. Topics will include: hydrology of the basin; plant and animal communities; history, culture, traditions, and celebrations; comparison of U.S., Mexico, and joint water management systems; priority issues and concerns; basin economy and future scenarios.

Discover a Watershed: The Columbia

(Available Fall, 2001)
Currently under development

in cooperation with outstanding educators and resource specialists, this 150-page guide provides background information on the hydrology of the Columbia River Basin, the cultural and natural history, tribal issues, and land uses. It also includes field-tested, ready-to-use teaching activities that invite children and adults to explore water issues, management challenges, and economic considerations in either a classroom or informal setting. Illustrated with high-quality graphics, informative maps and diagrams, the activities introduce learners to the wonder of Columbia's waters.

Discover a Watershed: The Missouri

(Available Spring, 2001)
Currently in production in cooperation with the Missouri River Roundtable, this 150-page guide features contemporary, unbiased, scientifically accurate, and educationally sound teaching activities along with pertinent background information on the natural and cultural history of the Missouri River Basin and modern water uses, issues and concerns. Illustrated with high-quality graphics, informative maps and diagrams, the activities introduce learners to the problems and prospects facing the "Big Muddy".

Supplementary Resources, continued

The Native Waters Educators Guide

A 150-page Native Waters Educators Guide for the Missouri will contain background information and innovative, interdisciplinary activities that are fieldtested, scientifically accurate, educationally sound, culturally grounded and easy to use. A reference section will discuss tribal water resources, ways of knowing about water, historic and modern water uses and tribal water issues. Guide activities, to be developed in partnership with tribal educators and resource professionals, will promote critical thinking and problem-solving skills to help young people gain the knowledge and experience they need to make informed decisions.

GROUND WATER
Ground Water Flow Model Package

The Ground Water Flow Model is a popular and easy-to-use teaching tool for both young people and adult educators. The model is constructed with a clear plexiglass front, allowing observers to watch water and contaminants introduced into the system move through underground rock formations. The model can also be adapted to demonstrate how surface sources like rivers or wetlands can be connected to ground water. The model enables students to learn

about porosity, permeability, water tables, confined aquifers, contamination, and other important ground water concepts. This package includes a model, users guide and video, and everything needed to conduct a ground water education class or workshop.

Geothermal Educators Guide
(Available in 2002)
GEO: The Great Earth Odyssey, an educators guide being developed through a partnership of The Watercourse, the Geothermal Educators Office, and the Idaho Water Resources Research Institute, features a worldwide exploration of the earth's geothermal resources. A set of activities will help educators and students explore the origins of geothermal resources and their surface manifestations, investigate cultural and historical beliefs and uses, and illustrate the potential of geothermal resources in the mix of renewable energy today and in the future.

CHILDREN'S FISHING SERIES
The Children's Fishing Series, Bass

This is a story and activity book for elementary children, their families, and teachers that provides accurate and up-to-date information on bass and highlights the family bonds that develop through fishing. Through the story, "Granddaddy Bass," hands-on

activities, fishing tips and equipment, readers learn the natural history of the species and related topics such as watersheds, water quantity and quality, habitat protection and restoration.

Other Suggested Resources

Project WET Curriculum and Activity Guide

More than 90 activities cover seven major topics: 1) Water has unique physical and chemical characteristics. 2) Water is essential for all life to exist. 3) Water connects all Earth systems. 4) Water is a natural resource. 5) Water resources are managed. 6) Water resources exist within social and economic settings. 7) Water resources exist within historical and cultural contexts. The Guide is only available through training workshops provided by state Project WET Coordinators. For more information, contact the national headquarters at (406) 994-5392.

Watershed Management Educator's Guide
(Available in 2001)
This Guide will be for educators and resource manager's use in teaching about important watershed management topics (i.e., basic water concepts; hydrology; water users; issues identification, analysis, and discussion; management options and strategies; and

Supplementary Resources, continued

planning). Each topic will be addressed in specific activities. These activities will include background information, creative teaching methods, and ideas for use with students in grades 6 to 12.

Healthy Water, Healthy People

The Watercourse and Project WET, in partnership with the Hach Scientific Foundation and the Hach Company have launched a national water quality education project called Healthy Water, Healthy People. This project will result in: the publication of the *Healthy Water, Healthy People Water Quality Educators Guide*; the creation of the Healthy Water, Healthy People Water Quality Training CD-ROM and Video; the development of a variety of Healthy Water, Healthy People Water Quality Testing Kits; and an extensive training program of seminars, workshops, and institutes.

These publications and products are available by visiting The Watercourse website, http://www.montana.edu/wwwwater, or by calling (406) 994-5392.

Cross Reference Charts

Subject Area Cross Reference

ACTIVITY	SOCIAL STUDIES					SCIENCE						
	Fine Arts	Language Arts	History/ Anthropology	Geography	Government	Math	Earth	Physical	Life	Environmental	Ecology	Health
Alligators, Epiphytes, and Water Managers		■		■					■		■	
Blue Traveller							■					
Conservation Choices					■					■		
Get the Ground Water Picture					■		■			■		
Hydrologic Primer						■		■				
Ins & Outs of Conservation	■	■	■	■	■	■	■	■	■	■	■	■
Irrigation Innovation			■				■			■		
Mrs. Alderson: Early Lessons in Water Conservation	■	■	■							■		
Pass the Jug	■	■	■		■					■		
Water Audit				■					■		■	
Water Conservation Celebration	■	■	■	■	■	■	■	■	■	■	■	■
Water Conservation Invention Convention		■					■					■
Water Vessels		■		■		■						
Water Works							■			■		
Xeriscape!									■	■		
Your Hydrologic Deck							■			■		

Cross Reference Charts, continued

Case Study-Activity Cross Reference

CASE STUDY ▶ / ACTIVITY ▼	Adrift	Native Landscapes	One Scoop or Two?	Operation Water Sense	Planning with Vision	Shuttle Water	The Problem with Silt	TRP in NYC	Used Up Country	Water Trouble on the High Plains
Alligators, Epiphytes, And Water Managers	■									
Blue Traveller	■				■					
Conservation Choices			■						■	
Get the Ground Water Picture										■
Hydrologic Primer	■	■								
Ins & Outs of Conservation	■	■	■	■	■	■	■	■	■	■
Irrigation Innovation							■		■	■
Mrs. Alderson: Early Lessons in Water Conservation									■	
Pass the Jug					■					
Water Audit				■						
Water Conservation Celebration	■	■	■	■	■	■	■	■	■	■
Water Conservation Invention Convention	■			■	■	■		■	■	
Water Vessels									■	
Water Works			■							
Xeriscape!		■								
Your Hydrologic Deck		■		■	■			■		

Index

Words in **bold** indicate section titles. Numerals in **bold** indicate the page on which the term is defined in the glossary.

W

washboard 107, 110, **293**

wastewater treatment 152, 187, 217, 254, 257, 264-265, 267-268, **293**

water allocation 123-126, **293**

Water Audit 147. *See* Activities

water bag 92, 101, 107, 109, 113

Water Conservation Celebration 211.
    See Activities

Water Conservation Invention Convention 201.
    See Activities

water cycle 27, 34-35, 41, 43-50, 147, 161, 201, 214, 217-218, 232, 236

water diversion 124, 147-148, **294**

water dowsing 101-102, **294**

water rights 27, 91, 96, 123-129, 132, 134, 211, 214, **294**

water table 66, 68, 71, 133-134, 139, **294**

Water Trouble on the High Plains 260.
    See Case Studies

Water Use, Water Users
    Alligators, Epiphytes, and Water Managers 75
    Water Works 85

Water Vessels 91. *See* Activities

Water Works 85. *See* Activities

water-stress 131, **294**

The Watercourse A-8, A-15
    Project WET A-8, A-15

waterlogging 131, 134, 262, **294**

watershed A-19, 66, 79, 161-163, 165-166, 214-216, 224, **294**

X

Xeriscape 27, 31, 37, 115, 195, 208, **294**.
    See Activities

xerophyte 75, 77, **294**

Y

Your Hydrologic Deck 161. *See* Activities

Z

zone of aeration 71
zone of saturation 71